Lecture Notes in Computer Science   **9051**

Commenced Publication in 1973
Founding and Former Series Editors:
Gerhard Goos, Juris Hartmanis, and Jan van Leeuwen

More information about this series at http://www.springer.com/series/7409

Boualem Benatallah · Azer Bestavros
Barbara Catania · Armin Haller
Yannis Manolopoulos · Athena Vakali
Yanchun Zhang (Eds.)

Web Information Systems Engineering – WISE 2014 Workshops

15th International Workshops IWCSN 2014, Org2 2014, PCS 2014, and QUAT 2014 Thessaloniki, Greece, October 12–14, 2014 Revised Selected Papers

 Springer

Editors
Boualem Benatallah
University of New South Wales
Sydney
Australia

Azer Bestavros
Boston University
Boston, MA
USA

Barbara Catania
University of Genova
Genova
Italy

Armin Haller
CSIRO ICT Centre
Canberra
Australia

Yannis Manolopoulos
Aristotle University of Thessaloniki
Thessaloniki
Greece

Athena Vakali
Aristotle University of Thessaloniki
Thessaloniki
Greece

Yanchun Zhang
Victoria University
Footscray
Australia

ISSN 0302-9743   ISSN 1611-3349 (electronic)
Lecture Notes in Computer Science
ISBN 978-3-319-20369-0   ISBN 978-3-319-20370-6 (eBook)
DOI 10.1007/978-3-319-20370-6

Library of Congress Control Number: 2015941159

LNCS Sublibrary: SL3 – Information Systems and Application, incl. Internet/Web, and HCI

Springer Cham Heidelberg New York Dordrecht London

Printed on acid-free paper

Springer International Publishing AG Switzerland is part of Springer Science+Business Media (www.springer.com)

Preface

Welcome to the proceedings of the Web Information Systems Engineering (WISE) Workshops. The conference series on Web Information Systems Engineering aims at providing an international forum for researchers, professionals, and industrial practitioners to share their knowledge in the rapidly growing area of Web technologies, methodologies, and applications. The 15th WISE event (WISE 2014) was held in Thessaloniki, Greece, during October 12–14, 2014. Previous WISE conferences were held in Nanjing, China (2013), Paphos, Cyprus (2012), Sydney, Australia (2011), Hong Kong, China (2010), Poznan, Poland (2009), Auckland, New Zealand (2008), Nancy, France (2007), Wuhan, China (2006), New York, USA (2005), Brisbane, Australia (2004), Rome, Italy (2003), Singapore (2002), Kyoto, Japan (2001), Hong Kong, China (2000).

This proceedings volume includes 19 selected and extended papers from the four workshops and the challenge held at the WISE 2014 conference. The four workshops reported on the recent developments and advances in contemporary topics in the related fields of:

- Computational Social Networks (IWCSN) with Maria Bielikova, Jaroslav Pokorný, and Václav Snášel as Workshop Chairs
- Enterprise Social Networks (Org2) with Mara Nikolaidou, Dimosthenis Anagnostopoulos, and Ourania Hatzi as Workshop Chairs
- Personalization and Context-Awareness in Cloud and Service Computing (PCS) with Yanbo Han, Jian Yu, and Guilang Wang as Workshop Chairs
- Data Quality and Trust in Big Data (QUAT) with Bo Sundgren, Deren Chen, William Song, Xiaolin Zheng, and Hasan Fleyeh as Workshop Chairs.

The conference also hosted a challenge on the theme "Multi-label classification of printed media articles to topics" organized by Apostolos Papadopoulos, Weining Qian, and Grigorios Tsoumakas. We are thankful to all the above colleagues who greatly contributed to the success of the event.

Many colleagues also helped toward the success of the workshops and the challenge. We would especially like to thank the local organization team from Aristotle University of Thessaloniki, namely: Nick Bassiliades, Eleftherios Angelis, and Yannis Karydis and all their helpers in the background, who made the conference a really pleasant experience and the work on these proceedings so much easier. Finally, we would also like to thank all the Program Committee members and external reviewers for their conscientious reviewing. We are also grateful to the WISE Society for generously supporting our workshops. We greatly appreciate Springer LNCS for publishing the WISE workshop proceedings.

May 2015   Boualem Benatallah
                                                                  Azer Bestavros
                                                                Barbara Catania
                                                                    Armin Haller
                                                         Yannis Manolopoulos
                                                                  Athena Vakali
                                                                Yanchun Zhang

Preface to The International Workshop on Computational Social Networks (IWCSN 2014)

The International Workshop on Computational Social Networks (IWCSN 2014) was organized in conjunction with the 15th International Conference on Web Information System Engineering (WISE 2014) on October 12th, 2014, in Thessaloniki, Greece.

The Workshop aimed at addressing the research issues associated with online social networks, including the topics of the design and use of various computational intelligence tools and software, simulations of social networks, representation and analysis of social networks, use of semantic networks in the design and community-based research issues such as knowledge discovery, privacy and protection, and visualization.

The Program Committee, comprised of eleven members from seven countries, evaluated ten submissions (received from six countries). Five papers were accepted for the presentation and from them three papers have been selected for publication in the proceedings.

In the paper "On the Information Diffusion between Web-based social networks", G. Haralabopoulos and I. Anagnostopoulos propose the concept of multilayer information ow, by considering every on-line social network as a separate layer and the information as links connecting these layers. Under such formalization, information is spread from a source layer, while it is diffused in multiple other layers.

J. Kubalík, J. Pokorný, M. Vita, and P. Vojtáš, in the paper "Generic Private Social Network for Knowledge Management", present the tool sitIT.cz which was developed to support communication of IT specialists (both from academia and business) using public funding. This tool is quite generic and can be used in different scenarios. The main use case is to use it as a private social network for knowledge management in a company.

In the paper "Analysis from Event Logs: Behavioral Graphs", the authors K. Slaninová, D. Vymětal and J. Martinovič present a new approach for analysing user behavior in applications like information systems, enterprise systems or e- commerce systems. The approach allows to find behavioral patterns and groups of users with similar behavior. The paper is focused on REA (Resources, Events, Agents) based simulation process log and proposes a new type of social network graph, behavioral graph, which represents the relations between the users on the basis of their occurrence in cases (not in particular transactions) in the system.

We sincerely thank all the authors who contributed to this event as well as the IWCSN 2014 Program Committee members and external reviewers, for their time in providing valuable reviews for the workshop. Special thanks belong to K. Slaninova and J. Martinovic from VSB - Technical University of Ostrava for their assistance with the workshop website.

Jaroslav Pokorný
Maria Bieliková
Václav Snášel

Preface to Towards Organization 2.0: Advancements in Enterprise Social Networks (Org2 2014)

The Org2 Workshop was organized in conjunction with the 15th International Conference on Web Information System Engineering (WISE 2014) on October 12th, 2014, in Thessaloniki, Greece.

The Workshop aimed at exploring novel frameworks, services and interaction models utilizing enterprise social networks to reach the vision of Organization 2.0. Current enterprise social network implementations focus on providing mostly services for information dissemination among members of an organization. Current trends indicate that enterprise social networks, in order to substantially improve the way enterprise members actually work, should not only facilitate information dissemination but also help participants collaborate to complete specific business tasks, which implies service provision and application execution. To elevate the impact of enterprise social networks, participants expect some sort of collaborative process execution, leading to Social BPM. Creating an enterprise social network environment that will effectively merge knowledge, gathering capabilities through social collaboration with task accomplishment features may prove promising for supporting employees in being more agile and efficient and consequently enhancing organizational work. The workshop focused on investigating the exploration of new interaction and collaboration models, the provision of new services frameworks and the integration of task execution in enterprise social networks, leading to Organization 2.0.

Org2 Workshop aspired to serve as a melting pot for researchers and practitioners both in the areas of social platform engineering and business process management, in order to discuss and combine best practices in these fields into novel ideas and frameworks for enterprise social networks. We have received eleven submissions, all of which underwent a rigorous review process by three Org2 PC members. Reviewers completed their evaluations based on originality, significance, technical soundness, and clarity of expression. From these submissions, five papers were selected for presentation and are included in this proceedings volume.

Accepted papers contributed on: alternative interaction models within Organizations ("Delineating Worker-centered Organizational Work: Blending BPMS and Social Software Features" by N. Alexopoulou, C. Stary, and S. Oppl); privacy and security issues when employing social networks for business purposes ("Compliance of the LinkedIn Privacy Policy with the Principles of the ISO 29100:2011 Standard" by A. Michota and S. Katsikas); social Business Process Management ("The Use of Social Tagging in Social Business Process Management" by M.E. Rangiha and B. Karakostas); social network data aggregations ("SocIoS API: A Data Aggregator for Accessing User Generated Content from Online Social Networks" by M. Kardara, V. Kalogirou, A. Papaoikonomou, T. Varvarigou, and K. Tserpes); case studies of Org2 in the public sector ("Integrating Social Media and Open Data in a Cloud-based Platform for Public Sector Advertising" by D. Pop, A. Echeverria, and J.V. Vidagany).

We are grateful to all Org2 Program Committee members for their help and high quality reviews. Foremost, we deeply thank all the authors for submitting their work in Org2 Workshop and contributing in its success. We also like to thank Barbara Catania and Armin Haller, WISE 2014 Workshop Co-chairs, as well as Yannis Manolopoulos, WISE 2014 General Chair for their cooperation and continuous support in organizing this workshop.

Mara Nikolaidou
Dimostenis Anagnostopoulos
Rania Hatzi

Preface to The Seventh International Workshop on Personalization and Context-Awareness in Cloud and Service Computing (PCS 2014)

The Seventh International Workshop on Personalization and Context-Awareness in Cloud and Service Computing Workshop was organized in conjunction with the 15th International Conference onWeb Information System Engineering (WISE 2014) on October 12th, 2014, in Thessaloniki, Greece.

The Workshop looks into and promotes the research on personalization and context-awareness in the areas of service, grid and cloud computing. This line of research is emerging as an important topic with the transformation of the Internet and Web from traditional linking and sharing of computers and documents (i.e., "Web of Data") to current connecting of people and things (i.e., "Web of People", "Web of Things", and "Web of People and Things"). Adopting Service-oriented Computing as a basic paradigm, the Grid and Cloud Computing approach focuses on the virtualization and transparent provisioning of software and people resources. Under such paradigm, information and service supply faces a number of new challenges. For example, how to smartly deal with large amounts of services based on user's personalized needs, how to handle personalized service composition in a dynamic environment, and how to customize business processes according to stakeholder's preferences. Personalization for processes and services in such a dynamic environment is one of the most exciting trends in Grid/Cloud Computing today that holds the potential to enrich user experiences and make our daily life more productive, convenient, and enjoyable.

The PCS workshop aims at promoting the discussion around the personalization and context-awareness issues in the service, grid, and cloud computing fields, ranging from theoretical foundations, supporting infrastructures, engineering approaches, to applications and case studies, and lead to new solutions to smarter services for the future ubiquitous world.

PCS 2014 is the seventh in a series of workshops started in 2008. The six full papers accepted for PCS 2011 represent a range of relevant topics. The papers were selected after a rigorous peer-review by the workshop Program Committee members and external reviewers.

The paper "A Survey on Approaches to Modeling Artifact-centric Business Processes", by J. Kunchala, J. Yu, and S. Yongchareon, reviews the major approaches to artifact-centric business process modeling and then discusses to what extent they align with the BALSA (Business Artifacts, Lifecycle, Services, and Associations) framework. The paper "A Connectivity-Based Recommendation Approach for Data Service Mashups", by S. Zhang, G. Wang, Z. Zhang, and Y. Han, proposes an approach to recommend useful suggestions for developing data service mashups based on the association relationship of data services. The paper "Using Incentives to Analyze Social Web Services Behaviors", by Z. Maamar, G. Costantino, M. Petrocchi, and F. Martinelli, discusses how incentives allow social networks to attract more members and reward those that are honest by retaining them. The paper "Creating and Modelling Personal Socio-economic Networks in On-Line Banking", by B. San Miguel, J.M. del Alamo, J.C. Yelmo, describes the architecture and implementation of the PosdataP2P service, which seeks to model the economic ties between the holders of university smart cards, leveraging on the social networks the holders are subscribed to. The paper "Cloud-based Video Monitoring Framework: An Approach based on Software-defined Networking for Addressing Scalability Problems", by N.M. Sandar, S. Chaisiri, S. Yongchareon, and V. Liesaputra, proposes a framework that applies stream aggregation (SA) and software-defined networking (SDN) for a cloud-based video monitoring (CVM) system in dealing with the scalability issue. Finally the paper "Context-awareness in Task Automation Services by Distributed Event Processing", by M. Coronado, R. Bruns, J. Dunkel, and Sebastian Stipković, proposes a system architecture that incorporates context- awareness and real-time coordination features for Task Automation Services in a heterogeneous mobile, smart devices, and cloud services environment.

We sincerely thank the PCS 2014 Program Committee members and external reviewers for their time in providing valuable reviews for the workshop.

Jian Yu
Guiling Wang
José M. del Álamo
Sira Yongchareon

Preface to The Second International Workshop on Data Quality and Trust in Big Data (QUAT 2014)

The Second International Workshop on Data Quality and Trust in Big Data (QUAT'14) was organized in conjunction with the 15th International Conference on Web Information System Engineering (WISE 2014) on October 12th, 2014, in Thessaloniki, Greece

This is second event in the series of this international workshop on Data Quality and Trust in Big Data (QUAT). The problem of data quality in data processing, data management, data analysis, and information systems largely and indistinctly affects every application domain, especially at the era of "Big Data". "Big Data" has the characteristics of huge volume in data and a great variety of structures or no structure. "Big Data" is increased at a great velocity every day and may be less trustable. The use of big data underpins critical activities in all sectors of our society. Many data processing tasks (such as data collection, data integration, data sharing, information extraction, and knowledge acquisition) require various forms of data preparation and consolidation with complex data processing and analysis techniques. Achieving the full transformative potential of "Big Data" requires both new data analysis algorithms and a new class of systems to handle the dramatic data growth, the demand to integrate structured and unstructured data analytics, and the increasing computing needs of massive scale analytics. The consensus is that the quality of data and the veracity of data have to span over the entire process of data collection, preparation, analysis, modelling, implementation, use, testing, and maintenance, including novel algorithms and usable systems

The QUAT workshop 2014 was a qualified forum for presenting and discussing novel ideas and solutions related to the problems of exploring, assessing, monitoring, improving, and maintaining the quality of data and trust for "Big Data". We accepted five papers for presentations, of which four are included in this workshop proceedings, among the total of nine submissions. Accepted papers contributed on: quality evaluation for data streams generated in the health domain ("Data Streams Quality Evaluation for the Generation of Alarms in Health Domain" by S. Fagndez, J. Fleitas, and Adriana Marotta); data fusion techniques for improving the quality of information transmission in wireless sensor networks ("Multilayer and Multi-agent Data Fusion in WSN information" by S. Zhang, X. Liu, X. Bao, and W.W. Song); data quality monitoring in business processes ("Strategies for Data Quality Monitoring in Business Processes" by C. Cappiello, B. Pernici, and L. Villani); business oriented geo-spatial data quality ("Quality Improvement Framework for Business Oriented Geo-Spatial Data" by X. Du and W. Song).

We would like to thank all the authors, who contributed to this event. We would also like to thank our invited keynote speaker, Prof. Barbara Pernici, Politecnico di Milano, Italy, who gave us an excellent keynote talk. We would like to thank the workshops organizers Barbara Catania and Armin Haller for all your kind support to make this event successful. Finally we would like to thank PC co-chair Prof. Xiaolin Zheng for doing all the work to organize reviewers and reviews during the hot summer in China.

Bo Sundgren
Deren Chen
William Song

Organization

Executive Committee

Workshops Co-chairs

Barbara Catania	University of Genoa, Italy
Armin Haller	CSIRO, Australia

International Workshop on Computational Social Networks (WCSN 2014)

Workshop Co-chairs

Maria Bielikova	Slovak University of Technology in Bratislava, Slovakia
Jaroslav Pokorný	Charles University, Czech Republic
Václav Snášel	VSB Technical University of Ostrava, Czech Republic

Towards Organization 2.0: Advancements in Enterprise Social Networks (Org2 2014)

Workshop Co-chairs

Mara Nikolaidou	Harokopio University of Athens, Greece
Dimosthenis Anagnostopoulos	Harokopio University of Athens, Greece
Ourania Hatzi	Harokopio University of Athens, Greece

International Workshop on Personalization and Context-Awareness in Cloud and Service Computing (PCS 2014)

General Chair Program

Yanbo Han	North China University of Technology, China

Committee Co-chairs

Jian Yu	Auckland University of Technology, New Zealand
Guiling Wang	North China University of Technology, China

Publicity Co-chairs

José M. del álamo	Universidad Politécnica de Madrid, Spain
Sira Yongchareon	Unitec Institute of Technology, New Zealand

Workshop on Data Quality and Trust in Big Data (QUAT 2014)

Honorary Chair

Bo Sundgren   Stockholm University, Sweden

General Chairs

Deren Chen   Zhejiang University, China
William Song   Dalarna University, Sweden

Program Committee Chairs

Xiaolin Zheng   Zhejiang University, China
Hasan Fleyeh   Dalarna University, Sweden

Organizing Chair

Johan Håkansson   Dalarna University, Sweden

Organizing Team

Xiaofeng Du   British Telecom, UK
Jun Li   Wenzhou University, China
Lin Zhen   Zhejiang University, China
Xiaoyun Zhao   Dalarna University, Sweden

Program Committees

IWCSN 2014

Ioannis Anagnostopoulos   University of Thessaly, Greece
Milos Besta   Google, New York
Jiří Dvorský   VSB Technical University of Ostrava, Czech Republic
Jan Martinovič   VSB Technical University of Ostrava, Czech Republic
Petr Musilek   University of Alberta, Canada
Suhail S. Owais   AL-Balaqa University, Jordan
Jaroslav Pokorný   Charles University in Prague, Czech Republic
Kateřina Slaninová   VSB Technical University of Ostrava, Czech Republic
Václav Snášel   VSB Technical University of Ostrava, Czech Republic
Jakub Šimko   Slovak University of Technology in Bratislava,
                               Slovakia
Katarzyna Wegrzyn-Wolska   ESIGETEL, France

Org2 2014

Nancy Alexopoulou   Johannes Kepler University Linz, Austria
Denise A.D. Bedford   Kent State University, USA
Marco Brambilla   Politecnico di Milano, Italy
Selim Erol   Vienna University of Economics and Business, Austria

Boughzala Imed	Telecom Ecole de Management, France
Paul Johannesson	Royal Institute of Technology, Sweden
Bill Karakostas	City University, UK
Michael Leyer	Frankfurt School of Finance & Management, Germany
Rodrigo Magalhães	Kuwait-Maastricht Business School, Kuwait
Andreas Oberweis	Universität Karlsruhe, Germany
Rainer Schmi	Munich University of Applied Sciences, Germany
Chris Stary	Johannes Kepler University Linz, Austria
Iraklis Varlamis	Harokopio University of Athens, Greece

PCS 2014

Alan Litchfield	Auckland University of Technology, New Zealand
Aviv Segev	KAIST, Korea
Bing Li	Wuhan University, China
Chen Ding	Ryerson University, Canada
Chen Liu	North China University of Technology, China
Feng Zhang	Shandong University of Science and Technology, China
Hongbing Wang	SouthEast University, China
Hong-Linh Truong	Vienna University of Technology, Austria
Jianwu Wang	University of California, USA
Jinhua Xiong	Institute of Computing Technology, CAS, China
Jun Wei	Institute of Software, Chinese Academy of Sciences, China
Lina Yao	University of Adelaide, Australia
Ma Bingxian	University of Jinan, China
Miao Du	Swinburne University of Technology, Australia
Michael Mrissa	Université de Lyon, CNRS, France
Mingdong Tang	Hunan University of Science and Technology, China
Nilufar Baghaei	Unitec Institute of Technology, New Zealand
Paolo Falcarin	University of East London, UK
Patricia Arias	Universidad Carlos III de Madrid, Spain
Pengcheng Zhang	Hohai University, China
Qi Yu	Rochester Institute of Technology, USA
Qingtian Zeng	Shandong University of Science and Technology, China
Raymond Wong	University of New South Wales, Australia
Roland Wagner	Beuth Hochschule für Technik Berlin, Germany
Ruben Trapero	Technische Universität Darmstadt, Germany
Shijun Liu	Shandong University, China
Shizhan Chen	Tianjin University, China
Sivadon Chaisiri	Shinawatra University, Thailand
Talal H. Noor	The University of Adelaide, Australia
Tong Mo	Peking University, China
Veronica Liesaputra	Unitec Institute of Technology, New Zealand

Weiping Li	Peking University, China
Yanhua Du	University of Science and Technology Beijing, China
Zaiwen Feng	Wuhan University, China
Zhiyong Feng	Tianjin University, China
Zibin Zheng	The Chinese University of Hong Kong, China

QUAT 2014

Deren Chen	Zhejiang University, China
Xiaofeng Du	British Telecom, UK
Hasan Fleyeh	Dalarna University, Sweden
Johan Håkansson	Dalarna University, Sweden
Jun Li	Wenzhou University, China
Yang Li	British Telecom, UK
Christer Magnusson	Stockholm University, Sweden
Kami Makki	Lamar University, USA
William Song	Dalarna University, Sweden
Bo Sundgren	Stockholm University, Sweden
Yoshihisa Udagawa	Tokyo Polytechnic University, Japan
Hua Wang	University of Southern Queensland, Australia
Sheng Zhang	Nanchang Hangkong University, China
Xiaolin Zheng	Zhejing University, China

Contents

Semi-supervised Learning Algorithm for Binary Relevance Multi-label Classification

Jan Švec[✉]

Department of Cybernetics, New Technologies for Information Society,
University of West Bohemia, Univerzitní 22, 306 14 Pilsen, Czech Republic
honzas@kky.zcu.cz

Abstract. The presented paper describes our model for the WISE 2014 challenge multi-label classification task. The goal of the challenge was to implement a multi-label text classification model which maximizes the mean F_1 score on a private test data. The described method involves a binary relevance scheme with linear classifiers trained using stochastic gradient descent. A novel method for determining the values of classifiers' meta-parameters was developed. In addition, our solution employs the semi-supervised learning which significantly improves the evaluation score. The presented solution won the third place in the challenge. The results are discussed and the supervised and semi-supervised approaches are compared.

Keywords: Multi-label classification · Semi-supervised learning · Linear model

1 Introduction

The subject of WISE 2014 challenge was the task of multi-label classification of Greek print media articles from May 2013 to September 2013. Each document is represented using the unordered set of type (bag of words approach) and TF-IDF (term frequency-inverse document frequency) statistics for each type. The feature vectors were unit-normalized. The total number of features (distinct tokens) was 301,561. The training set contained 64,857 documents and the test set 34,923. In addition, the test set was split in to public and private test data (ratio 70:30). Only the results on the public test data were available during the challenge. The final standings were determined using the private test data to avoid over-fitting to the public test data. The mean F_1 score was used as the evaluation metric.

This paper describes the solution which was submitted to the WISE 2014 challenge and won the third place on the private test data. Since we had no experience with multi-label text classification prior the competition, we modified our models used for a spoken language understanding (SLU) task [3,9].

The SLU is virtually the multi-label classification task; the labels represent semantic concepts. We used a very simple model called Semantic Tuple Classifiers

B. Benatallah et al. (Eds.): WISE 2014, LNCS 9051, pp. 1–13, 2015.
DOI: 10.1007/978-3-319-20370-6_1

(STC) [3] in the early stage of the challenge. Since the achieved result was very competitive we decided to continue in the challenge and to develop a new model for text classification. The STC model is a simple binary relevance model implemented using support vector machines. The STC does not model the inter-label dependencies nor the thresholding for selecting the relevant subset of labels. At the end of the competition other teams also reported that the SVM-based model would finish in the top 10 with score 0.77554[1].

We also considered the usage of the Hierarchical Discriminative Model (HDM) [9] which we use successfully in the SLU task. The HDM allows to model the inter-label conditional probabilities and also uses a search algorithm with the minimum cost to obtain the most probable set of labels. The HDM uses multi-label SVMs which are very hard to train in the case of training set size about 65k.

Therefore we developed a new training procedure which employs a set of linear binary relevance classifiers, iterative direct optimization of cross-validated mean F_1 score and semi-supervised learning. The paper is organised as follows: Sect. 2 describes a final model submitted to the challenge, Sect. 2.1 describes the basic linear classifier (denoted as label classifier) used in a binary relevance model. Section 2.2 presents an iterative direct optimization method used to optimize meta-parameters with respect to the cross-validated mean F_1 score. Section 2.3 discusses various approaches to threshold the label probabilities to obtain the subset of relevant labels for a given document. Section 2.4 presents the semi-supervised learning adapted for the use in the multi-label classification task. The obtained results are discussed in Sects. 3 and 4 concludes the paper.

2   The Model

The presented method was based on our experience with the STC and HDM models. Analogically to STC, M independent binary classifiers for each label were trained – each classifier predicts the posterior probability of the corresponding label assigned to the input feature vector – and, as in HDM, the posterior probabilities predicted by all M classifiers are combined into the final decision using a prediction strategy.

The model consists of M binary classifiers (in this paper we call them the *label classifiers*) predicting the posterior probability of a document being labeled by the given label. The training set consists of N training examples represented by the row vectors $\boldsymbol{X}^i, i = 1, 2, \ldots N$. Then the whole training set is represented by the matrix $\boldsymbol{X}$ with N rows and F columns, where F is the number of features. In the WISE 2014 challenge the feature vectors are sparse because the bag-of-words representation of text documents was used. Each element of the feature vector represents the normalized TF-IDF statistics for a given word. The value of F is 301,561 (the number of distinct types in the train documents).

---

[1] See discussion forum at Kaggle.com: https://www.kaggle.com/c/wise-2014/forums/ t/9773/our-approach-5th-place.

Lets assume that we have trained M binary label classifiers. Using such classifiers we can predict the posterior probabilities for each label. For an i-th document represented with $\boldsymbol{X}^i$ we can construct the row vector $\boldsymbol{P}^i = [p_j^i], j = 1, 2, \ldots M$, where p_j^i is the predicted probability of i-th document being labeled by the label j.

The row vector $\boldsymbol{P}^i$ is used as an input into the *prediction strategy* that makes the decision which labels are assigned to the i-th document. The prediction strategy performs a simple thresholding based on the maximum probability in the vector $\boldsymbol{P}^i$. At least one label is assigned to each input vector. The prediction strategy converts the soft output of classifiers (posterior probabilities $\boldsymbol{P}$) into the hard output (binary decisions $\hat{\boldsymbol{Y}}$). The predicted matrix $\hat{\boldsymbol{Y}} = [\hat{y}_j^i]$, $i = 1, 2, \ldots N, j = 1, 2, \ldots M$ has the same shape as $\boldsymbol{P}$. The values of $\hat{\boldsymbol{Y}}$ are assigned using the following rule: $\hat{y}_j^i = 1$ if the model predicts that i-th document should be labeled by j-th label and $\hat{y}_j^i = 0$ otherwise.

Now suppose that the real labels assigned to i-th document are stored in the reference row vector $\boldsymbol{Y}^i = [y_j^i]$, where y_j^i has similar meaning as $\hat{y}_j^i$ for the predicted labels: $y_j^i = 1$ if the annotator decided that i-th document has label j and $y_j^i = 0$ otherwise. Again, the row vectors $\boldsymbol{Y}^i$ form the matrix $\boldsymbol{Y}$.

The reference matrix $\boldsymbol{Y}$ and the predicted matrix $\hat{\boldsymbol{Y}}$ allows to directly evaluate the mean F_1 metric used in the WISE 2014 challenge. This feature is important since it allows to tune the meta-parameters of the particular label classifier with respect to the predictions of other classifiers (see Fig. 1).

The whole training process could be summarized using the following steps (see Fig. 1 top; supervised learning):

1. For each label $j = 1, 2, \ldots M$ train the classifier $clsf_j$ using the reference prediction $\boldsymbol{Y}_j$ (column label) and the matrix $\boldsymbol{X}$ containing the training feature vectors.
2. For an unknown example represented by the row vector $\boldsymbol{X}^u$ use all M classifiers to obtain the probabilistic output vector $\boldsymbol{P}^u = [p_1^u, p_2^u, \ldots p_M^u]$.
3. Use the prediction strategy to convert $\boldsymbol{P}^u$ into the binary decisions $\hat{\boldsymbol{Y}}^u$.

All these steps are described in more detail in subsequent sections.

2.1 Label Classifier

For each label $j \in \{1, 2, \ldots M\}$ exactly one binary label classifier $clsf_j$ was trained. It corresponds to the binary relevance decomposition of the multi-label classification task. No inter-label dependencies nor label-powerset classifiers were used. At the beginning of the WISE 2014 challenge we used the linear SVM classifiers trained using `liblinear` library [1]. A similar approach was also used to label text annotation errors. Such task corresponds to multi-label classification in that the number of positive examples is much lower than the number of negative examples [4]. The model showed a moderate accuracy in both these tasks.

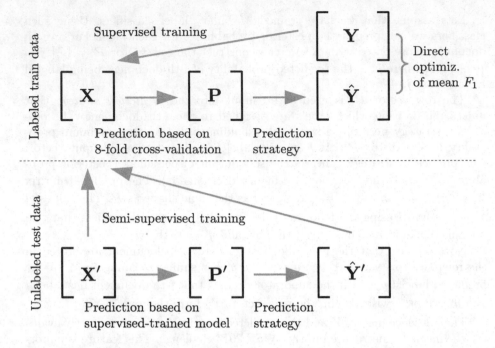

Fig. 1. Illustration of the training process. Top part of the figure shows the supervised learning with direct optimization of mean F_1 metric. In the bottom part of the figure the scheme of semi-supervised learning is depicted.

Then we replaced the label classifier with the linear model trained using the stochastic gradient descent (SGD) [5, 8, 11] from the `sklearn` library. By changing the underlying label classifier implementation we obtained an improvement in mean F_1 metric approximately 1.2 % absolutely (measured on public test data).

We used the modified Huber loss (smoothed hinge loss [12]) since in `sklearn` this loss function allows to predict the posterior probabilities. We tried the L_1, L_2 and elastic net regularization (convex combination of L_1 and L_2 regularization). In the final model we used the elastic net with L_1 weight 0.15 which leads to slightly better results than the L_1 regularization in our case.

For predicting the posterior probability the `sklearn` implementation of a method described in [10] was used. The method is based on isotonic regression and uses the algorithm called pair-adjacent violators which minimizes the mean-squared error criterion of probability estimates.

The classifiers were trained using the training vectors X^i provided by the challenge authors. No feature engineering nor feature transformation was performed.

Each SGD-trained linear classifier has a single meta-parameters α_j which weights the regularization term in the optimized loss function. The values of α_j were optimized using the *iterative direct optimization* method developed during the WISE challenge, which is described in the next section.

We also experimented with the number of SGD iterations performed during training. We started with 10 iterations and the final model was trained using 20 iterations. We did not observed any increase in cross-validation score if we advanced to 30 iterations.

2.2 Iterative Direct Optimization

Training the label classifiers for each label comprises determining the value of regularization meta-parameter α_j for each classifier $clsf_j$. We used simple grid-based search method[2] which selects the values from the logarithmic sequence $10^{-5.6}, 10^{-5.5}, 10^{-5.4}, \ldots 10^{-4.4}$ and uses the value which optimizes the selected criterion (the histogram of α_j values is shown in Fig. 2).

Since the WISE challenge uses the mean F_1 metric to evaluate the classification performance, we tried the directly optimize this metric with the *iterative direct optimization* (IDO) method. The IDO method assumes that the prediction strategy (see Sect. 2.3) is known and fixed. The prediction strategy allows to create the $\hat{Y}$ matrix from the P matrix and evaluate the mean F_1 score.

The IDO algorithm consists of the following steps:

1. Initialize the values of the P matrix.
2. Select label j for training the label classifier. Train the j-th classifier using the following sequence:
   (a) Iterate over the values of logarithmic sequence and set α_j.
   (b) Train $clsf_j$ using the α_j.
   (c) Use the 8-fold cross-validation predictions as the j-th row of the P matrix and evaluate the mean F_1 score.
   (d) Select the value of α_j which maximizes the mean F_1 score.
3. Continue with step 2 until all M classifiers are trained.

The described algorithm has two drawbacks:

– The order of labels (for which the label classifiers are trained) must be determined.
– Suitable initialization of P matrix must be used.

To solve the first drawback, we used the heuristics that the most frequent label is the most important. Therefore we trained the label classifiers from the most frequent to the least frequent label.

The second drawback causes the problem with training the j-th classifier which is trained with respect to the predictions of previously trained $j-1$ classifiers but it is not influenced by the predictions of classifiers trained subsequently. Therefore we run the algorithm several times and we are using the following initialization procedure:

– In the first run of the IDO algorithm the items of the P matrix are initialized to 0. Such initialization does not influence the prediction strategy.

---

[2] Similar to recommendation from **sklearn** documentation:
http://scikit-learn.org/stable/modules/sgd.html.

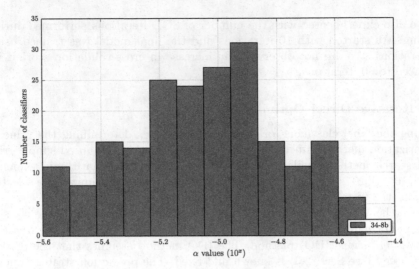

Fig. 2. The histogram showing the number of classifiers with a specific α_j value. The α_j values were selected from the sequence $10^{-5.6}, 10^{-5.5}, 10^{-5.4}, \ldots 10^{-4.4}$.

– Each subsequent run of the algorithm uses the P matrix from the previous run. It allows to optimize the α_j with respect to predictions of all other classifiers.

The IDO algorithm was typically repeated 3-times for a majority of our WISE challenge submissions.

Another option is to initialize the P matrix to be equal to the Y matrix (the reference assignment of labels). This approach could train label classifiers which replace the original columns of P (and Y respectively) with the minimal loss of the mean F_1. This kind of initialization gives promising results but we did not used it in the WISE challenge.

The effect of executing the algorithm several times is illustrated by the Fig. 4 (later in this paper). The plot shows the cross-validation mean F_1 score after training different number of label classifiers. The blue line shows the score for the first run of the IDO algorithm. This should be compared with the green line which shows the score for the third run of the algorithm. The difference after training all 203 classifiers is about 0.7 % absolutely.

2.3   Prediction Strategy

The *prediction strategy* constructs the set of relevant labels from the posterior probabilities of labels. It performs the thresholding of soft-predictions (probabilities) into a hard-decision (binary prediction). This section describes our prediction strategies used during the WISE 2014 challenge. The presented method for selecting the relevant subset of labels from the predicted label probabilities is one of several possible methods [6,7].

Formally, the prediction strategy constructs the set of relevant labels L^i for the i-th document based on the vector of posterior probabilities $\boldsymbol{P}^i$. Lets define two sequences l^i and q^i which are useful for the description of the prediction strategy. These sequences could be easily constructed from the vector $\boldsymbol{P}^i$ such that $l^i = (l_1^i, l_2^i, \ldots, l_M^i)$ and $q^i = (q_1^i, q_2^i, \ldots, q_M^i)$ satisfy the following equation (the index i is omitted for clarity):

$$p_{l_k} = q_k \quad \wedge \quad q_k \geq q_{k+1} \quad \text{for each } k \in 1 \ldots M \tag{1}$$

In other words, the labels in l^i are sorted in descending order according to the probabilities $\boldsymbol{P}^i$. The sequence q^i holds the corresponding probabilities.

Our early submissions into the WISE challenge used the simple rule, that all label l_k for which $q_k > 0.5$ are included in L. By using such prediction strategy, a large portion of documents does not have any labels assigned. It is consistent with a conclusion of [2].

Simple Thresholding. Our first successful strategy used the ratio q_k/q_1 (i.e. posterior probabilities normalized by the probability of the best label). Instead of using a single threshold we used three values t_A, t_B and t_C with the following prediction strategy (index i is again omitted):

$$L = \begin{cases} \{l_1, l_2, l_3, l_4\} & q_4 > t_C \cdot q_1 \\ \{l_1, l_2, l_3\} & q_3 > t_B \cdot q_1 \\ \{l_1, l_2\} & q_2 > t_A \cdot q_1 \\ \{l_1\} & \text{otherwise} \end{cases} \tag{2}$$

In cases where multiple conditions are satisfied (e.g. it is possible to assign two or four labels) the set with a larger cardinality is used.

The values of t_A, t_B and t_C are tuned using the $\boldsymbol{P}$ matrix corresponding to training data. To avoid biased predictions of posterior probabilities for training data, we used 8-fold cross-validation predictions. The method for finding the threshold is a simple greedy algorithm: start with $t_A = t_B = t_C = 1$, tune t_A first, then t_B and finally t_C to maximize the mean F_1 score.

Parameterized Thresholding. In the final stage of challenge, the prediction strategy was modified so that the number of positively classified labels (denoted by Q – the number of q_k which are greater than 0.5) is taken into account. The decision strategy selects first Q labels from l and in addition it adds the labels with lower probabilities if they satisfy the prediction strategy in Eq. 2.

In addition, the values for thresholds are parameterized using the number Q, so that the decision strategy has the following form:

$$L = \{l_1, l_2, \ldots l_{Q-1}\} \bigcup \begin{cases} \{l_Q, l_{Q+1}, l_{Q+2}, l_{Q+3}\} & q_{Q+3} > t_C(Q) \cdot q_Q \\ \{l_Q, l_{Q+1}, l_{Q+2}\} & q_{Q+2} > t_B(Q) \cdot q_Q \\ \{l_Q, l_{Q+1}\} & q_{Q+1} > t_A(Q) \cdot q_Q \\ \{l_Q\} & \text{otherwise} \end{cases} \tag{3}$$

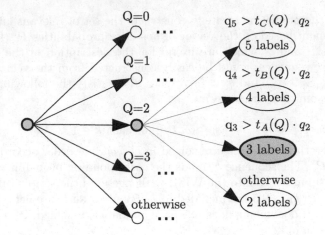

Fig. 3. Illustration of the prediction strategy decision tree. The number Q is the number of labels with posterior probability higher than 0.5. The branches for Q other than 2 are not shown since they have similar structure. The values q_k are the posterior probabilities ordered from the highest to lower ones according to Eq. 1. **Example:** Suppose that $l = (30, 12, 48, 64, 3)$, $q = (0.63, 0.61, 0.43, 0.05, 0.01)$, and the prediction strategy thresholds are $t_A(2) = 0.6$, $t_B(2) = 0.7$ and $t_C(2) = 0.5$. Then $Q = 2$ (the number of labels with posterior probability higher than 0.5) and $q_3 > t_A(Q) \cdot q_2$ is satisfied ($0.43 > 0.6 \cdot 0.61$). The prediction strategy says that the number of labels assigned to the document should be 3 and $L = \{30, 12, 48\}$.

The values $t_A(Q)$, $t_B(Q)$ and $t_C(Q)$ could be found using the same greedy algorithm described above. The only difference is that the algorithm is executed for different values of Q. We tuned the parameters for $Q = 1$, $Q = 2$, $Q = 3$ and $Q > 3$.

The prediction strategy from Eq. 3 is schematically illustrated in the form of decision tree in Fig. 3. The use of different values of thresholds for different values of Q caused the increase of cross-validation score from 0.81027 to 0.81140 with similar effect on the test data scores (0.77884 vs. 0.78003 on public test data).

Since the prediction strategy is based on the P matrix which is an outcome of the IDO training process, there is a circular dependency – IDO training needs the prediction strategy to be known and fixed. To solve this we started the IDO algorithm with hand-crafted values of thresholds. Then the resulting P matrix was used to tune the thresholds and the final model was trained.

2.4   Semi-supervised Learning

The multi-label classification tasks suffer from the data sparsity problem. In the WISE 2014 challenge, there were more than 100 labels with less then 100 training examples. We decided to explore the possibility to use the semi-supervised learning to improve the performance by using the unlabeled test data.

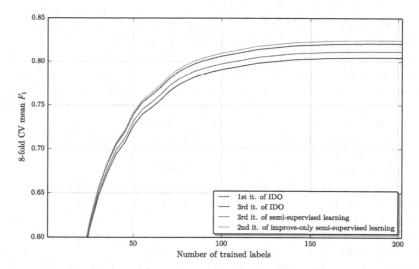

Fig. 4. The dependency of cross-validation mean F_1 score with respect to the number of trained label classifiers. The order of labels is from the most frequent to least frequent one. The performance improvement caused by repeated runs of direct optimization and semi-supervised learning is obvious especially between 50th and 100th most frequent label.

Semi-supervised learning is a technique which allows to use a set of feature vectors without target labels in the training process. The information about the distribution of feature vectors allows to increase the performance by better modelling the sparse classes and/or features.

The rules of the challenge disallowed to use other data then the data provided by the competition organizers. We therefore used the test data directly in the semi-supervised training. We started with our best supervised-trained model and we used it to predict the target labels for the test data. By the use of the described prediction strategy, all test documents were labeled by at least one label. This could lead to an improvement of the prediction performance since the document's labels are selected based on the posterior probabilities. It means that document with the most probable label with probability e.g. 0.1 is still labeled by that label because other labels are even less probable.

Formally, if we denote $\boldsymbol{X}'$ the matrix of T rows containing T test data feature vectors, then by using some supervised-trained model we can obtain the $\hat{\boldsymbol{Y}}'$ matrix (which is based on $\boldsymbol{P}'$) corresponding to thresholded predictions of M label classifiers. Then, the semi-supervised model training is performed using the feature vectors $\boldsymbol{X}$ and $\boldsymbol{X}'$ with corresponding target values $\boldsymbol{Y}$ and $\hat{\boldsymbol{Y}}'$ (see Fig. 1).

The semi-supervised model is trained using the iterative direct optimization described in Sect. 2.2. After each run of IDO, the matrix $\hat{\boldsymbol{Y}}'$ is updated based on the current values of the matrix $\boldsymbol{P}'$. Although the cross-validation is used to predict both P and P' (and $\hat{Y}$ and $\hat{Y}'$), the mean F_1 metric is evaluated only on $\hat{Y}$ (using Y). This is because only Y contains ground-truth target labels.

To prevent divergence of the semi-supervised learning, the search for optimal α_j values is slightly modified. In the supervised approach the label classifier $clsf_j$ is selected from the set of models trained with different α_j values based on the cross-validation mean F_1 score. In the semi-supervised approach the label classifier is selected from two such sets: the first one are the models trained using X only, the second one are models trained using both X and X'. In other words, if the semi-supervised label classifier has lower cross-validation score than the supervised one, only the supervised-trained model is used.

As with the standard IDO algorithm, the semi-supervised training was performed three times to refine the α_j values and the $\hat{Y}'$ matrix. The Fig. 4 shows the dependency of cross-validation score on the number of label classifiers trained. It directly compares the supervised-trained and semi-supervised-trained models. The effect of using the semi-supervised technique is evident starting from 50th most frequent label and the effect is increasing with decreasing label frequency.

Improve-Only Mode. We observed that after three IDO iterations the partial results for a specific label classifiers starts to oscillate – on even iteration the overall cross-validation score increased and on odd iteration it decreased. Therefore, we implemented a so called *improve-only* mode which tries to stabilize the semi-supervised training.

In the *improve-only* the training process is performed as a standard semi-supervised procedure described above. In the model selection phase of training the label classifier j the model is selected from three sets: models with different α_j trained from X only, models with different α_j trained from X and X' and model from the previous IDO iteration.

In this mode, the cross-validation score can be only improved, because if the supervised and semi-supervised classifiers are worse than the classifier from the previous IDO iteration, the corresponding column of the P matrix is left intact and cross-validation score does not decrease.

3   Summary and Results

The final challenge submission was trained using the following procedure: first, the initial supervised model was trained and the model was used to tune the parameters of the decision strategy. After this step the decision strategy was fixed and used in subsequent steps.

Then the supervised model was trained using three iterations of the iterative direct optimization algorithm (row *IDO* in Table 1). This model was used to predict the test data labels as the basis for the semi-supervised training of subsequent model.

The semi-supervised model was trained using the train data and the test data labeled by the supervised model trained in the previous step. Because

Table 1. Mean F1 scores for three different models. The table contains cross-validation score (cv-F1), the public test data score (pub-F1), the private test data score (priv-F1) and the difference between public and private test data (pub-priv).

Model	cv-F1	pub-F1	priv-F1	pub-priv
IDO	0.81140	0.78003	0.78181	−0.00178
IDO+semisup	0.81941	0.79023	0.78983	0.00040
IDO+semisup+impr	0.82458	0.79558	0.79463	0.00095
winning solution		0.79437	0.79685	−0.00248

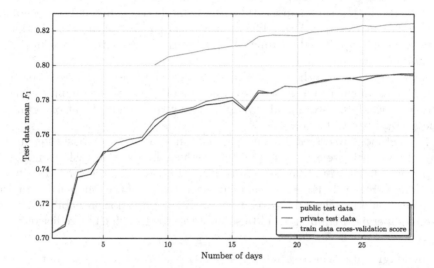

Fig. 5. The development of the performance of our model depending on the date. The x-axis shows the number of days since we joined the challenge. The results on public and private test data are shown as well as the train data cross-validation score.

the semi-supervised training algorithm is basically the IDO algorithm, three iterations of IDO were also performed. The only one difference is that the test data labels were updated after each iteration of IDO. The resulting model is denoted *IDO+semisup* in Table 1.

After training the semi-supervised model the *improve-only* training was performed. Two iterations in this mode were performed and the final model is denoted *IDO+semisup+impr*. The results are summarised in Table 1.

4   Conclusion and Future Work

This paper presents the solution, which won the third place in the WISE 2014 challenge. Our solution was the simplest of the three winning ones. The authors of both the first and the second solution used ensembles of classifiers with a number of different classifiers. The model described in this paper uses just a simple linear classifier for each label with fine-tuned prediction strategy.

The presented solution shows that the simple linear model could achieve competitive results by using the carefully designed training procedure. The procedure employs the direct optimization of target metric by tuning the meta-parameters of the partial label classifiers. The meta-parameters are tuned not only with respect to the prediction accuracy of the partial label but also the predictions of other classifiers are taken into account.

The novel method for semi-supervised training of the classification model was developed during the challenge. The overall improvement in prediction performance caused by the semi-supervised training method was about 1.3 % absolute (measured on private test data). The improvement consists of the contribution of the generic semi-supervised training (0.8 %) and the contribution of the improve-only mode (additional 0.5 %).

The Table 1 and also the Fig. 5 also show that the cross-validation score is a good indicator of the resulting score evaluated on the test data. An improvement in the cross-validated score is always followed by the improvement on both the public and private test data.

The methods described in this paper stands as a good basis for future research. Currently we are evaluating the methods in a similar task using Czech newspaper data. It would be also interesting to investigate the semi-supervised training in more depth. For example, by using a portion of the unlabeled data, the documents could be selected based on the predicted posterior probabilities. Then the semi-supervised training would use only the most confident predictions.

Acknowledgments. This research was supported by the Grant Agency of the Czech Republic, project No. GAČR GBP103/12/G084. Access to computing and storage facilities owned by parties and projects contributing to the National Grid Infrastructure MetaCentrum, (project No. LM2010005), is greatly appreciated.

References

1. Fan, R., Chang, K., Hsieh, C.: LIBLINEAR: A library for large linear classification. J. Mach. Learn. **9**, 1871–1874 (2008)
2. Godbole, S., Sarawagi, S.: Discriminative methods for multi-labeled classification. In: Dai, H., Srikant, R., Zhang, C. (eds.) PAKDD 2004. LNCS (LNAI), vol. 3056, pp. 22–30. Springer, Heidelberg (2004)
3. Mairesse, F., Gašić, M., Jurčíček, F., Keizer, S., Thomson, B., Yu, K., Young, S.: Spoken language understanding from unaligned data using discriminative classification models. In: 2009 IEEE International Conference on Acoustics, Speech and Signal Processing. ICASSP 2009, pp. 4749–4752. IEEE, Taipei (2009)
4. Matoušek, J., Tihelka, D.: Annotation errors detection in TTS corpora. In: Proc. Interspeech. Lyon, France (2013)
5. Pedregosa, F., Varoquaux, G., Gramfort, A., Michel, V., Thirion, B., Grisel, O., Blondel, M., Prettenhofer, P., Weiss, R., Dubourg, V., Vanderplas, J., Passos, A., Cournapeau, D., Brucher, M., Perrot, M., Duchesnay, E.: Scikit-learn: machine learning in python. J. Mach. Learn. **12**, 2825–2830 (2012)

6. Skorkovská, L.: Dynamic threshold selection method for multi-label newspaper topic identification. In: Habernal, I. (ed.) TSD 2013. LNCS, vol. 8082, pp. 209–216. Springer, Heidelberg (2013)
7. Tsoumakas, G., Katakis, I.: Multi-label classification: an overview. Int. J. Data Warehouse. Min. **3**(September), 1–13 (2007)
8. Tsuruoka, Y., Tsujii, J., Ananiadou, S.: Stochastic gradient descent training for L1-regularized log-linear models with cumulative penalty. In: Proceedings of the Joint Conference of the 47th Annual Meeting of the ACL and the 4th International Joint Conference on Natural Language Processing of the AFNLP, vol. 1, p. 477 (2009)
9. Švec, J., Šmídl, L., Ircing, P.: Hierarchical Discriminative Model for Spoken Language Understanding. In: 2013 Proceedings of IEEE International Conference on Acoustics, Speech, and Signal Processing, pp. 8322–8326. IEEE, Vancouver, Canada (2013)
10. Zadrozny, B., Elkan, C.: Transforming classifier scores into accurate multiclass probability estimates. In: Proceedings of the Eighth ACM SIGKDD International Conference on Knowledge Discovery and Data Mining KDD, vol. 2, pp. 694–699 (2002)
11. Zhang, T.: Solving large scale linear prediction problems using stochastic gradient descent algorithms. In: Proceedings of the Twenty-First International Conference on Machine Learning ICML 2004, p. 116. ACM, New York (2004)
12. Zou, H., Zhu, J., Hastie, T.: New multicategory boosting algorithms based on multicategory Fisher-consistent losses. Ann. Appl. Stat. **2**(4), 1290–1306 (2008)

On the Information Diffusion Between Web-Based Social Networks

Giannis Haralabopoulos[(✉)] and Ioannis Anagnostopoulos

School of Sciences, Department of Computer Science and Biomedical
Informatics, University of Thessaly, Lamia, Greece
{ghara, janag}@dib.uth.gr

Abstract. The topic of Information diffusion has been in the centre of sociology
interest for many years. Even before the rise of Online Social Networks (OSNs),
social ties and the way the information flows have been studied in traditional real-
life social networks. In this paper, we propose the concept of multilayer information flow, by considering every On-line Social Network (OSN) as a separate
layer and the information as links connecting these layers. Under such formalization, information is spread from a source layer, while it is diffused in multiple
other layers. In order to validate our proposal, experimentations are focused on
Reddit and its content, by observing the diffusion of its posts and related content
in ImgUr and YouTube.

Keywords: Information · Diffusion · On-line social networks

1 Introduction – Background

The notion that information flows, from mass media to opinion leaders and later on to a
wider population as final consumers, was firstly introduced during the middle of 40's
[1]. Almost a decade later, the authors in [2] revisited the subject by proposing their
theory of "Two step flow of communication", while, the authors of the work described
in [3] noted that analysis of social networks is suggested as a tool for linking micro and
macro levels of sociology theory. Similar conclusions were verified in OSNs after
nearly 40 years, while at the same time, the interest for social media analysis has
skyrocketed [4, 5].

Viral marketing was introduced in [6], acknowledging the importance of peer
communication in social networks. The authors in [7], found that provocative content
such as sexuality, humour, violence and nudity are crucial virality factors, in comparison with traditional TV advertising, where emotive content had always been the
key. In addition to virality, information diffusion became an important research subject.
As a result, the authors in [8], modelled outbreak detection via node selection, while
performing a two-fold evaluation of their model by using a water distribution network
as well as a blog network. In a work that dealt with word of mouth scenarios, it was
noted that 59 % of individuals frequently share online content [9]. Additionally, the
authors in [10] observed that positive content is more viral than negative.

© Springer International Publishing Switzerland 2015
B. Benatallah et al. (Eds.): WISE 2014, LNCS 9051, pp. 14–26, 2015.
DOI: 10.1007/978-3-319-20370-6_2

Social influence modelling was the scope of [11]. Using old diffusion data to create such models, the authors observed that viral marketing could leverage genuine influence. Similarly, the authors in [12], investigated the social influence in meme social graph.

The authors in [12] noted that content lifespan is very important to virality. For the same OSN, Sakaki et al. [13] study users as social sensors by monitoring information flow and dissemination during earthquake incidents. In [14], authors analyse the entire Twitter graph in order to assess its topological characteristics.

Rajyalakshmi et al. in [15], proposed a stochastic model for the diffusion of several topics. The authors discovered that strong ties play a significant role in virality, having homophily as a major contributor, as observed in [17]. Micro and macro scales of the network become relevant - similarly to [3] - and the authors noted that, acts within groups have a global impact.

Authors of [16], studied the dynamics of the spreading process. Furthermore in [4], Bakshy et al., address the problem of information diffusion in OSNs. The authors ended up with the statement -as seen in [3, 14, 14] that, strong ties are more influential but weak ties are responsible for diffusing novel information.

Guille et al. in [17], addressed the issue of information adoption in Twitter, based on the assumption described in [16] in respect to micro and macro level dynamics. Their results were similar with the ones described in [2].

In this work, we consider every OSN as a layer and the information as links connecting each layer, we propose the concept of multilayer information flow. In this concept, information is spread from a source layer and diffuses in multiple others. To test our proposal, we decided to focus on Reddit and its content.

Reddit is a social news and entertainment site powered by user generated content. Registered users submit content on the form of a descriptive link; namely a post. Posts that acquire a high (vote ratio in a short period after their submission, are moved to the front page. It is apparent that Reddit community, defines the content and determine its "success" or "failure". Across various content posted on Reddit, we focus on posts that link to an external domain and their traffic is measurable.

Content of posts on Reddit can be (amongst others) an image or a set of images hosted in ImgUr, or a video in YouTube. In ImgUr, content is usually created at the same time as the corresponding post in Reddit. While in YouTube, most posts in Reddit are linked to old videos. A short time after their creation and rise in terms of popularity within Reddit, users from different OSNs start mentioning that content, either by citing Reddit or the domain where the content is hosted (ImgUr or YouTube in our case).

For the purposes of our research, we wanted to use famous and heavily visited OSNs. In one hand, Twitter provided us with the ability to fully observe the impact of a front-paged Reddit post. On the other hand, since most content in Facebook and Google Plus is private, we only discovered a fraction of the total references, derived from search through public posts.

The rest of the paper is organised as follows. The next Section provides a detailed description in respect to our methodology. In Sect. 3, we thoroughly present the results derived from our analysis, while in the last two sections (4 and 5), we discuss evaluation issues and conclude our research.

2 Methodology – Dataset Description

Our research is focused in Reddit, a social news and entertainment site. Content is generated and ranked by users, based on positive/negative (up/down respectively) votes. Newly created posts with a high enough[1] rank, reach the front page. The submitted content often links to an external domain and varies from simple news posts, political articles, Ask Me Anything sessions, up to entertaining pictures. The view count on their original source is not always available (e.g. Wikipedia, News Sites), while it is also possible for a post to not be linked with any other external domain. Additionally, comments on posts also link to several other domains, yet this link relation is out of context of our research.

Since our initial idea was to be able to count viewership in various parallel social networks, the types of posts, hosted in domains without a view counter, were excluded from our analysis. Subsequently, we were able to monitor pictures in ImgUr and videos in YouTube, since in the front page of Reddit, there are always some posts that link to either one.

Generally, a post in Reddit consists of its title, content and comment section. Title part is self-explanatory; comment section is hosted within Reddit domain, while content is usually hosted in an external domain and rarely in Reddit. We focus on the hosting domain of a post, and more specifically on the content hosted on YouTube and ImgUr domains. We should note that our initial plan included the Quickmeme domain, which was a well-known meme creation site. Unfortunately, the use of Quickmeme in Reddit was banned in June of 2013.

In our work, we need domains that provide viewership counters in order to monitor and examine information diffusion features. In one hand, ImgUr and YouTube count views according to the user's IP address, while on the other hand, Reddit only provides the voting count of a post. As such, the sum of negative and positive votes is used as the Reddit views counter. We were aware that both the absence of an IP based view counter and the method Reddit uses to fuse voting (see Footnote 1) introduces some inaccuracy in our results. However, since our main aim is towards diffusion rather than viewership volume, such kind of inaccuracy does not affect our initial perception over multi-layer information flow.

In some preliminary tests we performed on Facebook and Google Plus, it was observed that both demonstrated a fairly low diffusion, even on viral content. This happens because both APIs, do not provide access to private posts. Thus, only public posts were taken into consideration. Additionally, the network usage of Google Plus is fairly low compared to Facebook. Considering these factors, we decided to only include Facebook in our analysis. Furthermore in order to provide a more detailed picture of how information is spread amongst Facebook users, we not only take into account the post count, but also the "Like" count of each post. This method yields greater numerical results, but still relatively small compared to Twitter mentions. In Twitter we counted the mentions of either the Reddit post, or of the content in its respective domain. Finally, in order to present our results in a consistent format between different OSNs, we address

---

[1] http://amix.dk/blog/post/19588.

all kinds of viewership count as "Units of Interest" (UoI). As such, a single Unit of Interest is equal to one content view in its domain (ImgUr or YouTube), one vote in Reddit, one mention in Twitter or one mention/like in Facebook.

During August and September of 2013, we scrapped two categories of Reddit (subreddits), named "new" and "rising", in an almost hourly-basis. The selection of these two categories was two-fold. Firstly, because we focus on diffusion of newly created content, and secondly, because in both Twitter and Facebook APIs only recent posts can be accessed in their entirety. In both selected subreddits, content is refreshed every 2 min. During the 60 days of our scraping, almost 1 million posts were obtained and further analysed.

These posts are separated into several topics such as "pictures", "gaming", "funny", "news", "videos", "music", etc. As mentioned, not all of them were used in our research. Out of more than 950.000 posts in total, nearly 102.400 met our domain scraping criteria, belonging to either ImgUr or YouTube. Each post was analysed every one hour (in most cases in a less frequent rate), in order to measure the accumulated "Units of Interest" in their hosting domains, Twitter, Facebook and Reddit.

Additionally, in order to discard content that is not gaining attention rapidly, we employed a simple rule (mentioned hereafter as check criterion). In this rule, we examined if "Units of Interest" in Reddit are doubled (in absolute values) on every check, for the first 4 checks after the post creation. We found out that only a small percentage of total posts reached such high viewership counts within such a short time span. Specifically, only 0.66 % of the tested posts passed this UoI check criterion among our dataset (682 out of nearly 102.400 posts).

3 Results

In this section, we present the results derived from our scraping procedure and the respective analysis. Data is separated based on their topic, subreddit category and the domain they are hosted in. So "new" and "rising" in every chart denotes the corresponding (subreddit) category, while ImgUr and YouTube defines the hosting domain. Reddit topics of posts are "AdviceAnimals", "Aww", "Eathpon", "Funny", "Gaming", "Gifs", "Movies", "Music", "Pics", "TIL", "Videos" and "WTF".

3.1 Posts and Counters

An important remark in our analysis was that "rising" category contained less posts linking to ImgUr and YouTube, compared to "new" category. This is perhaps due to the fact that more news and current events usually gain attention in a short timeframe, thus featured in "rising" subreddit. In total, we found nearly 45.000 ImgUr and YouTube posts in "rising" category and nearly 70.000 in "new" category. More specifically, the posts of the "rising" category revealed 40.966 links to ImgUr and 3.084 links to YouTube. Similarly, the distribution for posts of "new" category was 51.984 and 6.366 respectively. We also observed that "new" subreddit content is more prone to become viral, compared to content in "rising" subreddit. Content featured in "new" subreddit was twice as likely to pass our UoI check, while content in "rising" category presented a higher initial UoI count, but fell short on our criterion (of at least double UoI). Out of 40.966 posts linking to ImgUr in "rising" subreddit, only 200 surpassed our check criterion (0.48 %). As for posts linking to YouTube, out of 3.084 posts in total, only 14 went through our check (0.45 %). On the other hand, in "new" subreddit, out of the 51.984 posts that linked to ImgUr, 431 doubled their UoI in 4 subsequent checks (0.82 %). Similarly, the number of posts that linked to YouTube and successfully passed our UoI criterion, was 37 out of 6.366 (0.58 %).

We must note here that our UoI criterion should not be considered as a virality validation, yet it provides strong evidence that enough viewers, within a small time-frame, have viewed the analyzed posts and the interest is not diminishing. Among 682 highly viewed posts, 631 were linked to ImgUr and 51 were linked to YouTube. The topics spread, according to the subreddit categories and the employed social platforms, are illustrated in Fig. 1 and Table 1.

Table 1. Number of posts per topic (after the check criterion)

Topic	Rising category		New category	
	ImgUr	YouTube	ImgUr	YouTube
AdviceAnimals	27	0	73	0
Aww	18	0	38	0
Eathpon	2	0	5	0
Funny	84	0	158	0
Gaming	25	0	69	0
Gifs	4	0	8	0
Movies	3	2	5	2
Music	0	1	0	3
Pics	29	0	56	0
TIL	0	1	0	1
Videos	0	10	0	29
WTF	8	0	19	2
Total	**200**	**14**	**431**	**37**

Prior to discussing Fig. 1, let us examine the topic titles. As mentioned in [9, 10], positive and entertaining content was found as the most frequently shared topic. In our case, we could label "AdviceAnimals", "Funny" and "WTF topics", as entertaining content. "Aww" and "Eathpon" can be considered as containing emotive content, as described in [7]. "TIL" is mainly informative, while "Pics" and "Videos" characterise various content. Finally, "Gaming", "Movies" and "Music" contain user-centric and specific entertainment content.

As mentioned, entertaining and positive content is shared more frequently than anything else. Although provocative and controversial content can be created within Reddit and ImgUr, it rarely gets enough votes to appear in the front page. Most of the time, they appear in the form of a "news" or "TIL" post. The number of "gaming" posts that passed our check criterion is descriptive of the interests of Reddit users, especially

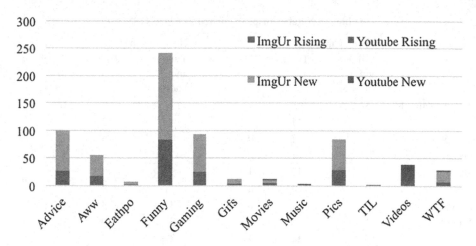

Fig. 1. Distribution of posts per topic (after the check criterion)

when compared to other forms of established entertainment, such as movies and music. Apart from the number of posts that passed our initial viewership test, we were strongly interested in their diffusion to Twitter and Facebook. Out of the 682 posts, 371 were mentioned in Twitter, 7 in Facebook and 172 in both OSNs. We observed that posts of "funny" topic are the most shared in both Twitter and Facebook. However, a closer look in the percentage of posts shared in these OSNs, reveals that "funny" is not included among the top-shared topics (see Fig. 2 and Table 2). Additionally, almost every category presents high Twitter and low Facebook sharing percentage (a direct result of the Facebook API limitations).

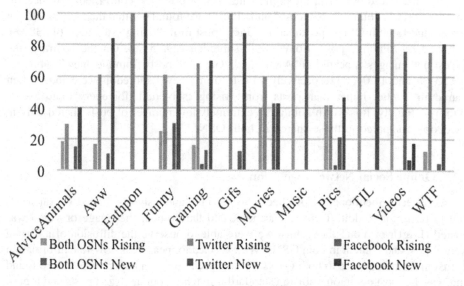

Fig. 2. Percentage of posts that diffused to OSNs

Table 2. Number of posts shared in tested OSNs

Topic	Rising category			New category		
	Twitter and Facebook	Twitter	Facebook	Twitter and Facebook	Twitter	Facebook
AdviceAnimals	5	8	0	11	29	0
Aww	3	11	0	4	32	0
Eathpon	0	2	0	0	5	0
Funny	21	51	0	47	87	0
Gaming	4	17	1	9	48	0
Gifs	0	4	0	1	7	0
Movies	2	3	0	3	3	0
Music	1	0	0	3	0	0
Pics	12	12	1	12	26	0
TIL	1	0	0	0	1	0
Videos	9	0	0	22	2	5
WTF	1	6	0	1	17	0
Total	**59**	**114**	**2**	**113**	**257**	**5**

By further analysing the sharing percentage, we notice that almost all posts of "Music" and "TIL" categories are shared in both OSNs. However, the number of total viral posts in those categories is less than ten. The only categories that present a high number of viral posts diffusing to other OSNs in a percentage level close to 50 %, are "Videos" and "Movies". This confirms the positive attitude of Internet users towards multimedia content. "Eathpon" posts, with photographs from around the world were 100 % shared in Twitter.

As far as the topics with the highest number of posts are concerned ("AdviceAnimals", "Aww", "Funny", "Gaming" and "Pics"), we found out that the highest sharing percentage to both OSNs, pertained to "Pics" post from "rising" subreddit (41.38 %), followed by "Funny" posts from "new" subreddit (29.75 %). On the contrary, the lowest percentages appeared to "Aww" and "Gaming" posts from the "new" subreddit (10.53 % and 13.04 % respectively). Posts from "new" subreddit were more often shared in Twitter rather than posts from "rising" subreddit, for every topic except "Funny". Finally, it is worth noting the extremely low number of posts shared only in Facebook compared to those shared in both OSNs.

3.2 Online Social Network Diffusion

As we already mentioned, UoI checks were simultaneously conducted on (at least) hourly-basis for Reddit, Twitter, Facebook and the domain the image or video was hosted (ImgUr or YouTube). Thus, we were able to observe the diffusion of a certain Reddit post and content in both OSNs. We expected to measure a slow-rate information diffusion from its source to both OSNs. In fact, such diffusion pattern was indeed found and was the most common diffusion standard throughout our analyzed posts and topics.

For evaluation purposes we use the mean values for every topic and for each subreddit. When the mean value of OSN diffusion is calculated, we do not take into consideration the posts that presented zero UoI variance in both OSNs. In other words, in our analysis we use the mean values of the posts that presented at least some variance in their UoI.

The time interval between subsequent checks performed in the tested domains (Reddit, ImgUr or YouTube, Twitter and Facebook) is at least one hour and the first check of every post has zero UoI. Each post is monitored for 7 days, yet we noticed that after 14 checks, the interest (in terms of UoI variation) declines significantly. The mean number of checks was 65 per post, while the 14th check happens within a 24-h period from the creation of the post. After the 14th check, we measured that the percentage level of UoI variation is lower than 0.1 %.

Furthermore, as we mentioned before, all posts are filtered to those that manage to double their UoI on Reddit in an hourly basis, for a 4 h timeframe. Consequently, every post we analyse presents high Reddit UoI variance for the first 5 checks, but only few of them present higher levels of variance after that point. As far as our OSN data scraping is concerned, we only had access on information from the public API of Facebook, while on Twitter we can only check messages within a timespan of a week, due to Twitter API limitations.

The most common pattern observed, corresponds to "AdviceAnimals" posts from the ImgUr domain in the "rising" subreddit. Domain UoI are growing at a high rate, concurrently with Reddit. Twitter is following with relatively small level of interest, while Facebook shows a delayed and low interest. Similar patterns appeared in several other categories; while in most of the cases Facebook presented nearly zero level of interest. This specific pattern was the most common in our research and appeared in 14 out of 18 ImgUr topics. Topics such as "AdviceAnimals", "Aww, "Funny", "Eathpon", "Gif" "Pics" and "WTF", followed this pattern - in both "rising" and "new" subreddits. However in both "Gif" categories, interest variation in Reddit is slightly higher than Domain.[2]

This is a good evidence that the most common diffusion flow of Reddit content, to the tested OSNs. Content hosted in the parent Domain is visible from many external sources and rapidly accumulates interest, whereas Reddit posts grow in the same time with a lower UoI count variance. In our tested OSNs, firstly Twitter increases its - initially high- UoI, presenting low variance, in contrast with Facebook where its UoI grow later with lower initial numbers and with very low variance.

Another interesting pattern was observed in "Movies" topic, in both subreddits. On every monitored post, we noticed interest spikes and, then sudden decreases in the UoI of all tested social media simultaneously, within few hours. This is mainly because the content shared is usually time sensitive (e.g. new trailers or news for upcoming movies). In other words, such posts seem not to be so persistent, since they do not interest users for long periods, but they rapidly diffuse to the tested OSNs. The concept of persistence in our analysis has to do with the ability of a post to retain interest for long periods of time, thus presenting positive UoI variation throughout that period.

---

[2] Every observed pattern can be found, in the appendix of a draft version of this paper, at http://arxiv.org/abs/1403.1486.

We should add that "Movies" and "Gaming" posts, as dealing with two of the most popular forms of entertainment, present the highest diffusion levels through OSNs. Posts about movies are generally diffusing faster, but gaming posts appeared to be more persistent.

Interestingly enough, in YouTube content, we encountered completely different diffusion patterns. In most cases, domain UoI was not seriously affected by the increased interest in OSNs and Reddit. This is mainly because shared content in YouTube is not usually a newly created video, but an instance of a video that existed for a long time and becomes mildly popular in time. In our evaluation, the videos under study presented a very high initial UoI count, which resulted in a low UoI variance. Apart from that, we observed high UoI variance in Reddit and Twitter, low UoI variance in Facebook, and practically zero UoI variance in the tested domain.

4 Discussion

Our analysis verified many observations of previous researches, mainly in respect to the micro and macro effects of information flows [1, 2, 17]. More specifically, a single post (micro effect) in the parent domain connected with a post in Reddit, starts to accumulate views (macro effect) up to a point where the information hops to OSNs (first in Twitter and then in Facebook) flowing through individuals, while eventually the interest dies off. Positive content is confirmed to be the mostly shared content in OSNs, as mentioned in [7, 10, 10]. Similarly to [12], we found out that a Reddit post is mostly popular within the first hours after its creation. This effect is also enhanced by the classification method of Reddit, where new posts need fewer votes (compared to old posts) to move to the first page.

In addition, we have observed that the most shared posts are of positive and entertaining content, also seen in [9, 10]. These categories, would include post from topics such as "AdviceAnimals", "Funny" and "WTF topics, while we also identified emotive posts, as described in [7], in topics such as "Aww" and "Eathpon". Unfortunately, not enough viral posts of such content were found, in order to safely identify their diffusion model. "Gaming", "Movies" and "Music" contain user-centric and very specific entertainment content, with low post appearance but great viral to total posts ratio, while, "TIL" is mainly informative and rarely used in posts linking to either ImgUr or Youtube.

Figure 3 illustrates the information flow scheme of the posts diffused to OSNs, according to our proposed method. Content creation in ImgUr is always tied to the respective post in Reddit occurring in t_0. Moreover, after approximately 3 h, links to ImgUr or Reddit are shared in Twitter. Finally, after nearly 12 h, the same links appear in public posts of Facebook. This results in the following user interest distribution: for each Facebook view or like, we have 8 Twitter posts, 19.231 Reddit votes and 426.656 views on ImgUr, which is the hosting domain. This reveals that ImgUr UoI are 22 times the UoI of Reddit. This is due to the fact that not every user votes on a post and we only count up and down votes of posts as user actions similar to views. Additionally, another factor is the large number of external sources that link directly to the hosting domain. Furthermore, total Reddit votes were found to be 2.403 more than the

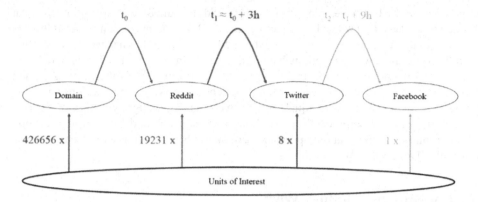

Fig. 3. Diffusion time and UoI allotment for ImgUr content of both subreddits

number of Twitter mentions, which is significantly lower than Domain to Reddit views ratio. Although these are mean values, views ratio (Domain to Reddit, Reddit to Twitter etc.) dispersion was fairly low.

Similarly, Fig. 4 illustrates the respective information flow for the YouTube case. However, t_0 does not correspond to the time of creation in YouTube, but instead is the time at which the post in Reddit appears. In one hand, we found out that Reddit posts with content linking in YouTube are rarely created at the same time as the video itself, since the video achieves a high number of viewers, far after its initial "viral" period. On the other hand, the first post in Twitter and Facebook appears much faster (approximately 2 and 3 h after the Reddit post respectively). For each Facebook view or like, we measured 9 Twitter mentions, 2.162 Reddit votes and almost 1.7 million YouTube views. This difference is because most videos, when used in Reddit posts, are already widely known.

Of course, these figures highlight the analysis of data from our tested domains and OSNs, during our experimentations. However, if we used a slightly different method, results would be significantly different. For example, if we would calculate the

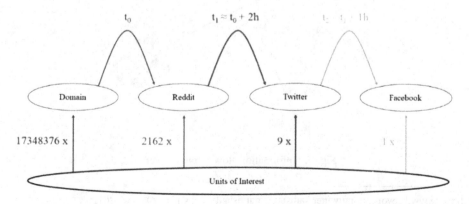

Fig. 4. Diffusion time and UoI allotment for YouTube content of both subreddits

exposure on both OSNs, UoI allotment would be smoother. According to "An Exhaustive Study of Twitter Users Across the World",[3] the mean number of followers in an average Twitter user has been estimated equal to 208. That would mean that Reddit votes and Twitter mentions having a ratio of almost 1 in YouTube content and 0.1 in ImgUr content (down from 240 and 2.403, respectively). Furthermore, if we add the mean number of friends in an average Facebook account, which according to the "Anatomy of Facebook"[4] is equal to 190, we would get slightly higher Twitter to Facebook ratio, but significantly lower Reddit to Facebook and Domain to Facebook ratios. Finally, the fact that only public Facebook can be scraped, is a big factor to those particular UoI allotments.

5   Conclusions – Future Work

Information starts within a domain and hops to various other OSNs within minutes. However, upon its initial diffusion to other networks, information flow within the domain does not halt - it just slows down. Positively emotive and entertainment focused content is the most "viral". Persistence was only found in gaming posts, while posts with movie content were the only ones that spread nearly simultaneously to every domain and OSN.

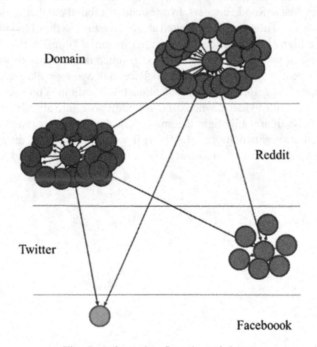

Fig. 5. Information flow through layers

[3] http://www.beevolve.com/twitter-statistics/, published results from October 2012.

[4] https://www.facebook.com/notes/facebook-data-team/anatomy-of-facebook/10150388519243859.

We should present a model of information flow, one that would accurately describe content sharing in modern OSNs. For example, let us consider a random Reddit post that follows a specific diffusion pattern, which has 30 domain UoI, 20 Reddit UoI, 7 Twitter UoI and 1 Facebook UoI. The UoI count used in this post, is obtained right after its first Facebook UoI appears, long before the 14th check. A single thread of information is spread into multiple concurrent users, spanning to various users of different OSNs simultaneously. Then, with a simple clustering the perception of layers (Fig. 5) is revealed. Information flows from the top layer towards the lower one, concurrently with the vertical flow where each layer expands.

Subsequently, we look forward into analysing a wider range of topics, in as many OSNs as we can. We believe that a predictive algorithm for viral posts will greatly benefit from our scraping findings. However, we would also benefit from such algorithms, because virality is hard to come by in modern OSNs.

In a different note of interest, we observed that various news posts in Reddit, have arisen to the first page before getting reported in dedicated news sites. As such, we could consider a different perspective, where OSNs could serve as a worldwide events station, similarly to what is proposed in [15]. Although we didn't discuss the great personalization options and properties of Reddit, we look forward into researching all these aspects of this modern OSN and its information flows in a future work of ours.

References

1. Lazarsfeld, P.F., Berelson, B., Gaudet, H.: The People's Choice: How the Voter Makes up his Mind in a Presidential Campaign. Columbia University Press, New York (1944)
2. Katz, E., Lazarsfeld, P.F.: Personal Influence. The Part Played by People in the Flow of Mass Communications. Transaction Publishers, New Jersey (1970)
3. Granovetter, M.S.: The strength of weak ties. Am. J. Sociol. **78**(6), 1360–1380 (1973)
4. Bakshy, E., Itamar, R., Cameron, M., Adamic, L.: The role of social net-works in information diffusion. In: Proceedings of the 21st International Conference on World Wide Web, pp. 519–528 (2012)
5. Rajyalakshmi, S., Amitabha, B., Soham, D., Tripathy, R.M.: Topic diffusion and emergence of virality in social networks (2012). arXiv:1202.2215
6. Jurvetson, S. Draper, T.: Viral Marketing: Viral Marketing Phenomenon Explained. DFJ Network News (1997)
7. Porter, L., Golan, G.J.: From subservient chickens to brawny men: a comparison of viral advertising to television advertising. J. Interact. Advertising **6**(2), 30–38 (2006)
8. Leskovec, J., Krause, A., Guestrin, C., Faloutsos, C., VanBriesen, J., Glance, N.: Cost-effective outbreak detection in networks. In: Proceedings of the 13th ACM SIGKDD International Conference on Knowledge Discovery and Data Mining, pp. 420–429 (2007)
9. Allsop, D.T., Bassett, B.R., Hoskins, J.A.: Word-of-Mouth research: principles and applications. J. Advertising Res. **47**(4), 398–411 (2007)
10. Berger, J., Milkman, K.: Social transmission, emotion, and the virality of online content. Wharton research paper (2010)
11. Goyal, A., Bonchi, F., VS Lakshmanan, L.: Learning influence probabilities in social networks. In: Proceedings of the 3rd ACM International Conference on Web Search and Data Mining, pp. 241–250 (2010)

12. Ienco, D., Bonchi, F., Castillo, C.: The meme ranking problem: maximizing microblogging virality. In: Data Mining Workshops, pp. 328–335 (2010)
13. Sakaki, T., Okazaki, M., Matsuo, Y.: Earthquake shakes Twitter users: real-time event detection by social sensors. In: Proceedings of the 19th International Conference on World Wide Web, pp. 851–860 (2010)
14. Kwak, H., Lee, C., Park, H., Moon, S.: What is Twitter, a social network or a news media? In: Proceedings of the 19th International Conference on World Wide Web, pp. 591–600 (2010)
15. Rajyalakshmi, S., Bagchi, A., Das, S., Tripathy, R.M.: Topic diffusion and emergence of virality in social networks (2012). arXiv:1202.2215
16. Guille, A., Hacid, H.: A predictive model for the temporal dynamics of information diffusion in online social networks. In: Proceedings of the 21st International Conference Companion on World Wide Web, pp. 1145–1152 (2012)
17. Guille, A., Hacid, H., Favre, C.: Predicting the temporal dynamics of information diffusion in social networks (2013). arXiv:1302.5235

Generic Private Social Network
for Knowledge Management

Jiří Kubalík[1], Jaroslav Pokorný[2(✉)], Martin Vita[3], and Peter Vojtáš[2]

[1] Department of Cybernetics, Czech Technical University,
Prague, Czech Republic
kubalik@labe.felk.cvut.cz
[2] Faculty of Mathematics and Physics, Charles University,
Prague, Czech Republic
{pokorny,vojtas}@ksi.mff.cuni.cz
[3] NLP Centre, Faculty of Informatics, Masaryk University,
Brno, Czech Republic
info@martinvita.eu

Abstract. The main motivation of this paper is a support of knowledge management for small to medium enterprises (business). We present our tool sitIT.cz which was developed to support communication of IT specialists (both from academia and business) using public funding. The main message of this paper is that this tool is quite generic and can be used in different scenarios. Particularly significant is its use as a private social network for knowledge management in a company. Our system is quite rich on actors, knowledge classification schemes, search functionalities, and trust management.

Keywords: Social network · Knowledge management · Conceptual multigraph · Structured profile

1 Introduction

In today's world, popular online social networks represent a new class of information networks comparing to the traditional Web. Unlike the traditional Web, which is largely organized by content, online social networks embody users as first-class entities. Users join a network, publish their own content, and create links to other users in the network, e.g. friends, co-workers, projects, companies, etc. Social networking systems become de facto portals for both personal and commercial online interactions. Today's social networking portals offer also services like searching, news, and e-commerce services. An important part of many social networks is a possibility of advertising. It uses social networks to communicate and promote the benefits of products and services. Advertising strategies include direct advertising (via banners on social networking website, etc.) and advertising using an individual's network of friends, since people frequently make decisions based on output from their close group of users (e.g., friends). A significant use of social networks can be found in the hiring process. What is still missing is wide use of social networks for knowledge sharing inside companies.

© Springer International Publishing Switzerland 2015
B. Benatallah et al. (Eds.): WISE 2014, LNCS 9051, pp. 27–41, 2015.
DOI: 10.1007/978-3-319-20370-6_3

1.1   Categorization of Social Networks

The numbers of people involved in social networks are high. The numbers from 2014 talk about 1.35 billion monthly active users on Facebook and 284 million on Twitter. The Student Room has over 1.35 million members; Academia.edu involved nearly 16 million researchers.

The scope of social networks offers more options than well-known websites like Facebook, LinkedIn[1], or ResearchGate[2]. In 2008, M.G. White[3] distinguished seven major social network categories:

1. *Social connections* - focused on friends and family members connected by various associations. This category includes popular social networks like Facebook, Twitter, MySpace[4], and Google+[5].
2. *Multimedia sharing* - serving to share video and photography content online. Platforms like YouTube[6], Flickr[7], and Picasa[8] belong to this category.
3. *Professional social networks* - designed for professional forums serving to professionals with specific occupations or interests. We often talk also about *business networking communities* in this case. They include, e.g., LinkedIn, ResearchGate and Classroom 2.0[9].
4. *Informational communities* - using forums focused on answering to specialized everyday problems, e.g., HGTV Discussion Forums[10] (for home design improvement), Do-It-Yourself Community[11], etc.
5. *Educational networks* - for students and their collaborations on projects, interactions with professors and teachers via blogs and classroom forums, see, e.g., The Student Room, The Math Forum[12].
6. *Hobbies*. When people find a website based on their favorite hobby, they discover a whole community of people from around the world who share the same interests. Hobby-focused social networking sites include, e.g., Oh My Bloom[13] dedicated to gardening, and Sport Shouting[14] for sports fans.

---

[1] https://www.linkedin.com/.

[2] http://www.researchgate.net/.

[3] http://socialnetworking.lovetoknow.com/What_Types_of_Social_Networks_Exist.

[4] https://myspace.com/.

[5] https://plus.google.com/.

[6] https://www.youtube.com/.

[7] https://www.flickr.com/.

[8] http://picasa.google.com/.

[9] http://www.classroom20.com/.

[10] http://boards.hgtv.com/eve.

[11] http://www.diychatroom.com/.

[12] http://mathforum.org/students/.

[13] http://www.ohmybloom.com/.

[14] http://www.sportshouting.com/.

7. *Academic networks* - determined for researchers to share their research. For example, Acadamia.edu, and ResearchGate belong there.

So far the classification of M.G. White.

1.2 Professional and Enterprise Social Networks

Some social connection networks have received criticism[15] on a wide range of issues, including its treatment of its user's privacy, online privacy, child safety, hate speech, and the inability to terminate accounts without first manually deleting the content.

As a result, many companies removed their advertising from such sites because it was being displayed on the pages of individuals and groups they found controversial. This leads us to the point, that professional and business networks have to be studied and developed separately.

From our point of interest, a significant category of social networks is professional social networks. They are focused exclusively on business relationships and interactions. Perhaps the most known professional social network is LinkedIn. Indeed, 80 % of all jobs in United States filled through LinkedIn [2]. In professional social networks we can find services like analytics on profiles and papers, possibilities to follow other people active in a given field. They are usually managed from portals for science, research, and innovation. In some features these networks overlap with academic networks. A detailed analysis of ResearchGate, SciSpace[16], Epernicus[17], and ScienceStage[18] is presented in the work [11]. Here we have to mention also our implementation of a professional social network sitIT.cz we will deal in detail later.

The last category, which is not covered in M. White's list and which has appeared just recently, is commercial business software *Enterprise social networks*. To mention at least few, we refer to following representatives of this category: Coyo enterprise social network[19] and Jive social business software[20]. Another example is IBM Connection[21], a social network platform which helps improve knowledge sharing, decision-making and innovation. All of these are large scale, expensive solutions which are behind possibilities of a small to medium enterprise.

1.3 Social Networks and Knowledge Management

Professional and academic social networks contain also huge stored data which can be exploited as new resources to automatically derive valuable information for

---

[15] http://en.wikipedia.org/wiki/Criticism_of_Facebook.

[16] http://www.scispace.com/.

[17] http://www.epernicus.com/.

[18] http://sciencestage.com/.

[19] https://www.coyoapp.com/.

[20] www.jivesoftware.com/.

[21] http://www-03.ibm.com/software/products/cs/conn.

decision-making. In what follows, we will mention natural language processing approach to increase information for automated processing (e.g., from CV when applied for a job). Nevertheless not all information is written somewhere, some are in people's heads, memories, etc. A typical motivation example can be as follows:

A company is facing a communication problem with a banking system which is coded in Cobol. Is there any employer which is familiar with COBOL?

Or another example:

A new competitor emerged. Is there an employee which has some knowledge related to this?

So we argue that both social, professional and enterprise dimension are relevant for an enterprise social network. Both automated and human assisted knowledge management are important.

Sensitive information of companies is shared neither on the net nor in cloud. Mostly it is kept internally in e-mails and not keen to automate processing. Business oriented use of social networks is mostly limited to contact customers. Many large companies, as opposite to small and medium ones, public institutions and non-profit organizations have resources dedicated to internal knowledge management (KM) efforts, often as a part of their business strategy, information technology, or human resource management departments. Several consulting companies provide strategy and advice regarding KM to these organizations [1]. KM efforts typically focus on organizational objectives such as improved skills, performance, competitive advantage, innovation, sharing of lessons learned, integration, and continuous improvement of the organization [5]. These technologies are practically available only for large companies. The problem we would like to deal with is how to support KM for small to medium companies (enterprises, business, but also non-profit organizations). In Sect. 4 we present more statistical data in support of this claim.

1.4 SitIT Web Portal – a Professional Network Suitable for Knowledge Management

Within the SoSIReČR project[22] we developed sitIT Web portal[23] for a social network of ICT specialists in the regions of the Czech Republic [12, 14] serving for academic sphere, companies, students, and to the wider IT professional community. The portal is applicable both for professional and academic social networks. In this paper we will argue that it is also suitable for KM in small to medium enterprises. The main argument is that our network has functionality extended by features which make KM easier. The functionality differs from the others in at least the following ways:

- Unlike other existing Web portals oriented mainly on social connections between people such as LinkedIn or ResearchGate which operate with a single entity type, a User, and all other information is treated as a users' features, our portal offers

---

[22] http://www.strukturalni-fondy.cz/Programy-2007-2013/Tematickeoperacni-programy/OP-Vzdelavani-pro-konkurenceschopnost?lang=en-GB.

[23] https://www.sitit.cz/.

besides the standard User also other entity types such as Group, Project, Company, Offer/Demand, etc.

- sitIT uses so called *structured profiles* (SP) representing, e.g., a professional profile or a knowledge profile. The SP defines a hierarchically structured set of domain specific expertise. An important thing is that profiles of all entity types can be extended with these SPs defined for the specific domain. For example, an ACM (see ACM Computing Classification System[24]) professional profile from ICT community might look as {(D.2.1, 2), (D.2.4, 3), D.2.8, 1), (D.2.m, 5)}. Identifiers D.2.1, D.2.4, D.2.8, and D.2.m are associated to categories Requirements/Specifications, Software/Program Verification, Metrics/Measurement, and Miscellaneous, respectively. The numbers 2, 3, 1, and 5 can be interpreted as grades associated with topics.

1.5   Goal of the Paper

Because of the characteristics described in Sect. 1.3 and also certain application domain adaptability we have found that sitIT can be used for changing the way people within the business communicate with each other. In other words, sitIT could be used both as a social intranet and employee network. In this paper, we present principles of sitIT and attempt to propose and discuss possibilities how to use this network to KM, particularly in small and middle enterprises (SME).

The paper is organized as follows. Section 2 describes some basic notions. Section 3 provides more details about the sitIT portal including its conceptual schema expressed as a conceptual multigraph. Section 4 discusses a social network as platform for internal communication and knowledge sharing in SME company. Section 5 mentions shortly the architecture and implementation of the social network software. Finally, Sect. 6 contains conclusions and provides some suggestions for a future research.

2   Basic Notions

We start with the simplest model of a *social network*, e.g. when the network is represented by an undirected graph $G = (V, E)$, where V, $|V| = n$, is the nonempty set of nodes representing *actors* and E, $|E| = m$, is the set of edges representing the *relationships* among them. There is always an alternative to represent a social network by a directed graph, depending on whether actors' connections are symmetric or not. A more real model of social networks is based on the notion of *multigraph*, where more edges are allowed between two nodes. Such multigraph must have edges named.

Different social networks should be specified on a conceptual level, that specifies which actor and relationship types are implemented. For our purpose we will use typed multigraphs. This is motivated by conceptual modelling known from database area (object-oriented approach, ER modelling). To index class and relationship hierarchies we use a tree structure of sequences of natural numbers (in our case classes split into a

---

[24] http://www.acm.org/about/class.

small number of subclasses, hence e.g. 2212 is a subsequence of length 4 with entries 2, 2, 1, 2). Assume, we have a forest T of non-empty-sequences of natural numbers ordered by prefix relation (our trees grow top-down – $s < t$, means s is higher than t, if s is a prefix of t). Further assume, we have a set A of *attributes*. In terminology of social networks we talk also about *features*. We consider a tuple $H = ((V_t, A_t), (E_{t,s}, A_{t,s}): s, t \in T))$. Here V_t's are different *actor types* (classes, entities) and $A_t \subseteq A$ are their attributes. $E_{t,s}$'s are edges from V_t's to V_s's, i.e. *relationship types* and $A_{t,s} \subseteq A$ are their attributes. We assume, for each $s < t$, s, $t \in T$ there is a distinguished relation *sub-ClassOf$_{t,s}$* $\in E_{t,s}$ representing an edge in associated ISA hierarchy and $U \in A$ a distinguished feature ($U \in A_s$ denotes V_s is a union of immediate successors).

A tuple H is called a *conceptual multigraph* if it preserves inheritance:

- for every $s < t$ we have $A_s \setminus \{U\} \subseteq A_t$,
- for every $s < s_1$, $t < t_1$ we have $A_{s,t} \subseteq A_{s1,t1}$ and $E_{s,t} \subseteq E_{s1,t1}$.

Note, $V_1,..., V_k$ for $1,...k \in N$ represent different actors superclasses.

Assume, H is a conceptual multigraph and for each $A \in A$ there is D_A domain of A. A *multiactor social network* G_H is an instantiation of H if there is a function defining extensions of actor types (objects) and relational types. Each actor type V_t has assigned an extension (objects) $Ext(V_t)$. If V_t subClassOf V_s, then $Ext(V_t) \subseteq Ext(V_s)$. Extension of relationship type $E_{t,s}$ is a subset of $Ext(V_t) \times Ext(V_s) \times E_{t,s}$, i.e. edges have names from $E_{t,s}$. For example, a triple $(v_1, v_2, e) \in Ext(V_t) \times Ext(V_s) \times E_{t,s}$ is interpreted as an named relationship, an edge from v_1 to v_2 tagged e. This is same as in the RDF data, where v_1 is the subject, v_2 is the object and e is the property.

In other words, the extensions of a conceptual multigraph enable to express an associated social network as a multigraph for H. Its nodes are actors and its edges represent relationships. Two actors can be connected by more edges of different types. Each actor contained in an ISA-hierarchy is represented only by one node in the multigraph.

Extension also assigns each object (actor, relationship) attribute values from respective *domain* appropriately to A_s, $A_{s,t}$. We will suppose only single-valued attributes here. In practice, a multi-valued attribute is a more real case, e.g. hobby = {reading, chess, music}. Then, e.g. the employee's expertise will be expressed by a set of topics (categories) not as value of a multivalued attribute, but via relationships of a special type. Also each feature could be optionally an aggregation of single-valued attributes (e.g. date of birth = [day, month, year]).

Users are often using profiles of some actors in today's online social networks, consisting of attributes like geographic location, interests, and schools attended. Such profile information is used as a basis for grouping users, for sharing content, and for recommending or introducing people who would likely benefit from direct interaction. To take *actors' profiles* into account, let $A_t \subseteq A$ (different actors will/can have different features) be the set of features describing the actors from V_t of the social network.

According to Sect. 1.3 a special profile case is an SP. It can be expressed, e.g., as a set of couples $\{(T_1, w_1),...,(T_m, w_m)\}$, where T_i are the terms (e.g., topics) that describe the actor and w_i denote the importance of T_i in describing the actor. In our system we call them *grades*. They enable to order results of a search by relevance.

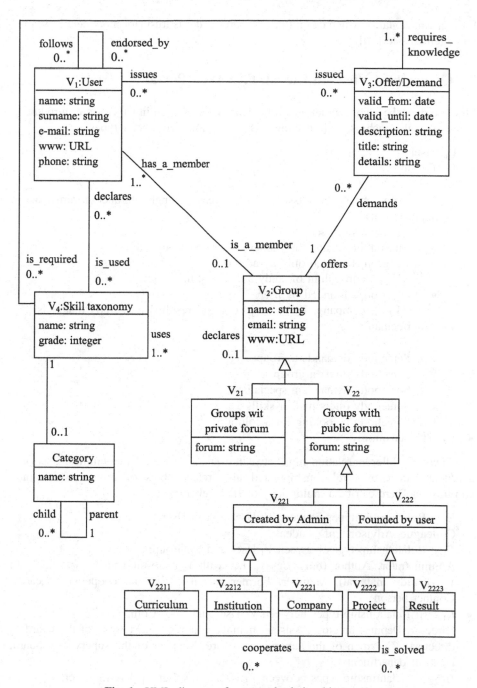

Fig. 1. UML diagram of actor and relationship types

Further functionality which can influence search order is trust (for more details on trust management see [10]).

3   Conceptual View on the sitIT.cz Web Portal

First we describe a conceptual view on social network used in sitIT portal introducing its actors, relationships, and attributes. There are four basic actor types:

- V_1: User
- V_2: Group

  - V_{21}: with private discussion forum (e.g., trough intranet forums or in management)
    - V_{211}: groups of users
  - V_{22}: with public (inside the framework) discussion forum
    - V_{221}: groups created only by admin
      - V_{2211}: curriculum of study and V_{2212}: institution
    - V_{222}: groups founded by user
      - V_{2221}: company, V_{2222}: project, V_{2223}: result, V_{2224}: study materials, ...
- V_3: Offer/demands

  - V_{31}: Somebody demands a group
  - V_{32}: Somebody offers a group
  - V_{33}: Somebody demands a specialist
  - V_{34}: Somebody offers his/her skills
  - V_{35}: Somebody is looking for a solution
- V_4: Skill taxonomy

There are different relationships between users, groups and other entities. Users can add/delete their own relationships and also relationships of groups which they administer. There can be a multiplicity of such relationships.

- $E_{1,1}$: Relationship types between V_1:User and V_1:User:
  Colleague, Advisor, PhD student
- $E_{1,2}$: Relationship types between V_1:User and V_2:Group:
  Administrator, Author (only $E_{1,2223}$, i.e. with V_{2223}:result and $E_{1,2224}$, i.e. with V_{2224}:study material), Member, Former member, External cooperator, Leader, Contact person
- $E_{1,2221}$: Relationship types between V_1:User and V_{2221}:Company:
  Director, Deputy director, Assistant manager, Employee, Member of the board of directors, Chairman of the supervisory board, Member of the supervisory board, Head of department
- $E_{1,2222}$: Relationship types between V_1:User and subgroup V_{2222}:Project:
  Coordinator, Project team member, Subteam leader
- $E_{2*,2221}$, $E_{2*,2222}$: Relationship types between all types of groups, Project, and Company:
  Cooperation

- $E_{1,3*}$: Relationship type of a User to Offer/Demand:
  Administrator
- $E_{1,4}$: Relationship type of a User to Skill taxonomy:
  Knows
- $E_{2,4}$: Relationship type of a Group to Skill taxonomy:
  Somebody in the group knows
- $E_{3,4}$: Relationship type of an Offer/Demand to Skill taxonomy:
  Requires knowledge
- *Features of the User* (also called *user profile*): Address, Education and training, Occupational experience, Contact, Domain knowledge, Current position, Web sources
- *Features of the Group* (also called *group profile*): Detailed description, Web sources, Contact person, Others, Key words, Abbreviations
- *Features of the Offer/Demand* (also called *Offer/Demand profile*): Detailed description, Web sources, Addresses, Others, Key words
- *Features of Skill taxonomy:* Name, Grade

In Fig. 1 we present UML version of a simplified conceptual multigraph used for implementation of sitIT. Only main relationships types are involved there. Attributes of relationship types are not described there. Also only partial sets of Actor's attributes are shown.

There are two SPs supported in the portal – *professional profile* and *knowledge profile*. The professional profile uses the ACM Classification as one of universally accepted standard classifications of ICT disciplines. Conceptually, the classification has a tree structure with general topics on upper layer and more specific topics on deeper layers. One can use this profile to express his/her expertise or subject of a project or focus of a research group by simply choosing relevant terms within the ACM classification tree and assigning a proper level of the expertise (see Sect. 1.3). It enables to formally express a focus of a given entity on different parts of the domain expertise classification. The power of SPs is their internal vector-based machine-readable representation. Having such information, the portal is able to offer more exact search results, better characterization of offers and demands in the network. For instance, a structured profile of the ICT specialist can be matched against the project requirements, the similarity between required skills for given position in companies, etc.

The knowledge profile, suggested by University of Economics in Prague, has a simple flat structure of 16 dimensions describing Software engineering, Data and information engineering, etc., on one side, and soft skills as ICT market knowledge, Sales and marketing or Law, on the other side. Unlike the ACM classification the knowledge profiles suite for different type of purposes. Using them, profiles representing study programs, classes, students, alumni, as well as working positions in companies can be described in terms of provided or required knowledge level in given areas.

An important thing is that the two mentioned SPs have been implemented into the sitIT portal just for the purposes of the social network of ICT specialists. However, any other SP can easily be proposed and implemented into the portal either for ICT or for other knowledge domain (just replace an associated XML file).

A particular problem of social networks is user's profiles matching required in several scenarios. One of them consists of linking data corresponding to two actors, particularly coupling a project and appropriate researchers, and searching for suitable job seekers based on an offer described as a professional profile [12]. A testing of the portal is summarized in [10].

4 Social Network as Platform for Internal Communication and Knowledge Sharing in SME Company

In this section we describe our main motivation for using sitIT portal as a tool for knowledge sharing.

There are several reasons to look for an internal solution of the problem. First is data security (see [6]). Second is the price of the solution. There are commercial tools for KM which are behind possibilities of a small to medium company. Here our system comes.

We would like to describe how sitIT can be used in a company. Main motivation is to use different classes with attributes and functionalities for company interests.

Assume we run our system in a company isolated from the rest of the world. The class company can be used to create a virtual model of a company of interest – and collect information about it.

4.1 Organized Enterprise Communication – Current State

In the SME segment we can observe a markedly stronger focus on the external communication than the internal. This fact can be illustrated on the ratio of companies that use applications for organized external communication, e.g., communication to (potential) customers, business partners, suppliers, etc., and the ratio of companies that use applications for smart internal communication and knowledge sharing, such as internal social networks or wiki type Webs, etc. In what follows, we illustrate this finding using data from European and Czech statistical office.

In Table 1, we describe distribution of European enterprises regarding various forms of usage of social media. For total percentage of enterprises using any form of organized communication, we show quartiles (values taken at regular 25 % intervals from the inverse of the cumulative distribution function of data). One of our main motivations is that our country is at the very end of the list. Moreover, in all countries, only a small fraction of enterprises uses these for exchange of views inside the company – this is one of the key elements of KM.

Figure 2 depicts usage of special types of media separately for different size of companies. Here we can see that situation of small enterprises is worst.

In the last Fig. 3, a finer classification of reasons of use of social media is given. We can see that external activities PR, questionnaires, customer-involved innovation. B2B collaboration, recruiting new employees – all are used in higher ration of Czech enterprises than internal exchange of opinions, etc.

Table 1. Organized communication in European countries – overview [3]

		Total	by type of social media				by reason of use		
			social networks	corporate blogs	sharing multimedia Web content	Wiki type Web	recruit new employees	exchange of views in the company
			As a percentage of the total number of enterprises in given country					
maximum	Netherlands	49.8	45.2	27.1	23.0	7.1	25.1	17.1
¾ quantile	Denmark	40.4	36.2	8.2	14.0	4.8	18.3	13.0
median	Spain=EU28	31.5	28.8	13.2	14.8	5.0	5.6	9.1
¼ quantile	Romania	18.9	17.2	3.3	5.9	1.6	6.9	6.7
minimum	Czech Republic	16.2	14.8	3.4	5.5	2.5	4.4	4.1

One of the main disadvantages of traditional forms of internal communication – based mainly on the email communication and/or mass mailing – is that the knowledge contained inside these messages is hardly accessible for others, to new team members for instance. Other difficulties are caused by missing meta-information related to data files on shared drives. Obviously, it is also relatively hard to measure the impact of these inefficiencies.

In the last years we can observe a dramatic positive impact of social media on internal communication in companies (see, e.g., [7] motivated by the book [13]). The communication is both vertical (i.e. between different levels of organizational

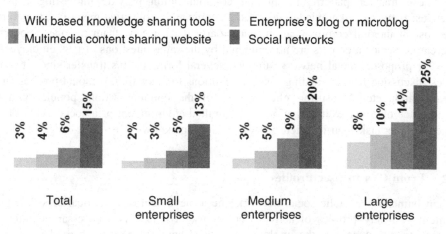

Fig. 2. Types of social media used by enterprises in 2013 (Source [3])

hierarchy, for example between CEOs and employees) and horizontal communication, (i.e., communication across different functional areas, such as sales and marketing). Companies even use social media to increase their speed of decision making.

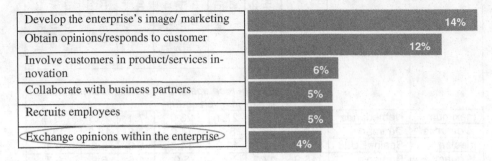

Develop the enterprise's image/ marketing	14%
Obtain opinions/responds to customer	12%
Involve customers in product/services in-novation	6%
Collaborate with business partners	5%
Recruits employees	5%
Exchange opinions within the enterprise	4%

Fig. 3. Reasons for the use of social media by enterprises (as a percentage of all enterprises in a given size and industry class (in %)) in 2013 (Source [3])

In companies in the knowledge based society era and quickly changing environment, there is a need for more sophisticated solutions that support efficient sharing of knowledge which is not so dependent on activities of relevant employees. In the last years we can see a progress in forms of internal communication that can be illustrated in the following shifts from traditional to modern forms [7]:

e-mail → discussion
mass mail → blog
word processor → wiki
shared disk drive → portal
company contact list → personal profiles/social networks

These transfer patterns in internal communication provide interesting consequences: they create knowledge nets and a "company's collective memory", therefore the cost of internal communication, particularly when a new team member appears, decreases. Senior members are not hindered by the same questions of new employees.

Our proposed social network supports several forms of this transfer since it provides discussion forums, adding text contributions functionality, personal profiles and their search, etc. Measuring effectiveness of the communication, popularity and importance of concrete information in the unified environment of a social network is much simpler task than in heterogeneous sources of knowledge.

4.2   From CVs to User Profiles

When launching a public social network, the achievement of a "critical mass" of the content – mainly profiles of active users or useful data – is a necessary condition leading to the success of the implemented social network. Due to internal rules and internal culture can be the process of filling in the empty social network completely different and more efficient – in contrast to internet environment, it can be done "on command".

As already mentioned, one of the keystones of a social network are the user profiles. Filling forms during the registration process in an internal social network is, of course, a time consuming activity. But most of these data is typically already stored in heterogeneous databases and collections of documents (CVs of employees on shared discs, internal information systems, etc.). Obviously, the CVs contain very relevant information for building the content of a "skill-oriented" social network (skills of each employee, work history – relationships to companies, work, etc.). These semi-structured data (CVs) can be parsed in order to extract named entities (company names, position names, educational institutions, etc.). This information extraction can be based upon using machine learning methods [15], see also [4].

Nowadays, there are several applications/web services – for example Extract![25] from Textkernel BV company – implementing these methods for CV parsing. The import of these extracted data belongs to implementation issues of the proposed social network.

5 Architecture and Implementation

The implementation of the sitIT portal is built on the Spring 3.0 library, which connects individual parts and realizes processing of HTTP requests (Spring MVC). The whole application is built using the Maven 3 system, which also manages binding of all external dependencies. The persistence layer is implemented using by standard means of SQL database and Java Persistence API. Extensions are implemented directly in Java. The structure of the database tables is automatically generated by the Hibernate library according to the entities implemented in Java, their dependencies and additional annotations in compliance with the JPA2 specification. The system incorporates 55 libraries under the following license types: Apache License 1.1, Apache License 2.0, BSD, BSD (3-clause), CC BY 3.0, CDDL 1.0, Common Public License 1.0, EPL 1.0, MIT License, LGPL 2.1.

SW requirements for installation of the application are Java Run Environment 1.6 or higher, Apache Tomcat 6 Web server (or any other supporting Java Servlets), PostgreSQL database version 8.4 or higher, Apache+PHP (for MyBB forum that realizes support for messaging and discussions). Of course, everything can be running behind a firewall.

The sitIT portal can be implemented for other than the ICT community as well or as a system supporting a KM in companies. It would require several changes to the source code such as renaming the actor types and accordingly renaming the attributes of the actor types and relationships and modifying texts in all dialog windows and messages. However, the functionality of the respective actor types and the respective relationships

---

[25] www.textkernel.com.

between actor types would stay unchanged. So, for example the actor type "company" can be used under a name "department" that would have the same functionality as it has implemented for the company (i.e., the list of attributes and relationships). Obviously, the skill taxonomies would have to be changed as well. Since the skill taxonomies (i.e., the ACM professional profile and the knowledge profile) are defined in an XML files, a new type of skill taxonomy can easily be defined just by replacing the current XML files with new ones.

6   Conclusion and Future Work

We have presented our software sitIT.cz which was developed to support communication of IT specialists (academic sphere, companies, students, and to the wider IT professional community). SiIT.cz is a non-commercial tool developed from public EU funding. We have tried to show that that this tool is quite generic and can be used in different scenarios. The portal is applicable both for professional and academic social networks and as an enterprise social network, particularly in medium companies.

SitIT functionality differs from the others in at least the following ways: our portal offers besides the standard User also other entity types such as Group, Project, Company, Offer/Demand, etc.; sitIT enables KM using SPs and weighted claims about skills. Specific search functionality enables search and output is ordered by relevance, weights, and trust.

Application domain adaptability makes our system generic. The main goal is changing the way people within the business communicate with each other. SitIT can be used both as a social extranet and company social intranet.

Concerning future work, we have already started to clone the English version. In our academic research we plan to use our portal as an experimental tool for testing different hypotheses about social network which cannot be tested on large social network which are not under our control. The main problem which is still present is how to attract users to use a new network. Main possibilities for this we see in well-organized licensed communities and companies.

In future work, we would like to provide a more detailed comparison with commercial business software Enterprise Social Networks e.g. Coyo, Jive and IBM Connection, just to mention a few. We would like to combine methods of [7] and [8] to improve analytics on network data.

Acknowledgments. This paper has been partially supported by the grant of GACR No. P103/13/08195S and Prvouk P-46.

References

1. Addicot, R., McGivern, G., Ferlie, E.: Networks, organizational learning and knowledge management: NHS cancer networks. Pub. Money Manag. **26**(2), 87–94 (2006)

2. Ahmed, E.B., Nabli, A., Gargouri, F.: Group extraction from professional social network using a new semi-supervised hierarchical clustering. Knowl. Inf. Syst. **40**, 29–47 (2013)
3. Cesky statisticky urad: Information technologies in the business sector. XSL file 3, Table 6, pdf file ICT in enterprises of individual EU countries – results for January 2013. http://www.czso.cz/csu/redakce.nsf/i/podnikatelsky_sektor, English version. http://www.czso.cz/csu/2014edicniplan.nsf/engt/E4003C6C12/$File/061005-14_D.pdf
4. Dedek, J., Vojtáš, P., Vomlelová, M.: Fuzzy ILP classification of web reports after linguistic text mining. Inf. Process. Manag. **48**(3), 438–450 (2012)
5. Gupta, J., Sharma, S. (eds.): Creating Knowledge Based Organizations. Idea Group Publishing, Boston (2004)
6. Hardesty, L.: Who's using your data? New Web technology would let you track how your private data is used online. MIT News 13 (2014)
7. Hora, P., Mrázek, M.: Era of symbolic-analytical services. IDG CIO Business World.cz, International Data Group (2009) (in Czech)
8. Horváth, T., Vojtáš, P.: Induction of fuzzy and annotated logic programs. In: Muggleton, S.H., Otero, R., Tamaddoni-Nezhad, A. (eds.) ILP 2006. LNCS (LNAI), vol. 4455, pp. 260–274. Springer, Heidelberg (2007)
9. Kazienko, P.: Relational classification for uniplex and multilayer social networks. In: Keynote talk at IWCSN International Workshop on Computational Social Networks Within WISE 2014 - The 15th International Conference on Web Information System Engineering, Thessaloniki, Greece, 12–14 October 2014
10. Kopecký, M., Pokorný, J., Vojtáš, P., Kubalík, J., Matoušek, K., Maryška, M., Novotný, O., Peška, L.: Testing and Evaluating Software in a Social Network Creating Baseline Knowledge. Frontiers in Artificial Intelligence and Applications, vol. 251, pp. 127–141. IOS Press, Amsterdam (2013)
11. Kubalík, K., Matoušek, K., Doležal, J., Nečaský, M.: Analysis of portal for social network of IT professionals. J. Syst. Integr. **2**(1), 21–28 (2011)
12. Pokorný, J.: Profiles in professional social networks. In: Linger, H.; Fisher, J.; Barnden, A.; Barry, C.; Lang, M.; Schneider, C. (eds.) Building Sustainable Information Systems, pp. 387–399. Springer, New York (2013)
13. Reich, R.B.: The Work of Nations: Preparing Ourselves for 21st Century Capitalism. Vintage, New York (1992)
14. Vojtáš, P., Pokorný, J., Skopal, T., Nečaský, M., Matoušek, K., Kubalík, J., Novotný, O., Maryška, M.: SoSIReČR – IT professional social network. In: Abraham, A., Corchado, E., Alhaj, R., Snasel, V. (eds.) Proceedings of 2011 International Conference on Computational Aspects of Social Networks (CASoN), October 19–21, Salamanca, pp. 108–113. IEEE press, Piscataway (2011)
15. Rotaru, M.: Textkernel NL from tokens to text entities: line-based parsing of resumes using conditional random fields. In: 21st Meeting of Computational Linguistic in the Netherlands, Ghent, p. 46 (2011)

Analysis of Event Logs: Behavioral Graphs

Kateřina Slaninová[1][(✉)], Dominik Vymětal[1], and Jan Martinovič[2]

[1] School of Business Administration in Karviná, Silesian University in Opava,
Univerzitnínáměstí 1934/3, Karviná, Czech Republic
{slaninova,vymetal}@opf.slu.cz

[2] Department of Computer Science, FEECS, VŠB - Technical University of Ostrava,
17. Listopadu 15/2172, 708 33 Ostrava-poruba, Czech Republic
jan.martinovic@vsb.cz

Abstract. Analysis of event logs is very important discipline used for the evaluation of performance and control-flow issues within the systems. This type of analysis is typically used in process mining sphere, where information systems, for example workflow management systems, enterprise resource planning systems, customer relationship management, supply chain management systems, and business to business systems record transactions and executed activities in a systematic way. Social network analysis takes part of process mining techniques, focused on activity performers, on users. The authors present a new approach to analysis of user behavior in the systems. The approach allows to find behavioral patterns and to find groups of users with similar behavior. An observer can obtain relations between the users on the basis of their similar behavior. The visualization of relations between the users is then presented by so called behavioral graphs. The approach was tested for event log analysis of a virtual company model developed as a multi-agent system by modeling environment MAREA.

Keywords: Business process modeling · Business process analysis · Complex networks · User behavior · Behavioral patterns · Behavioral graphs · MAREA

1 Introduction

Modern applications like information systems, enterprise systems or e-commerce systems record transactions and executed activities in a systematic way. Due to this reason, they produce a large amount of data, often systematically recorded into databases or logs. Such information, if presented in a transparent way, can be used as support for the administration of systems, for system optimization, for personalization in recommended systems, as support in decision making for management, or in other areas (e.g. marketing campaigns).

Analysis of event logs is a very important discipline used for the extraction of valuable information from log files. This type of analysis is typically used in process mining sphere, where information systems, for example workflow management systems (WFM), enterprise resource planning systems (ERP),

© Springer International Publishing Switzerland 2015
B. Benatallah et al. (Eds.): WISE 2014, LNCS 9051, pp. 42–56, 2015.
DOI: 10.1007/978-3-319-20370-6_4

customer relationship management (CRM), supply chain management systems (SCM), and business to business systems (B2B) systems, record transactions and executed activities in a systematic way. Process mining techniques typically focus on performance and control-flow issues. A standard log file usually consists of records with information about executed events that have occurred in the system. These records may contain various attributes such as timestamp (date and time when the event happened), an originator, the type of event and additional information. If an originator of such event is a person, we can extract the relevant records and obtain information about his/her behavior. Social network analysis then takes part of process mining techniques, focused on activity performers, on users.

Process mining techniques focused on performers' activities have been developed several years yet. For example knowledge based semantification of business communications is presented in [15]. Thus, fundamental approaches related to social network analysis are mentioned in Sect. 3. The main motivation of the presented research is to find a new type of relation between the users for the analysis of users' behavior in the system. The paper is focused on REA based simulation process log, see Sect. 4.1, and proposes a new type of social network graph, *Behavioral graph*, which represents the relations between the users on the basis of their occurrence in cases (not in particular transactions) in the system. Such approach is useful especially if the analysis of business processes is focused on the model structure, when it is important to know which types of processes are used in the system and what users execute the activities within these processes. The approach allows to find behavioral patterns and to find groups of users with similar behavior. An observer can obtain relations between the users on the basis of their similar behavior. The visualization of relations between the users is then presented by so called behavioral graphs. The approach was tested for event log analysis of a virtual company model. The analysis was used for the model verification.

The paper is organized as follows. Section 2 presents an introduction to business process modeling and simulation. Section 3 is focused on typical methods of social network analysis from event logs. The new approach to analysis of user behavior is presented in Sect. 4. Section 5 describes the application of new approach to analysis of event logs from a virtual company model developed as a multi-agent system by modeling environment MAREA. Finally, Sect. 6 with conclusions closes the paper.

2 Business Process Modeling and Simulation

Due to globalization bringing about rapid changes in the market environment, new decision support systems tools garner much attention both by researches and in the industry. Some of these tools comprise modeling and simulation methods. The reason for this is that the management of business companies try to increase the flexibility of business processes by means of decisions, which often does not allow to foresee the impacts of their decisions due to the complexity or time schedule.

This is where the modeling and simulations find their place. Simulations supporting decision support systems are typically based on business process modeling treated by many researchers [3,4,6,12,18,23]. While analytical modeling approaches are based mostly on the mathematical theories [2,9,13] most approaches are based on experimental simulations using various generic business process models.

Most of business process modeling methods use the process and control flow paradigm [1,2,11]. Alternative enterprise modeling methods are value chain oriented models treating value flows as a complement to process control flow modeling. Value chain modeling idea, originally based on well-known Porter's model, concentrates on the value flows both inside the enterprise and on the value exchange with the environment. Currently, the most popular value chain enterprise methodologies are e3-value [8], and the REA (Resources, Events, Agents) ontology [5,7,10,14]. REA was proposed by McCarthy with the aim to resolve issues specific to the double-entry bookkeeping [18]. It was gradually expanded upon by Geerts and McCarthy into the enterprise ontology. It is generally accepted that the REA concept has a potential to be implemented within the design of new ERP systems and recently also to auditing [26].

However, typical business process and value chain modeling methods tend to omit the real situation within the business companies and in the market environment. Namely, there are also social interaction forces to be taken into consideration during the modeling and simulation of business processes. Social behavior elements may comprise negotiation, management specific methods, market disturbances and others. In such cases, some local intelligence within a business process model can be of advantage. This challenges lead to a new software modeling paradigm - the multi-agent modeling approach. By definition, software agents can act to some extent independently and use their own targets, aims and cooperation in order to achieve the global target of the modeled system [27].

2.1   Verification

When modeling and simulating complex business processes, the model verification can be a very challenging task. At least two main problem areas have to be taken into the verification process:

- The correspondence between the real data acquired from the real company processes and the simulation outputs,
- The model structure itself.

The first verification task is connected mainly with various real input and output data pre-processing needed for model parametrization and control in order to achieve sufficient quality of the model outputs allowing for various predictions. The second verification problem represents the core of the verification itself. No correspondence of real and model output data can be achieved without a correct model structure consisting not only of the 'static' structures (the modeled structure items) but also of correct processes, their interrelations and roles played by the process performers. The question arises, how to ensure this verification. The third paradigm of the business process modeling can be advantageous here, namely the principle of process mining introduced by van der Aalst et al. [19,22]. This type of data mining is based on analysis of process log files. Process mining techniques allow for the discovery of information usually not apparent from the log files.

The most prominent process mining tool is the open source software ProM, developed by Eindhoven University of Technology[1]. ProM uses special formatted process log files as an input and delivers various types of control flow and social network diagrams such as Petri nets, Working together, Subcontracting and other social networks as outputs. Hence, the ProM outputs can be looked upon as ideal model structure verification tools. The Petri nets, generated from the model log files can be used for general model structure verification, while the social network diagrams obtained from the analysis can help to verify and correct the actual process structure and process participant relations.

The motivation of presented research is to find new types of networks using pro-cess log (and new type of output presentation) using file analysis and to compare the results with the ProM outputs. As an input file for the comparison, the business company simulation outputs are used, that was generated by the company simulation work-bench MAREA presented in several papers before [16,24,25].

3   Social Networks Derived from Event Logs

Process mining is a discipline focused on the extraction of information about processes from event (or transaction) logs [21]. Event logs contain events, each event refers to an activity (activity is a step in the process), each event refers to a case (i.e., a process instance), each event refers to an originator, and events are totally ordered. An event log is then a collection of events.

Techniques, generally known as organizational mining, are focused on the organizational perspective of process mining. Alongside typical information such as event, case, activity or the time when an event was performed, we can also find information about the originator (device, resource, or person) who initiated the event (activity). These events from the log file can be projected onto their resource and activity attributes. By using this approach, we can learn about people, machines, organizational structures (roles, departments), work distribution and work patterns.

Social network analysis is one of many techniques used in organizational mining [20]. Event logs with attributes describing person as an originator are used in order to either discover real process work flow models of the organization or just generally allow us to construct models that explain some aspects of an individual's behavior. Using principles from workflow management and social network analysis, it is possible to discover and analyze social networks.

---

[1] For more information, see http://www.processmining.org/.

Social networks are represented by graphs $G(V, E, w)$, where vertices (nodes) V relate to the organizational entities (persons, groups of persons) within organizational mining. In some cases, the nodes can be assigned multiple organizational entities such as roles, groups or departments. Edges E (ties) in a social network correspond to relationships between such organizational entities. Social networks can be weighted, as both nodes and ties can have their weights w assigned to represent their importance in the network or the intensity of the relation.

3.1   Relationship Determination from Event Logs

Relationship between the users derived from event logs can be set from various points of view, and therefore, the weight can be defined by several ways. According to van der Aalst [21], the weight is usually determined on the basis of (possible) causality (handover of work, subcontracting), joint cases, joint activities, or special event types. Therefore, a resulted graph of social network with each type of weight has different meaning.

Weight determined by (possible) causality represents how work flows among users within particular cases. As an example, we can mention handover of work, which represents handover from user u_i to user u_j. Another one is subcontracting, which is described by number of times user u_j executed an activity in-between two activities executed by user u_i. Both examples have also their modifications. The visual representation of such relation type can be for example by Subcontracting graph.

Relation weight determined by joint cases ignores causal dependencies in a case (transaction). It is only based on a frequency of activities that users performed in a common case (transaction). The more frequent is common work of both users on cases, the stronger the relationship between them is. We can mention Working together graph as an example of such type of relation.

Social networks, respectively graphs representing social networks can be analyzed by social network analysis tools, for example GraphViz, Gephi, UCINET etc. However, the derivation of relations from event logs is a very specific problem, which can be solved only by specialized tools. Here we must mention for example MiSoN, a tool by Song, Aalst, and Reijers, which contains the derivation of all the previously mentioned types of graphs from event logs (now a plug-in of ProM software).

4   New Approach to Analysis from Event Logs

As mentioned in Sect. 2.1, the motivation of presented research is to find a new type of relation between the users. The new type of relation is based on users' behavior in the system. It is focused not only on the common work on the transactions, but on the similar working habits, resp. on similar behavioral patterns they performed in the system.

A detailed process of the proposed approach was described in our previous work [17]. Let $u_i \in U$ be a set of users, so that $i = 1, 2, \ldots, n$, where n is number of users u_i. Then, transactions (traces) are sequences of events $\sigma_{ij} = \langle e_{ij1}, e_{ij2}, \ldots, e_{ijm_j} \rangle$ executed by the user u_i in the system, where $j = 1, 2, \ldots, p_i$ represents type of the sequence, and m_j is length of j-th sequence. Thus, set $S_i = \{\sigma_{i1}, \sigma_{i2}, \ldots, \sigma_{ip_i}\}$ is a set of all sequences executed by the user u_i in the system, and p_i is number of that sequences.

Then, let us define matrix $B \in N^{|U| \times |S|}$, where b_{ij} is a frequency of sequence $\sigma_{ij} \in S$ for user u_i. Then, base user profile of user u_i is a vector $b_i \in N^{|S|}$ represented by row i from matrix B.

4.1 Working Together Graph

Base user profile represents user behavior in the system. It is a vector of all the sequences of events (transactions), which user executed in the system. This approach had to be modified to business process analysis, because in this area, the users execute only such activities, which are assigned to them depending on their roles. One transaction usually consists of events related to different user roles according to the defined process in the system. Therefore, it is common that in one sequence (transaction) we can find several users. Thus, base user profile in business process analysis represents all the sequences on which user has participated.

The relations between the users are defined as a similarity between base user profiles. The similarity can be set by cosine measure or by other similarity measure suitable for vector comparison. Matrix similarity of users can be visualized by weighted undirected graph $G = (V, E, w)$, where vertices V (nodes) represent users, edges E represent relations between users and weight w defines similarity between users on the basis of their behavior. This type of graph is usually called *Working together graph*. Common Working together graph (for example in ProM) takes into account the occurrence of event performer in the trace (transaction). However, we work with the communication and with the user interaction, on which the REA model is based. Therefore, not only an event performer (message sender), but also a recipient occurs in one event. Both senders and recipients are users of the system, and due to this reason, they both should be included in Working together graph. Section 5 shows a difference between the Working together graph constructed by ProM tool and our modification of this type of graph.

4.2 Behavioral Graph

In many cases, especially if the analysis of business processes is focused on the model structure, it is important to know which types of processes are used in the system and which users execute the activities within these processes. We propose a new type of social network graph, *Behavioral graph*, which represents the relations between the users on the basis of their occurrence in cases (not in particular transactions) in the system. Sequences σ_{ij} extracted with relation to certain user u_i are mapped to set of sequences $\sigma_c \in S$ without the relation to users: $\sigma_{ij} = \langle e_{ij1}, e_{ij2}, \ldots, e_{ijm_j} \rangle \rightarrow \sigma_c = \langle e_1, e_2, \ldots, e_{m_c} \rangle$, where $e_{ij1} = e_1$,

$e_{ij2} = e_2, \dots, e_{im_c} = e_{m_c}$. Such sequences σ_c then refer to cases in business process analysis.

According to this mapping, let us define matrix $B_c \in N^{|U| \times |S|}$, where b_{il} is a frequency of sequence $\sigma_l \in S$ for user u_i if $\sigma_l \in S_i$. Then, base user profile of user u_i is a vector $b_i \in N^{|S|}$ represented by row i from matrix B_c.

The relations between the users are then defined as for previous type of graph (Working together) and similarity matrix of users can be also visualized by weighted undirected graph $G = (V, E, w)$. Such graph we call Behavioral graph. This type of graph represents groups of users according to cases they participated in.

Section 5 shows a case study, in which the outputs of the proposed approach and the usage of Behavioral graph is presented for verification of an analysis of event logs from virtual company model simulation.

5   Case Study: Analysis of Simulation Model Event Logs

The principle proposed herein above was applied as a case study on a generic company model, presented in Fig. 1. The experiments presented here should confirm the hypothesis that the proposed approach in comparison with common methods allows to find latent ties between the users on the basis of their behavior in the system, which usually are not noticeable.

The company consists of controlling, measuring and controlled subsystems. The controlled subsystem sales realizes the sales of the product to customers.

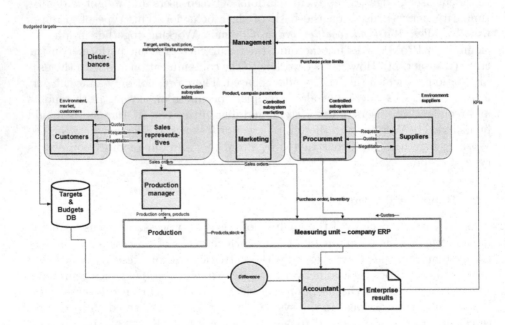

Fig. 1. Generic company model used for event log analysis

The customers communicate with the sales representatives. On customer sales request, the sales representative sends a sales quotation, which starts price negotiations. In a case, the negotiations end with an agreement a stock or production order and sales orders are generated. After the product is shipped, the invoicing starts. Next controlled subsystem is the procurement subsystem. Procurement can be looked upon as a mirror image of sales. The purchase representatives place purchase requests to suppliers and after (possible) negotiation, the purchase order is realized and the product or its components are put into the stock. The next controlled subsystem is the marketing subsystem realizing marketing actions. The movements within sales, procurement, inventory and marketing are registered by company ERP system. Using ERP system, the accountants regularly evaluate the company results characterized by Key Performance Indicators (KPIs) and report the differences to management, the controlling subsystem. Based on KPIs developments, the managers take decisions in order to keep the company system at the proximity of targets.

5.1   MAREA

The company model presented in Fig. 1 was transformed into a multi-agent system by means of MAREA workbench. MAREA (Multi-Agent, REA based system) is a complex modeling environment consisting of REA Based ERP system used for registration of the all economic activities modeled in a simulation run (see measuring unit in Fig. 1) multi-agent system simulating activities both controlling and controlled subsystems of the modeled company. Each grey-colored square in Fig. 1 was transformed into a MAREA agent with appropriate parameters. The general principles and features of the MAREA workbench are presented in detail in [25].

During simulation design, the intelligent agents were programmed in such a way, that they can simulate the human activities in the model company. So, the sales representatives and the customers can negotiate on the price the manager can decide on management actions such as marketing campaigns etc. Each action of the agents is represented by accompanying message which is simultaneously registered in the event log. The messages are presented by means of MAREA message viewer and can be compared with other ERP outputs. For the event log, the XES[2] format was used. This format was used in order to be able to use ProM procedures for comparison if the proposed analysis results correspond with ProM outputs [19]. The ERP system outputs enable to see the development of sales/purchase quotations and orders, main Key Performance Indicators development, management action results etc. An example of XES format is presented in Example 1.

---

[2] XES standard:
  http://www.xes-standard.org/_media/xes/xesstandarddefinition-1.4.pdf.

Example 1 (Example of XES file).

```
<event>
  <string key="concept:name" value="Sales request" />
  <string key="concept:instance" value="10000" />
  <string key="org:resource" value="Customer 75" />
  <date key="time:timestamp" value="2014-06-01T02:02:02" />
  <int key="Id" value="10000" />
  <int key="Correlationid" value="10000" />
  <string key="MessageType" value="Sales request" />
  <string key="Sender" value="Customer 75" />
  <string key="Recipient" value="Peter Hanson" />
  <date key="SentDate" value="2014-06-01T02:02:02" />
  <date key="ReadDate" value="2014-06-02T14:14:14" />
  <date key="Date" value="2014-06-01T02:02:02" />
  <float key="Budget" value="707.86" />
  <string key="SalesRequestLine-1" value="">
    <string key="Item" value="UTP cable" />
    <float key="Quantity" value="95" />
  </string>
</event>
```

An important feature of MAREA workbench is the REA based ERP system. Due to REA principles used here, the registration of economic events does not require double entry bookkeeping. These results in a very short simulation experiments as far as the simulation time are concerned. A normal simulation run consisting of 365 simulation steps (one year) takes up to four minutes depending on the customer count. Hence, a large number of simulation runs could be realized during the research.

5.2 Experiment Description

A real data from one high tech company selling IT accessories was used. A single product (UTP cable sales statistics) was put into the ERP base indicators such as product market share, selling price limit, average purchase price, estimated market volume in the region where the company is active etc. The main parameters used in the simulation experiment sums up Table 1.

Table 2 shows basic statistics of analyzed event log from the simulation.

Table 1. Global Parameters of Simulation

Parameter	Value	Remark
Number of iterations	365	One year
Number of customers	100	Up to several thousand possible
Number of vendors	5	As a rule
Mean quantity in one sales order (m)	40	From real sales statistics
Maximum quantity in one sales order (m)	305	From real sales statistics
Management action period (days)	30	Typically one month
Number of sales representatives	2	For this report
Sales representative ability to sell	1	For this report
Maximum days of negotiations	10	The negotiation is canceled after

Table 2. Basic Statistics of the Simulation

Attribute	Value
Transactions	1.378
Events in transactions	9.937
Unique events	587
Unique sequences (cases)	415
Users	117
Management action period (days)	30
Number of sales representatives	2
Sales representative ability to sell	1
Maximum days of negotiations	10

5.3   Working Together Graph

The event log from the simulation has been used for the analysis with the aim to construct Working together graph, see Fig. 2. This graph was constructed using the approach described in Sect. 4.1.

The nodes represent the users in the simulation, the relations represent the similarity between user profiles. An example of user profiles is presented in Example 2. The size of nodes is determined by node degree.

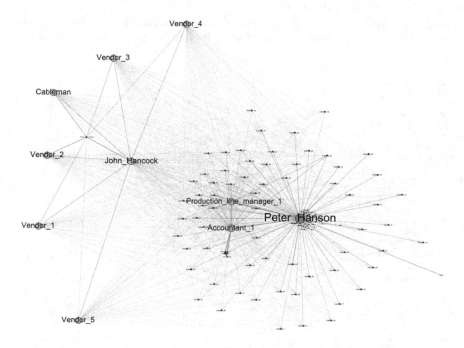

Fig. 2. Working together graph: proposed modification

Example 2 (Example of UserProfile for Working Together Graph).

```
3|1|Sales_request^;Sales_quote^;Sales_quote_rejection^;Sales_quote^;Sales_quote_re
jection^;Sales_request_revoked^;Stop_sales_request^;|0;1;2;1;2;3;5;
14|1|Sales_request^;Sales_quote^;Sales_quote_rejection^;Sales_quote^;Sales_quote_r
ejection^;Sales_quote^;Sales_quote_rejection^;Sales_quote^;Sales_request_revoked^;
Sales_quote_ignored^;Stop_sales_request^;|0;1;2;1;2;1;2;1;3;4;5;
#user:Peter_Hanson
```

This type of Working together graph is a modification of a common approach, see Sect. 4.1. A comparison with this common approach has been done,
using tools for social network analysis of ProM software. The output from ProM
software is presented in Fig. 3. The graph presents similar output as Fig. 2: nodes
represent users, relations are defined on the basis of common occurrence in the
transactions. Both approaches show two main clusters of users (customers and
vendors), as well as users Peter Hanson and John Hancock, who had special roles
in the negotiation processes in the system. Also Production line manager and
Disturbance manager can be seen in both graphs. However, Working together
graph created by ProM software did not visualize several users, for example
Accountant, Marketing agent and Manager 1 (the users with stronger relation
to the Accountant in Fig. 2) and Market share manager (a small node with relations to vendors and John Hancock in Fig. 2). These users have relations to other
users due to their participation on the common transactions with them, however
they were only recipients of the messages (in the events). This is the reason,
why common type of Working together graph (created by ProM software) did
not included them into the graph.

REA approach to business process modeling is based on communication
between users (agents), which means that each event in the process has its sender

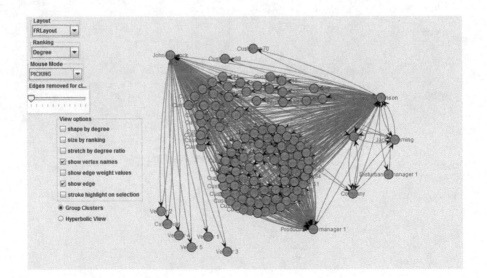

Fig. 3. Working together graph: ProM

and recipient, see Sect. 4. It is important to capture the communication between them and to include such users into Working together graph. Our modification presented in Fig. 2 can be a solution.

Working together graphs were constructed with the aim to compare our methods with ProM software. This type of graph is useful if we need to know who cooperates with whom during the working process. Thus, this type of graph represents the relation between the users on the basis of their common occurrence in the trace (transaction). However, it is often necessary to know on which type of transaction (case) the user has participated. It is very important for example for the verification of the set business process model or of the processes themselves. Therefore, our new approach represents a different view to the relation between the users, based on their behavior in the system with the focus to the business processes. Section 5.4 shows Behavioral graph, a new type of graph which visualizes this new type of relation between the users.

5.4   Behavioral Graph

Behavioral graphs show relation between the users given by their similar behavior in the system with the focus on the business processes. The relation is based on similar cases they were participated in, not traces (transactions). The relation weight is given by the similarity of base user profiles, while the profiles are constructed using the cases the users were participated in, see Fig. 4. A detailed description of this type of graph was presented in Sect. 4.2 and an example of such user profiles are presented in Example 3.

Example 3 (Example of User Profiles for Behavioral Graph).

```
131|4|Sales_request^S:Customer_75^R:Peter_Hanson^;Stock_level_too_low^S:Peter_Hanso
n^;Sales_request_revoked^S:Customer_75^R:Peter_Hanson^;|0;20;3;
258|1|Sales_request^S:Customer_75^R:Peter_Hanson^;Sales_quote^S:Peter_Hanson^R:Cust
omer_75^;Sales_quote_rejection^S:Customer_75^R:Peter_Hanson^;Sales_quote^S:Peter_Ha
nson^R:Customer_75^;Sales_quote_rejection^S:Customer_75^R:Peter_Hanson^;Sales_reque
st_revoked^S:Customer_75^R:Peter_Hanson^;Stop_sales_request^S:Peter_Hanson^;|0;1;2;
1;2;3;5;
```

Behavioral Graph presented in Fig. 4 clearly divided users into several groups on the basis of their participation with similar processes (cases).

We can see the two dominant groups of the users, customers and vendors. As we can see, Customer 99 had a completely different behavior than other customers. Behavioral graph also depicted other users with their specific behavior, for example all the types of managers, or the user dealing with material purchase requests for all the vendors (John Hancock). The cases they have participated in are presented in Table 3.

Table 3 shows examples of user profiles; each profile consists of the cases the users have participated in. Each case consists of activities, each activity has its unique ID. These users are very important for the verification of the users with specific roles in the systems or for finding the users with deviations (for example the users who do not respect the set roles in the system).

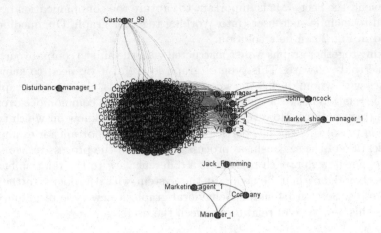

Fig. 4. Behavioral Graph

Table 3. Example of User Profiles

User	Cases
Manager 1	26;27;28;
	26;27;29;30;31;32;31;32;28;33;34;33;
	26;27;
Company	26;27;28;
	26;27;29;30;31;32;31;32;28;33;34;33;
	26;27;
Marketing agent 1	26;27;28;
	26;27;29;30;31;32;31;32;28;33;34;33;
Jack Flemming	26;27;29;30;31;32;31;32;28;33;34;33;
Market share manager 1	16;17;18;19;20;
John Hancock	0;1;7;8;9;10;11;12;13;14;14;14;14;14;14;15;15;15;15;15;15;
	16;17;18;19;20;
	16;17;21;22;23;
	0;1;7;8;9;10;11;14;14;14;14;14;14;15;15;12;13;15;15;15;15;
	16;21;17;23;22;
	...
	0;1;7;8;9;10;11;14;14;14;14;14;14;15;15;15;15;15;15;12;13;
Disturbance manager 1	24;25;
Customer 99	0;1;2;1;2;3;5;
	0;1;7;8;9;10;11;14;14;14;14;14;14;15;15;15;12;13;15;15;15;

6   Conclusion

The main goal of this paper was to present the new approach to visualization of relations between the users on the basis of the principles of complex network analysis and analysis of social network with the focus on users' behavior in the system. The description of the new approach was provided, and the comparison to other common approaches from the area of social network analysis was described. The case study presented in Sect. 5 described the verification of simulation of general company model, in which the new approach was used. The presented approach was tailored to MAREA approach to business process modeling, which is based on communication between the users (agents).

The results showed that the presented approach brings us a new perspective of the analysis of users' behavior in the systems, which record the users' activities performed in the system into the event logs, and allows us to find latent ties between the users. As discussed in Sect. 5, the presented approach successfully depicts the important users on the basis of their behavior, and it helps to find the users with behavior deviations in the system.

Acknowledgments. This work was supported by the grant of Silesian University no. SGS/6/2013 'Advanced Modeling and Simulation of Economic Systems' and by the Ministry of Education, Youth and Sports within the Institutional Support for Long-term Development of a Research Organization in 2014 and co-financed by SGS, VSB - Technical University of Ostrava, Czech Republic, under the grant No. SP2014/110 Big data parallel processing.

References

1. Aris. Aris - architecture of integrated systems. workflow management within the aris framework. (2000). http://www.pera.net/Methodologies/ARIS/ARIS.html
2. Baden-Fuller, C., Haefliger, S.: Business models and technological innovation. Long Range Plan. **46**(6), 419–426 (2013)
3. Bucki, R., Suchánek, P.: The method of logistic optimization in e-commerce. J. Univ. Comput. Sci. **18**(10), 1238–1258 (2012)
4. Davenport, T.: Process Innovation: Re-engineering Work through Information Technology. Harvard Business School Press, Boston (1992)
5. Dunn, C., Cherrington, O., Hollander, A.: Enterprise Information Systems: A Pattern Based Approach. McGraw-Hill/Irwin, New York (2004)
6. H. E. Eriksson and M. Penker. Business Modeling with UML. John Wiley & Sons Inc, 2006
7. Geerts, G., McCarthy, W.: Policy-level specification in rea enterprise information systems. J. Inf. Syst. **20**(2), 37–63 (2006)
8. Gordijn, J., Akkermans, J.: Value-based requirements engineering: exploring innovative e-commerce ideas. Requirements Eng. **8**(2), 114–134 (2003)
9. Gries, M., Kulkarni, C., Sauer, C., Keutzer, K.: Comparing analytical modeling with simulation for network processors: a case study (2011). http://www.eecs.berkeley.edu/IPRO/VIF/Papers/GKSK_date03.pdf

10. Hruby, P., Kiehn, J., Scheller, C.: Model/Driven Design Using Business Patterns. Springer Verlag, Berlin Heidelberg (2006)
11. Initiative, B.P.M.: Business process modeling notation. working draft (1.0). Technical report, Object Management Group - OMG (2003)
12. Janakova, M.: Visualization and simulation in data processing with the support of business intelligence. In: Snasel, V., Platos, J., El-Qawasmeh, E. (eds.) ICDIPC 2011, Part I. CCIS, vol. 188, pp. 151–159. Springer, Heidelberg (2011)
13. Liu, Y., Triverdi, S.: Survivability quntification: the analytical modeling approach. Technical report, Department of Electrical and Computer Engineering, Duke University, Durham, NC, USA (2011)
14. McCarthy, W.: The rea accounting model: a generalized framework for accounting systems in a shared data environment. Acc. Rev. **57**, 554–578 (1982)
15. Meimaris, M., Vafopoulos, M.: Knowledge-based semantification of business communications in erp environments. Lect. Notes Comput. Sci. **7652**, 159–172 (2013)
16. Slaninová, K., Martinovič, J., Dráždilová, P., Vymětal, D., Šperka, R.: Analysis of agents behavior in multiagent system. In: Proceedings of the 24th European Modeling and Simulation Symposium. EMSS 2012, pp. 169–175 (2012)
17. Slaninová, K., Martinovič, J., Šperka, R., Dráždilová, P.: Extraction of agent groups with similar behaviour based on agent profiles. In: Saeed, K., Chaki, R., Cortesi, A., Wierzchoń, S. (eds.) CISIM 2013. LNCS, vol. 8104, pp. 348–357. Springer, Heidelberg (2013)
18. Suchánek, P., Vymětal, D.: Security and disturbances in E-commerce systems. In: Proceedings of the 10th International Conference Liberec Economic Forum (2011)
19. van der Aalst, W.M.P.: Process Mining: Discovery. Conformance and Enhancement of Business Processes, 1st edn. Springer, Heidelberg (2011)
20. van der Aalst, W.M.P., Reijers, H.A., Song, M.: Discovering social networks from event logs. Comput. Support. Coop. Work **14**(6), 549–593 (2005)
21. van der Aalst, W.M.P., van Dongen, B.F., Herbst, J., Maruster, L., Schimm, G., Weijters, A.J.M.M.: Workflow mining: a survey of issues and approaches. Data Knowl. Eng. **47**(2), 237–267 (2003)
22. van der Aalst, W. et al.: Process mining manifesto. www.win.tue.nl/ieeetfpm/lib/ exe/fetch.php?media=shared:process_mining_manifesto-small.pdf
23. Šperka, R., Spišák, M., Slaninová, K., Martinovič, J., Dráždilová, P.: Control loop model of virtual company in bpm simulation. Adv. Intell. Syst. and Comput. **188**, 515–524 (2013)
24. Šperka, R., Vymětal, D.: Marea - an education application for trading company simulation based on rea prin-ciples. In: Proceedings Advances in Education Research of Information, Communication and Education Application, vol. 30, pp. 140–147 (2013)
25. Vymětal, D., Scheller, C.: Marea: multi-agent rea-based business process simulation framework. In: Conference proceedings of International Scientific Conference ICT for Competitiveness, pp. 301–310 (2012)
26. Weigand, H., Elsas, P.: Model-based auditing uinternational journal of accounting information systemssrea. Int. J. Account. Inf. Syst. **13**(3), 287–310 (2012)
27. Wooldridge, M.: MultiAgent Systems : An Introduction. 2nd edn, Wiley, Hoboken (2009)

Delineating Worker-Centered Organizational Work: Blending BPMS and Social Software Features

Nancy Alexopoulou[✉], Christian Stary, and Stefan Oppl

Department of Business Information Systems – Communications Engineering,
Johannes Kepler University, Linz, Austria

Abstract. Nowadays, companies seek for new technological enablers and adopt new business models to cope with the frenetic pace of change. Such an effort is depicted in the Enterprise 2.0 initiative. Knowledgeable workers should be empowered so that they can help, through their knowledge, the organization they work for to thrive in the today's highly demanding business environments. Empowerment concerns supporting them to easily gather the knowledge they need as well as to efficiently execute required tasks to accomplish business goals. To provide an efficient working aid, knowledge gathering and task execution should be supported through a unified environment. Towards identifying the features of such a unified environment, we conduct in this paper a two-phase analysis, which leads to the development of a coarse-grained conceptualization of this environment, reflecting a worker-centered organizational work model. This conceptualization is named Worker-Centered Organizational Work Wheel. The Wheel adopts features from both BPMS and social software to enable the integration of knowledge gathering and task execution. Apart from delineating how a knowledgeable worker should work, the Wheel also provides a roadmap showing what features should be offered by any implementation targeting this work model.

Keywords: BPMS · Social software · Social BPM · Knowledgeable worker · Organizational work

1 Introduction

The world is changing. The signs for this change are around us, reflected upon every human aspect, like consuming, travelling, learning, socializing, etc. Companies are obliged to follow this change pace in order to remain competitive or even alive. In alignment with these new demands, modern workers have to be knowledgeable [1] more than ever before. This means that they should be able to adapt and cope with change effectively, which, in turn, implies that they should be more functionally and

The research leading to these results has received funding from the European Commission within the Marie Curie Industry an Academia Partnerships & Pathways (IAPP) programme under grant agreement n° 286083.

© Springer International Publishing Switzerland 2015
B. Benatallah et al. (Eds.): WISE 2014, LNCS 9051, pp. 57–71, 2015.
DOI: 10.1007/978-3-319-20370-6_5

cognitively fluid and able to work across many tasks and situations. Thus, not only will they have to keep their technology skills up-to-date, but also they will need to be continuous learners in their knowledge fields.

To foster employees in being knowledgeable, it should be ensured that they are able to discover the knowledge they need fast and easily. Such knowledge should not concern only explicit information found in books, documents, data bases etc. It should also include tacit knowledge. Tacit knowledge [2] resides in peoples' heads. Thus, it is bound to persons and consists of their mental models, beliefs and experiences. For this reason, it is difficult to be explained and shared, as opposed to explicit knowledge which is usually formal, systematic and easy to codify, communicate and share [3]. Tacit knowledge can be even more important than explicit knowledge as, in rapidly changing environments, explicit knowledge may quickly become obsolete and consequently new or unexpected situations could only be effectively tackled based on the experience and intelligence of specific workers.

To endorse knowledge discovery and sharing through organizational collaboration, enterprises are moving towards the Enterprise 2.0 [4] business model, although the definition and understanding of this model is still in some flux. Enterprise 2.0 basically promotes the utilization of social software in organizational environments for efficient collaboration and knowledge sharing but it additionally represents a fundamental change in how businesses operate. In the traditional corporate environment, information flows through an ordered path from the top to the bottom, and suggestions are made from the bottom flow towards the top. Enterprise 2.0 changes this structured order and allows information to flow laterally as well as up and down, since it promotes a flat organizational logic as opposed to the currently established hierarchical model [5]. In alignment with Enterprise 2.0 model, work in organizations should become more worker-centered than merely be determined by top management. In this way, employees will become empowered and using their knowledge will help the organization to thrive in the today's highly competitive business environment.

As signified by the Enterprise 2.0 initiative, it has already been discerned that the introduction of social software in entrepreneurial environments may help workers with knowledge gathering [6–8]. Task execution, on the other hand has been traditionally supported through Business Process Management Systems [9]. To be true enablers for workers, however, these two environments should not function in an isolated manner. In contrast they should be integrated in a unique environment. Consider, for example, social networking platforms. By their nature, they can considerably contribute to faster discovery of relevant information and expertise (i.e. knowledge), helping workers to become more agile. However, uncontrolled social interactions may result in chaotic situations that may in turn lead to the opposite end, hindering significantly the on-time accomplishment of tasks and ultimately the effective pursuit of business goals. Therefore, it is necessary for workers to function under a guiding umbrella so that they know when and how to use social networking capabilities and thereby effectively utilize the benefits gained from changing work technologies. Such a guiding umbrella would prevent them from getting lost in perpetual communications and unfocused interactions and facilitate them to effectively pinpoint what they need in terms of informational resources and people with the appropriate knowledge and expertise. One way to achieve this is to tightly link social collaboration to business activities so that employees can have as a compass the business tasks they have to carry out and the business goals they wish to satisfy [10].

To this end, we consider that workers within an agile organization either engage themselves in discovering and acquiring knowledge concerning the tasks they have to accomplish or in actual doing to execute a task. These two happen interchangeably, both utilizing and augmenting organizational knowledge, as depicted in Fig. 1.

Creating an integrated environment that will achieve such a linkage between knowledge gathering and task execution is not straightforward [11]. However, it may prove promising for enhancing organizational work and supporting employees in being agile and therefore, it is worthwhile further investigating it. This potential has already been identified by the research community, as revealed by a recently established field called *Social BPM* [12], which investigates the adoption of social features in the Business Process Management discipline.

Fig. 1. Aspects of worker-centered organizational work

Towards identifying the features of such an integrated environment supporting both knowledge gathering and task execution in a seamless fashion, we conduct in this paper a two-phase analysis, which leads to a coarse-grained conceptualization of such an environment, reflecting a worker-centered organizational work model. This model is built utilizing features from both BPMS and social software. Therefore, in the *separation-of-concerns* first phase, well-established BPMS and social software features are juxtaposed based on specific business process modeling perspectives proposed in [13, 14]. Subsequently, in the *integration-of-concerns* phase, the identified traits are fused into a single structure, yielding a high-level functional view called *Worker-Centered Organizational Work Wheel*. This view as implied by the word "wheel" was inspired by a wheel's structure and function.

The Worker-Centered Organizational Work Wheel depicts how prominent features identified in both software types, social software and BPMS, can be combined in a unified environment, and reflects a working model from the employee's perspective. Therefore, the purpose of the Wheel is threefold: (1) it prescribes a working model, delineating how a knowledgeable worker should work using the aforementioned integrated environment, (2) it helps towards a deeper understanding of the requirements for such an integration and (3) it provides a roadmap showing what features should be offered by any implementation targeting this working model. To this end, issues regarding the implementation of the integrated environment that were extracted from the Wheel are also mentioned in the paper.

The rest of the paper is organized as follows. Section 2 includes related efforts of combining social software with BPMS and, in general, of adopting social features in BPM discipline. The two-phase analysis is presented in Sect. 3, where it is also unfolded how a knowledgeable employee should work using the unified environment. Conclusions and future work are given in Sect. 4.

2 Related Work

Business Process Management utilizing social software concepts has recently gained momentum, due to social software characteristics like weak ties and mutual service provision, which fulfill requirements of collaborative environments [15, 16].

In practice, although the phenomenon of social networking within an organization, as provided by enterprise social networks [17], is growing, as investigated by Richter and Riemer in [18], its usage is restricted in communication and information sharing. That is, the social software infrastructure is used only for exchanging information or performing trivial tasks, such as arranging a meeting, and not for integrated BPM solutions, which seems to be the step forward. Current trends indicate that enterprise social networks should not only facilitate communication but also help participants cooperate and substantially improve the way they work; for this reason, advanced services which target business task execution are required [17, 19].

On the other hand, literature is rich in contributions concerning the adoption of social software features in the BPM discipline. A part of this research focuses on how social software can be used to support collaborative business process modeling [20–22]. Other approaches focus on using social tagging mechanisms for relating models dynamically [23] or managing them in a model repository [24]. Collaborative business process modeling is also supported by commercial tools like IBM Blueworks (www.ibmblueworks.com) and Signavio Process Editor (www.signavio.com).

Blending the two software types for supporting business process execution has also been explored in various research endeavors. Brambilla et al. [25] have proposed a notation for social BPM defined as a BPMN 2.0 extension. It enables the annotation of specific tasks as collaborative ones and their potential execution within a social network environment. In [26] a BPM infrastructure bearing social software features is proposed, targeting both collaborative modeling as well as business process execution in a fashion that mashes up definition and operation of business processes. The corresponding tool, called AGILIPO, is currently under development and testing. In [27] the authors examine how the architectural principles behind BPMS and social software can be combined in order to develop a unified infrastructure supporting features of both software types. In [28] an approach for using wikis in an organizational context is presented along with a prototype implementation for developing a wiki-based workflow system. Xie et al. [29] examine the potential of combining social software with BPM through process-oriented mashups in order to enable users to easily build applications encompassing workflow logic. Khalaf et al. [30] focus on social production of workflows. Johannesson et al. [31] suggest a set of guidelines for augmenting

BPMS with social software features, which may be effective for knowledge-intensive process modeling, though the execution model is not clearly defined. Neumann and Erol [32] propose a wiki-based implementation of a workflow system. Moreover, Motahari-Nezhad et al., [33] introduce a framework for supporting Adaptive Case Management [1] in social networking environments.

All the aforementioned approaches towards the integration of task execution and social software features may serve the concept of a worker-centered working model, though they are based on different technologies and technical solutions. Furthermore, they usually focus on effectively extending an existing working paradigm with specific new or advanced features, targeting the solution of the technical problems raised. Thus, they do target on specifying and supporting an alternative working model for worker-centered organizations, although they may support partial features of it. In practice, they contributed to the feasibility of the implementation of an integrated environment linking both task execution and knowledge gathering, as discussed in the following, and provide sound solutions for specific implementation issues that may arise.

3 Delineating Worker-Centered Organizational Work Through a Two-Phase Analysis

The provision of an integrated environment, supporting both knowledge gathering and task execution in a seamless fashion, is promising for promoting a worker-centered working model taking advantage of knowledgeable workers and, therefore, enhancing organizational work. Towards identifying the features of such environment, prominent characteristics of both social software and BPMS should be integrated, taking into account existing efforts, presented in the previous paragraph, to enhance task execution with social features. To do so, a two phase analysis was conducted.

In the first phase, notable features of both software types that should be offered in the integrated environment to support a worker-centered working model, are separately identified and presented in a juxtaposing manner [34]. Thus, it is characterized as a separation-of-concerns phase. It should be noted that the characteristics of social software are examined in the context of Enterprise 2.0 vision.

Subsequently, in the integration-of-concerns phase, the identified features are brought together in an integrated structure to prescribe a working model, delineating how a knowledgeable worker should work utilizing organizational knowledge and identify requirements and issues that should be resolved towards implementing such an integrated environment.

3.1 Separation of Concerns

To identify prominent features of both software types in a systematic manner, the business process modeling perspectives proposed by Curtis et al. [13] were adopted. According to Curtis et al. [13], a business process model can be viewed from a functional, behavioral, organizational and informational perspective. The functional perspective depicts what activities are performed. When and how activities are performed constitutes the behavioral perspective, while where and by whom they are executed corresponds to the organizational perspective. What information entities are created and processed during each activity is examined in the informational perspective. We also include an intentional perspective, corresponding to the business process context perspective suggested by List and Korherr in [14], which focuses on the goals satisfied through a business process, reflecting the rationale behind it. We considered such a perspective important to clarify the intension of workers choosing to use either social software or BPMS in the enterprise environment.

Table 1 juxtaposes BPMS and social software characteristics distinguished in the aforementioned perspectives. As BPMS and social software have a different orientation, they reasonably bear diverse traits, which can even be regarded to a large extent contradictory. In the following, features of both software types are briefly discussed from each perspective.

Functional Perspective. The functionality of a business process is described through business-specific activities often called tasks [35], although a hierarchical relationship may also be defined between these two terms. A business activity can be anything performed within the context of a specific business process. However, there are strict descriptions of its input and output as well as the roles/participants responsible for its execution, which constitute parts of its definition. Activities supported in social software, on the other hand, have a more narrowed scope. They mainly regard information sharing and context creation. Context creation involves creation of metadata for the existing data. This can be accomplished through tagging (i.e. using keywords to classify data), evaluating (e.g. through rating or endorsing) and annotating.

Table 1. Juxtaposing features of social software and BPMS from five business process modeling perspectives

Business process perspectives	Social software	BPMS
Functional perspective	- information sharing - context creation	- business-specific activities (tasks)
Behavioural perspective	- wisdom of the crowds - social interaction - social production	- wisdom of the expert - prescribed task execution - predefined input from each participant
Organizational perspective	- egalitarianism - weak ties - public access	- role hierarchy - strong ties - access policies specified by top management
Informational perspective	- content or context information concerning artifacts or physical objects	- business or physical objects
Intentional perspective	- learning	- achieve business goal

Behavioral Perspective. Two fundamental features of social software are social inter-action and social production. The first concerns the communication between individuals without predefined rules (e.g. Facebook), while the second is about the creation of artifacts by combining the input from independent contributors without a priori spec-ification of the way doing this (e.g. Wikipedia). In contrast, using a typical BPMS, the interactions among participants are usually prescribed through rigid or flexible process models, specifying the order of tasks as well as the way each participant is involved, so that a certain business goal is reached [36]. Social software is based on "collective intelligence" [37] of many people that may sometimes lead more effectively to the solution of a problem than the knowledge of an expert who is sometimes difficult to be identified. This adheres to the "wisdom of the crowds" idea introduced in [38].

Organizational Perspective. Weak ties are formulated through social networks, as opposed to strong ties which are developed through relationships based on hierarchy and team structure. As indicated in [16], weak ties are spontaneously established contacts invoked not by management but by individuals. Egalitarianism [16] is about giving all participants the same rights to contribute, in contrast to organizational environments, where well-defined roles and role interrelationships determine respon-sibilities within the context of the organization, which in turn are depicted within BMPS environment. Access to information is also determined by roles and policies specified by top management, while social software environments allow for a wider access to information.

Informational Perspective. Information in social software regards objects like photos, songs, e-books etc. associated with metadata developed by participants using tagging, evaluating and annotating (see above). Utilizing the "wisdom of the crowds", partic-ipants may also classify information, formulating folksonomies, which may help others to seek the information they need. Thus, context information is available for the content created by participants. In contrast, information in BPMS is depicted onto business objects such as order forms, receipts, invoices, etc., which are strictly related to activities as input or output data. Creation of business objects is highly controlled and therefore a high quality can be better ensured in case of such information compared to the information produced in social software environments.

Intentional Perspective. Regarding BPMS, the intentional perspective implies the business goals that are meant to be satisfied through business processes [14]. In case of social software when considered within the Enterprise 2.0 initiative, the goal is learning, both individual and group learning, which contributes to organizational knowledge [6, 7].

3.2   Integration of Concerns

In the following, we identify the features of the two software types that should be integrated within the unified environment to promote a worker-centered working modeling and discuss related decisions on how to utilize them. The discussion is made progressively, by exploring the different perspectives discussed above.

As already mentioned, workers are continually engaged in their everyday work, either in the acquirement and exchange of knowledge regarding the business goals they need to satisfy or in actual task execution (see Fig. 1). But how should workers be represented? The concept of the profile, popular in social software, is adopted. However, compared to typical social software profiles, worker profiles should convey richer semantics. Identity, background, skills and experience are attributes of one's personality, typically found in professional-oriented social networks like LinkedIn (www. linkedin.com), for example. Concerning reputation [39], it is also a factor that may considerably affect knowledge discovery in terms of identifying, for example, who is more competent or trustworthy to consult or refer to for the accomplishment of a specific task. However, apart from those common profile aspects already found in existing social networks, a profile in the integrated environment should include also roles, responsibilities and working data which constitute work-oriented parameters. The concept of role is used as defined within the Business Process Management community [40]. Responsibilities explicitly describe what an employee is accountable for performing within the company, based on his/her roles. It should be noted that two employees may bear the same role but have different responsibilities. Working data reflect runtime information of the employee's current activities. Essentially, the profile constitutes a representation of the employee's 'micro-world' in the broader organizational environment. In this respect, in their profiles, workers should be able to view their responsibilities, the goals and tasks that they should and/or could accomplish, data resources that they are allowed to access and events that are of interest to them, as well as run time information about the tasks under execution. Such an augmented profile essentially reflects the integration between the two software types.

To depict the interchangeable states of acting and knowledge gathering (see Fig. 1), a wheel's function has been used as a metaphor and the framework is named *Worker-Centered Organizational Work Wheel*, as depicted in Fig. 2.

Fig. 2. Worker-centered organizational work wheel

The hub of the Wheel is worker's profile, which is how the employee is represented in the unified environment. The spokes of the Wheel stand for the aspects mentioned above, which represent information related either to the workers themselves or the activities they are engaged in. This information is enriched as the wheel is turning, i.e. the person is working. In practice this information is part of the organizational knowledge related to the specific person, may be produced by him/her or others and may represent explicit or tacit knowledge (see Fig. 2).

Based on Table 1, which depicts the separation-of-concerns analysis, bringing together social software with BPMS from a functional perspective means that users may both execute business-specific tasks as well as engage themselves in context creation and information sharing, utilizing the content of their profile. Likewise, both types of interaction should be supported, predefined, according to specific process patterns and information access policies, or social, based on knowledge creation and sharing and social interaction, as indicated by the behavioral perspective. Both predefined and social interaction should be supported in either task execution or knowledge gathering.

Regarding the organizational aspect, it indicates that constraints stemming from organizational policies and business rules implemented in BPMSs should also be taken into account into the integrated environment. Social software does not dictate constraints from an organizational perspective, although, when considering the informational perspective in an enterprise environment, constraints associated with content quality and trust are imposed to social content production.

Lastly, the intentional aspect implies that the integrated environment should provide for both the accomplishment of business goals as well as individual and group learning. Figure 3 depicts the Organizational Work Wheel to a lower level of abstraction encompassing features directly or indirectly derived from Table 1.

Fig. 3. The worker-centered organizational work wheel at a lower level of abstraction

What a worker can do in the corporate environment is depicted along the tire. The upper part of the tire shows the acting parameters, i.e. goal specification and task accomplishment, while the lower part illustrates the knowledge gathering aspects, i.e. information sharing, individual and group learning and context creation.

In Fig. 3, organizational policies and business rules are considered as some kind of "brakes" for the interaction among the employees, which may be to some extent predefined. Timing and resource management constraints may also be incorporated in them. "Brakes" herein refers to regulating entities, that determine the worker's access to, contribution to and/or involvement in the activities denoted in the outer area of the wheel. In contrast, social interaction which takes place when the stakeholders interact with each other, in order to exchange views, ideas, information and knowledge, is much looser [41].

During social interactions, workers augment their skills and knowledge [16]. In other words, they learn. Learning can be intensified through participation in groups sharing similar interests and responsibilities, creating thereby the stimuli for the externalization of tacit knowledge. Moreover, workers may create context by tagging, evaluating and annotating, contributing to information sharing and discovery. However, for a system to be both reliable and useful effectively supporting knowledge discovery, content quality and trust should be taken into consideration [41]. Content quality and trust are two parameters that can be considered brakes for the social interaction dimension of the wheel. Content quality to this respect addresses both, the idea that high quality content (i.e. well structured and written) can be more easily augmented with additional information and the idea that the quality of the content has impact on the willingness to access and share knowledge. Trust refers to the quality of interpersonal relationships which influence how and to which extent workers are willing to participate in knowledge sharing activities.

Organizational knowledge [42] constitutes the background of the Wheel, encompassing files and business objects as well as social production [15] data. Organizational knowledge constantly changes as the Wheel goes round, either because business data change during acting or as learning evolves within the enterprise. Moreover, along the Wheel's turning, organizational knowledge is shared. Sharing includes both exchanging existing knowledge and creating new knowledge in collaboration. During this process, individual knowledge is translated into organizational knowledge.

What should be made clear about the Wheel's turning is that as the hub with the spokes and tire are turning, the brakes remain stable, as indicated in Fig. 4. This has the following implications. Regarding acting, it means that during task accomplishment, the interactions may be predetermined (when acting is above the brakes referring to organizational policies and business rules) or ad hoc based on social interactions (when the acting part is above social interaction and social production). Likewise, depending on its current position, knowledge gathering may involve predetermined steps when the information sources already exist as part of the organizational knowledge and are known to the person that needs them or it may involve social interactions, for instance, for the acquirement of tacit knowledge.

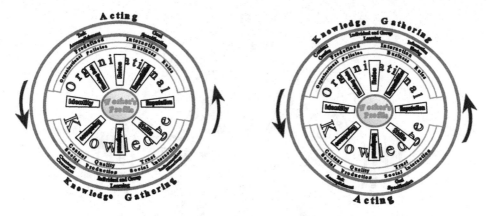

Fig. 4. The wheel's turning function

Enhancing the Worker-Centered Organizational Work Wheel

As agility is a very important aspect of the knowledgeable employee's work, the integrated environment should also enable the worker to handle events. Event streams should be fed into the environment and get instantly analyzed and recorded. Such capability may allow direct response to undesired situations as well as the uncovering of opportunities that could be exploited for competitive advantage. A CEP (Complex Event Processing) [43] mechanism should also be supported for the detection of meaningful patterns that could contribute to the organizational knowledge.

Furthermore, a worker might need to find the appropriate person to refer to for the accomplishment of a task or to get information on how to carry out a task. In a sense, identifying "whom-to-ask" and "how-to-do" worker activities may directly reflect an intertwined view of acting and knowledge gathering perspectives.

In simple words, this means that while trying to accomplish a goal, a worker might need right before executing a task to use the social features of the integrated environment in order to acquire knowledge on how to proceed with the specific task. For instance, an employee may use the searching mechanism to identify the suitable person to refer to based on information found on workers' profiles and even take into account possible ratings or endorsements existing on the profiles. In another case, a worker might need to employ advanced recommendation mechanisms [21], which would explore what steps have been followed by other workers in the past for the accomplishment of the specific task. Alternatively, the worker, depending on how urgent the execution of a specific task is, may be engaged in discussions/forums with the other stakeholders in order to sort out how to carry out the task. A newly encountered situation from the perspective of a specific employee, for example, may trigger such intertwined task execution and knowledge processing activities. To this end, mining capabilities should be provided to the worker. More specifically, "whom-to" mine and "how-to" mine should also be performed by the knowledgeable worker. Figure 5 presents the enhanced version of the Wheel.

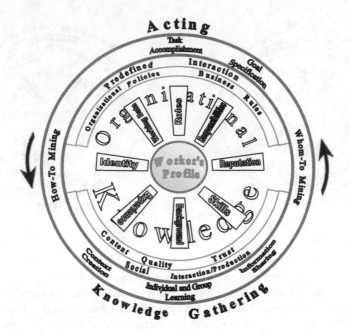

Fig. 5. The enhanced worker-centered organizational work wheel

4   Conclusions – Future Work

In alignment with initiatives like Enterprise 2.0, companies should adjust their organizational work practices in order to empower knowledgeable workers. Empowering
knowledgeable workers means to support them in efficient knowledge gathering and
task execution. For an efficient work however, knowledge gathering and task execution
should be supported through a unified environment. Towards identifying the features of
such a unified environment, we conducted in this paper a two-phase analysis, which
resulted in the development of a coarse-grained conceptualization of this environment,
reflecting a worker-centered organizational work model. This conceptualization was
named Worker-Centered Organizational Work Wheel.

The Wheel may constitute a reference framework, illustrating in a compact and
organized way the features of an environment that integrates knowledge gathering with
task accomplishment by adopting features from social software and BPMS. Guided by
this framework, we will elaborate our research by identifying research issues that need
to be resolved for the implementation of the integrated environment. Based on the
identified issues, we intend to specify an architecture for the implementation of the
unified environment and ultimately to develop a prototype so as to verify the correctness and applicability if the Wheel framework. For the implementation of the
prototype, enterprise social networks could be a candidate technology, which should
be, of course, appropriately augmented with task execution capabilities. The first steps
towards this direction would be to enrich user profile data to encompass working data
information, as indicated by the Wheel, and also to enable task execution and

input/output data exchange between tasks within the social networking environment. Lastly, it should be noted that concepts from Adaptive Case Management [1] will be also closely examined, as they may be relevant to the implementation of a part of the Wheel's functionality regarding non-routine activities.

References

1. Keith, S.: Mastering the Unpredictable. Meghan-Kiffer Press, Tampa (2010)
2. Polanyi, M.: Personal Knowledge - Towards a Post-Critical Philosophy. The University of Chicago Press, Chicago (1958)
3. Hopfenbeck, W., Müller, M., Peis, T.: Wissensbasiertes Management: Ansätze und Strategien zur UnternehmensführungInternet-Ökonomie (in German). Verlag Moderne Industrie, Landsberg (2001)
4. McAfee, A.P.: Enterprise 2.0: The Dawn of Emergent Collaboration. MIT Sloan Manag. Rev. **47**(3), 21–28 (2006)
5. Polaschek M., Zeppelzauer W., Kryvinska N., Strauss C.: Enterprise 2.0 integrated communication and collaboration platform: a conceptual viewpoint. In: AINA Workshops, pp. 1221–1226 (2012)
6. Fahd, Z.O., Ahmad, G.: Knowledge sharing and collaboration through social media. the case of IBM. In: Proceedings of the MCIS (2012)
7. Lester, H., Drury, J.L., Daniel, W., Damianos E.L., Donna, C.: Evaluating the uses and benefits of an enterprise social media platform. J. Soc. Media Organ. **1**(1) (2009)
8. Forrester: Social networking In The Enterprise: Benefits and Inhibitors. A commissioned study conducted by Forrester Consulting on behalf of Cisco Systems (2010)
9. Dumas, M., Aalst, W., Hofstede, A.: Process-Aware Information Systems. Wiley, Hoboken (2005)
10. Sandy, K.: Leveraging social BPM for enterprise transformation. In: Fischer, L., (ed.) Book Chapter in Social BPM: Work, Planning and Collaboration under the Impact of Social Technology. BPM and Workflow Handbook Series (2011)
11. Michael, L., Nina, C.: Toward an agile knowledge connection of employees with regard to business processes. In: HICSS, pp. 3436–3445 (2013)
12. Keith, S., et al.: Social BPM: work, planning and collaboration under the impact of social technology. In: Fischer, L. (ed.) BPM and Workflow Handbook Series (2011)
13. Curtis, B., Kellner, M., Over, J.: Process modeling. Commun. ACM **35**(9), 75–90 (1992)
14. List, B., Korherr, B.: An evaluation of conceptual business process modeling languages. In: SAC (2006)
15. Schmidt, R., Nurcan, S.: BPM and social software. In: Ardagna, D., Mecella, M., Yang, J. (eds.) Business Process Management Workshops. LNBIP, vol. 17, pp. 649–658. Springer, Heidelberg (2009)
16. Giorgio, B., Frank, D., Ben, J., Rania, K., Selmin, N., Michael, P., Marcello, S., Rainer, S., Rito, S.: Key challenges for enabling agile BPM with social software. J. Softw. Maint. **23**(4), 297–326 (2011)
17. DiMicco, J., Millen, D. R., Geyer, W., Dugan, C., Brownholtz, B., Muller, M.: Motivations for social networking at work. In: Proceedings of the 2008 ACM Conference on Computer Supported Cooperative Work, CSCW 2008. ACM, New York, pp. 711–720 (2008)
18. Richter, A., Riemer, K.: Corporate social networking sites –modes of use and appropriation through co-evolution. In: 20th Australasian Conference on Information Systems, Melbourne, p. 34, (2009)

19. Bruno, G.: An approach to defining social processes based on social networks. In: Handbook of Research on Business Social Networking: Organizational, Managerial, and Technological Dimensions, pp. 272–286. IGI (2012)
20. Dengler F., Lamparter S., Hefke M., Abecker, A.: Collaborative process development using semantic MediaWiki. In: Proceedings of the 5th Conference of Professional Knowledge Management. Solothurn, Switzerland (2009)
21. Qu H., Sun J., Jamjoom H. T.: Scoop: automated social recommendation in enterprise process management. In: IEEE International Conference on Services Computing, vol. 1, pp. 101–108 (2008)
22. Koschmider, A., Song, M., Reijers, H.A.: Social software for modeling business processes. In: Ardagna, D., Mecella, M., Yang, J. (eds.) Business Process Management Workshops. LNBIP, vol. 17, pp. 666–677. Springer, Heidelberg (2009)
23. Fengel J., Rebstock M., Nüttgens M.: Modell-tagging zur semantischen verlinkung heterogener modelle. In: EMISA, pp. 53–58 (2008)
24. Reich, J.: Supporting the Execution of Knowledge Intensive Processes by Means of Expert and Best- Practice Mediation. Dr. Hut, München (2008)
25. Brambilla, M., Piero, F., Carmen, K., Vaca, R.: Combining social web and BPM for improving enterprise performances: the BPM4People approach to social BPM. In: WWW (Companion Volume), pp. 223–226 (2012)
26. Silva, A.R., Meziani, R., Magalhaes, R., Martinho, D., Aguiar, A., Flores, N.: AGILIPO: embedding social software features into business process tools. In: Rinderle-Ma, S., Sadiq, S., Leymann, F. (eds.) BPM 2009. LNBIP, vol. 43, pp. 219–230. Springer, Heidelberg (2010)
27. Bider, I., Johannesson, P., Perjons, E.: A strategy for merging social software with business process support. In: Muehlen, M., Su, J. (eds.) BPM 2010 Workshops. LNBIP, vol. 66, pp. 372–383. Springer, Heidelberg (2011)
28. Rossi, D., Vitali, F.: Workflow enactment in a social software environment. In: Ardagna, D., Mecella, M., Yang, J. (eds.) Business Process Management Workshops. LNBIP, vol. 17, pp. 716–722. Springer, Heidelberg (2009)
29. Xie, L., de Vrieze, P., Xu, L.: When social software meets business process management. In: Proceedings of the Fourth. International Conference on Computer Sciences and Convergence Information Technology, pp. 238–243 (2009)
30. Khalaf, R., Subramanian, R., Mikalsen, T., Duftler, M., Diament, J., Silva-Lepe, I.: Enabling community participation for workflows through extensibility and sharing. In: Rinderle-Ma, S., Sadiq, S., Leymann, F. (eds.) BPM 2009. LNBIP, vol. 43, pp. 207–218. Springer, Heidelberg (2010)
31. Johannesson, P., Andersson, B., Wohed, P.: Business process management with social software systems – a new paradigm for work organisation. In: Ardagna, D., Mecella, M., Yang, J. (eds.) Business Process Management Workshops. LNBIP, vol. 17, pp. 659–665. Springer, Heidelberg (2009)
32. Neumann, G., Erol, S.: From a social wiki to a social workflow system. In: Ardagna, D., Mecella, M., Yang, J. (eds.) Business Process Management Workshops. LNBIP, vol. 17, pp. 698–708. Springer, Heidelberg (2009)
33. Motahari-Nezhad, H.R., Bartolini, C., Graupner, S., Spence, S.: Adaptive case management in the social enterprise. In: Liu, C., Ludwig, H., Toumani, F., Yu, Q. (eds.) Service Oriented Computing. LNCS, vol. 7636, pp. 550–557. Springer, Heidelberg (2012)
34. Alexopoulou, N., Nikolaidou, M., Stary, C.: Blending BPMS with social software for knowledge-intense work: research issues. In: Nurcan, S., Proper, H., Soffer, P., Krogstie, J., Schmidt, R., Halpin, T., Bider, I. (eds.) BPMDS 2013 and EMMSAD 2013. LNBIP, vol. 147, pp. 18–31. Springer, Heidelberg (2013)

35. OMG: Business Process Management Notation. Version 2.0 (2011)
36. Martinho, D., Silva, A.R.: An experiment on the capture of business processes from knowledge workers. In: Lohmann, N., Song, M., Wohed, P. (eds.) BPM 2013 Workshops. LNBIP, vol. 171, pp. 113–124. Springer, Heidelberg (2014)
37. Selim, E., Michael, G., Simone, H., Sami, J., Ben, J., Paul, J., Agnes, K., Selmin, N., Davide, R., Rainer, S.: Combining BPM and social software: contradiction or chance? J. Softw. Maint. Evol.: Res. Pract. 22(6–7), 449–476 (2010)
38. Surowiecki, J.: The Wisdom of Crowds: Why the Many are Smarter than the Few and How Collective Wisdom Shapes Business, Economies, Societies and Nations. Doubleday, New York (2004)
39. Nathaniel, P.: The role of trust and reputation in social BPM. In: Fischer, L., (ed.) Book Chapter in Social BPM: Work, Planning and Collaboration Under the Impact of Social Technology. BPM and Workflow Handbook Series (2011)
40. Martyn, O.: Business Process Management: A Rigorous Approach. Meghan Kiffer Press, Tampa (2005)
41. Shankar, K.: Social Process Design, Execution and Intelligence for a better Customer Experience. Infosys, white paper (2011)
42. Ikujiro, N., Philippe, B., Chester, B., Noboru, K.: Organizational knowledge creation theory: a first comprehensive test. Int. Bus. Rev. 3(4), 337–351 (1994)
43. David, L.: The Power of Events. Addison-Wesley, Boston (2002)

Compliance of the LinkedIn Privacy Policy with the Principles of the ISO 29100:2011 Standard

Alexandra Michota[✉] and Sokratis Katsikas

Systems Security Laboratory, Department of Digital Systems,
School of Information and Communication Technologies, University of Piraeus,
150 Androutsou Street, 18532 Piraeus, Greece
{amichota, ska}@unipi.gr

Abstract. Sharing personal information in online social networks can be risky, considering that unauthorized users can get access to this information and use it for purposes other than those intended to by the data subjects or those specified by the privacy policy of the online social network. The role of Social Networking Site (SNS) privacy policies is to make clear to the users what information is collected and how it will be used. In this paper we focus on examining whether the current LinkedIn Privacy Policy complies with the privacy principles specified in the ISO 29100:2011 standard. We investigated this conformance by mapping the ISO privacy principles to the privacy policy of the sharing content on LinkedIn, building upon our previous work on Facebook [1]. The results of this examination indicate serious mismatches and can be used for making suggestions that might help the Service Providers to redesign a more privacy respectful LinkedIn.

Keywords: ISO 29100:2011 · Standardization · Social networks · Privacy policy · Privacy principles

1 Introduction

SNS services are being used by millions of people worldwide. Privacy issues related to SNS data find their way to the media routinely, despite the fact that SNS have stated their privacy policies. This is because SNS privacy policies provide little protection against the risk of data leakage [2]. Thus, more attention needs to be paid to the privacy offered by SNS, in order to allow individuals to take informed decisions about what they post online. If the privacy policies continue on their current trajectory, without emphasizing organizational accountability and marginalizing data minimization and transparency, SNS users could become subject to increasingly stifling digital oversight.

Guidelines for developing and operating information security management systems, including risk assessment and management frameworks, have been and are being used to support businesses in setting up adequate control infrastructures for their information systems [3]. More recently, in response to the growing importance of privacy by design and by default, the International Standards Organization (ISO) issued the ISO 29100:2011 Privacy framework standard [4].

B. Benatallah et al. (Eds.): WISE 2014, LNCS 9051, pp. 72–83, 2015.
DOI: 10.1007/978-3-319-20370-6_6

When considering the ways in which SNS Service Providers (SNSSP) protect the SNS users' privacy, and the capabilities of the end users to ensure the protection of their data, we see a combination of fundamental data protection techniques (e.g. user-driven privacy setting menus) and policy statements. The SNSSP will usually claim that, because they publish their privacy policy, SNS users are well informed on how their data is used and how it is protected.

While all SNS have clear links to their privacy policies from their home pages, this does not necessarily mean that people will read these policies before they login or sign-up; even if they do read them, it does not necessarily follow that they will understand them fully. Similarly to the Facebook case, the LinkedIn example illustrates the users' challenge of understanding the SNS privacy policies. Hence, the privacy policies are often criticized for being too verbose and complex to allow end users to appreciate the implications of divulging their Personally Identifiable Information (PII) while using the service. These issues have been studied, particularly in the context of P3P policies, in [5, 6].

Our previous study of the Facebook privacy policy highlighted the gap between the SNS privacy policy and information privacy framework as suggested by the ISO 29100:2011 standard [1]. In this paper we investigate whether the ISO 29100:2011 privacy principles are satisfied by the current LinkedIn Privacy Policy, as revised in March 2014. This policy is separated into parts; these are examined separately, with the aim to facilitate compliance in a sense of assessing and enforcing privacy controls.

The paper is structured as follows: The privacy principles in ISO 29100:2011 are presented in Sect. 2. Section 3 describes the roles and the interactions in SNS as well as their relation to PII. Then, the LinkedIn Privacy Policy [7] is introduced and its conformance to the ISO 29100:2011 principles is examined in Sect. 4. Finally, the paper concludes with Sect. 5.

2 Privacy Principles in ISO 29100:2011

The ISO 29100:2011standard defines privacy safeguarding requirements as they relate to PII processed by any information and communication system in any jurisdiction. It is applicable on an international scale and sets a common privacy terminology, defines privacy principles when processing PII, categorizes privacy features and relates all described privacy aspects to existing security guidelines. The standard also serves as a basis for desirable additional privacy standardization initiatives, for example a technical reference architecture; the use of specific privacy technologies; an overall privacy management; assurance of privacy compliance for outsourced data processes; privacy impact assessments; and engineering specifications. It is necessarily general in nature; it puts organizational, technical, procedural and regulatory aspects in perspective; it addresses system-specific issues on a high-level; and it is closely linked to existing security standards that have been widely implemented into practice. The main aim of this standard is to provide guidance concerning information and communication system requirements for processing PII to contribute to the privacy of people on an international level, regardless of the particular national or regional laws and regulations and no matter which data systems are used.

As SNS are also widely used as marketing tools, it would be of significant importance for the privacy-related processes used by organizations to comply with privacy and data protection legislation and relevant good practice. The risks arising because of the use of social media marketing techniques for promoting the entrepreneurial activities will also need to be managed. The treasure of the SNS users' sharing data is used for marketing processes, like marketing campaigns. More specifically, LinkedIn profiles that include real information of the users' curriculum vitaes are considered to be targets for the marketers' data mining activities. Thus, the compliance of the LinkedIn Privacy Policy with the principles of the ISO 29100:2011 would also give solutions to the risks of data leakage and misuse of SNS users' PII, by providing privacy enhanced services in the entrepreneurial world.

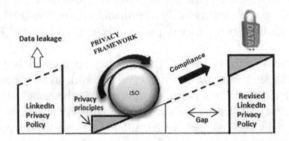

Fig. 1. ISO 29100:2011 privacy framework incorporation to the LinkedIn privacy policy

In Fig. 1, the privacy principles are the motivating force in order to move the wheel that symbolizes the privacy framework that is defined by the ISO standard. However, there is a gap in this route, between the ISO standard and the LinkedIn Privacy Policy. This gap is considered to be the difficult step of this "uphill path". If this gap can be somehow overcome, the incorporation of the privacy framework as defined by the ISO 29100:2011 standard to the LinkedIn privacy architecture will be accomplished and the privacy principles will be fully implemented into the LinkedIn Privacy Policy.

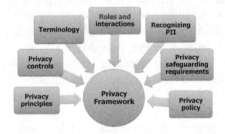

Fig. 2. ISO 29100:2011 privacy framework components

Figure 2 depicts the components that relate to privacy and the processing of PII in Information Communication Technology (ICT) systems. These make up the privacy framework described in this International Standard.

Figure 3 depicts the 11 privacy principles as suggested by the standard; these are to guide the design, development and implementation of privacy policies and controls.

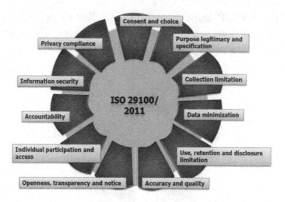

Fig. 3. ISO 29100:2011 privacy principles

- **Consent and choice:** PII principal has choice on and has Opt-In to PII processing and implementing the PII principal's preferences as expressed in his consent.
- **Purpose legitimacy and specification:** Processing complies with laws, giving notice before processing.
- **Collection limitation:** It should be done to what is legal and necessary for specified purposes.
- **Data minimization:** Minimize the processing of PII.
- **Use, retention and disclosure limitation:** It also applies to limitation on cross-border transfers.
- **Accuracy and quality:** Measure to assure validity and correctness of PII processing.
- **Openness, transparency and notice:** Clear, complete and accessible information on PII processing.
- **Individual participation and access:** PII principal access to review their PII and correct inaccuracies.
- **Accountability:** Demonstrate care in duty toward PII principal for PII stewardship.
- **Information security:** Protecting PII under its authority with appropriate controls.
- **Privacy compliance:** Verifying and demonstrating adherence to laws with internal or 3rd party audits.

3   Roles and Interactions in SNS

The ISO 29100:2011 standard defines as PII any information that (a) can be used to identify the PII principal to whom such information relates, or (b) is or might be directly or indirectly linked to a PII principal. The SNS user plays the role of the PII principal as, according to the ISO standard, this term defines the person to whom the PII relates. The SNS user also provides all the necessary information that is shared with her SNS audience. Figure 4 depicts in detail the Privacy Data Lifecycle that consists of five stages. As seen in Fig. 4, apart from the SNS users, the SNSSP team participates in the stages of the Privacy Data Lifecycle. PII controllers and processors are considered to be members of the SNSSP team. The PII Controller or privacy stakeholder is the entity that determines the purposes and means of processing the user's PII other than natural persons who use data for personal purposes [8].

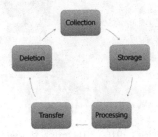

Fig. 4. Privacy data lifecycle

4   The LinkedIn Privacy Policy and the ISO 29100:2011 Standard Privacy Principles

LinkedIn has split its data use (privacy) policy down to four parts, namely "Information collected" or "What information we collect"; "Uses & sharing of personal information" or "How we use your personal information"; "Your choices & obligations"; and, last but not least, the part that includes "Important information". In the introduction of this policy, it is clarified that LinkedIn is a platform for posting and viewing content and that content may be available to unregistered users (called "Visitors"). It is also noted that the LinkedIn SP may disclose users' information to third parties only when they believe that it is required by law, subpoena, or other legal process, not when they merely believe that such disclosure is permissible.

In this study, we investigated whether each of the first three parts of the privacy policy covers the eleven legal principles outlined in Sect. 2; the fourth part provides details for the LinkedIn usage. Figure 6 depicts the mapping process we followed.

The privacy policy naturally applies to a social networking data flow system. As seen in Fig. 5, "PII" and "Visibility" are the main factors we took into account to do this mapping. The privacy principles provide guidelines on how the privacy policies should have been composed and how these principles should have been applied to the privacy control mechanisms of the SNS. Privacy policies specify the PII that is being collected by the SNSSP, as well as the uses and recipients (visibility) of that PII. In this study, we examined each statement in all parts of the LinkedIn Privacy Policy, noting whether or not the statement mentioned a particular data item. We then analyzed what this statement said about whether or not the PII involved was required or optional, what the SNSSP would do with that PII (PII processing procedures), and whether or not that PII is visible to individuals with no authorized access. Finally, we cross-referenced this information with the ISO privacy principles (guidelines), and verified whether or not the actions pertaining to that PII and its visibility could be mapped to any privacy protection guidelines (Fig. 5).

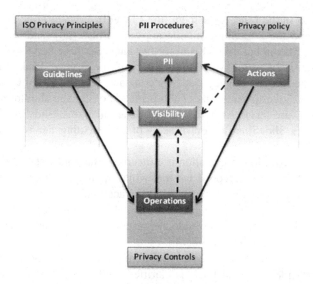

Fig. 5. Mapping process

Our results were obtained by mapping the detailed description of each part of the data use policy to each of the ISO 29100:2011 standard principles, by using the methodology presented in the previous paragraph. The following Tables show this mapping. In order to evaluate the mappings between the privacy policy and the ISO privacy policy parts principles, we needed to establish a mapping scale. Two symbols were used in the mapping. The symbol "+" designates that a principle is covered to a large extent, whereas the symbol "O" designates that a principle is covered to some extent. In order for the mapping to be considered complete, the privacy policy should meet all the policy parts aspects of each privacy principle, as specified by the ISO 29100/2011. A mapping is marked as partial if a concrete link cannot be established between the information presented in a privacy policy and the ISO privacy principles. Complete lack of principle coverage is not considered, as all the data use policies are formulated in a way such that even partial coverage can always be claimed. The workflow for this examination is presented below in Fig. 6.

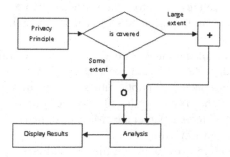

Fig. 6. Workflow for mapping study

As highlighted in the User Agreement, the LinkedIn Privacy Policy now applies to SlideShare [9] (and the SlideShare mobile app) and Pulse [10] (and the Pulse mobile app). The LinkedIn team has done this to further integrate these services into LinkedIn.

In the "What information we collect" part of the policy, LinkedIn "Terms of Service" are defined as this privacy policy accompanies the LinkedIn User Agreement. If a user does not agree to the terms of the privacy policy, she should not use any of LinkedIn products and services (including mobile applications, SlideShare or Pulse). A user may close her SlideShare or Pulse account by revisiting her account settings in those products.

As far as the registration information is concerned, the policy states that a user may still register for a SlideShare account and that while she may no longer register for new Pulse accounts, she may continue to use her Pulse account. There is no requirement for direct consent from a user to share her PII when she is requested to fill in the registration form as, if she does not provide the necessary information, she will not be allowed to create an account on LinkedIn.

In the section "Profile Information", the difference between an account on LinkedIn and accounts on SlideShare and Pulse is clarified. SlideShare profiles are meant to be public. LinkedIn may use the information that a user provides in a SlideShare or Pulse profile in the same manner as information in a LinkedIn.com profile, subject to the Terms of Service. Providing additional information may not only help recruiters find the user, but also others offering business opportunities. It easily follows that LinkedIn try to make the users to be addicted to over-sharing. Hence, a user is giving her direct consent to share all this additional information knowing that some of it may be made public. As seen in the following paragraphs, a LinkedIn user also agrees to share her PII even with Third Parties, Sites and Applications that are incorporated in the LinkedIn and Advertise Service Providers.

The LinkedIn Privacy Policy also states that SNSSP may provide and the users might use other mechanisms similar to the contacts importer, allowing users to upload individual contacts or their entire address book. The mobile applications may permit the SNS users to synchronize their calendar, email, or contacts apps with LinkedIn to show meeting attendees, email correspondents and contacts.

Additionally, it is clarified that SlideShare and Pulse are not considered third-party sites or applications.

"Cookies" is an issue for criticism by the research community. The LinkedIn team has clarified that mobile application identifiers are used rather than mobile device identifiers to help recognize the user across their services. Moreover, the SNS users are required to give their consent to placements of beacons in LinkedIn HTML emails to them.

For Advertising Technologies and Web Beacons, it is clarified that ads may be targeted to both LinkedIn Members and to Visitors. Furthermore, social actions on SlideShare, such as liking content are public, unless it is explicitly stated that the action is not public. It is clearly noted that a LinkedIn user can opt-out of this, using information from advertising partners to target ads. More information is provided about how to opt out of advertising on LinkedIn.

Last but not least, with regards to the log files, IP addresses, and information about users' computer and mobile device, it is clarified that the LinkedIn Team may receive the URL of the site a user visits immediately before or after she accesses any of the LinkedIn services.

Both the "Advertising technologies and web beacons" and "Log files, IP addresses, and information about users' computer and mobile device" parts of the policy cover the principle of "Purpose legitimacy and specification" because the data subjects are fully informed about the information they choose to share and about which pieces of this information are visible to the public.

With respect to design pattern coverage, we observe that the "What information we collect" part of the LinkedIn Privacy Policy covers only some principles to a large extent. It is evident by Table 1 that the principles of "Accuracy and quality", "Openness, transparency and notice" and Individual participation and access" are fully implemented by the majority of the LinkedIn Privacy Policy parts. This is due to the following reasons: First, there is no processing action that could "harm" the data. The policy ensures that the users' PII is accurate, up-to-date and relevant for the purpose. Second, during the PII processing, proper notices by the data controllers keep the data subjects informed of the processing. Third, the LinkedIn users can access, review or correct their PII whenever they wish.

Table 1. Mapping of the LinkedIn Privacy Policy "What information we collect" onto the privacy principles of the ISO 29100:2011

ISO 29100:2011 Privacy Principles

LinkedIn Policy Part	Consent and Choice	Purpose legitimacy and specification	Collection limitation	Data minimization	Use, retention and disclosure limitation	Accuracy and quality	Openness, transparency and notice	Individual participation and access	Accountability	Information security	Privacy compliance
Data Controllers	+	+	O	+	O	+	+	+	O	O	O
Registration	O	O	O	+	O	+	+	+	O	O	O
Profile information	+	+	O	O	O	+	+	+	O	O	O
Address book & other services that sync with LinkedIn	+	O	O	O	O	+	+	+	+	O	O
Customer service	O	O	O	O	O	+	+	+	O	O	O
Sites & Apps	+	O	O	O	+	+	+	+	O	O	O
Third Party services & sites	+	O	O	O	+	+	+	+	O	O	O
Cookies	+	O	O	O	+	+	O	+	+	O	O
Ad technologies &Web beacons	+	+	O	O	O	+	+	+	O	O	O
Log files, IP addresses & Information about your device	O	+	O	O	O	+	+	O	O	O	O
Other	O	O	O	O	O	+	O	O	O	O	O

On the contrary, the "Collection limitation", "Information security" and "Privacy compliance" ISO privacy principles are implemented only to some extent by all the parts of the policy. This is not surprising, as not only is much more data collected but the users are also encouraged to share even more PII. It is claimed that by over-sharing users can help the SNSSP to improve their services and make the SNS more user friendly. As seen in Tables 1, 2 and 3, the "Information security" and "Privacy compliance" principles are not covered to a large extent by almost all the parts of the LinkedIn Privacy Policy. This is because PII integrity, confidentiality and availability are difficult to guarantee when there are SNS interactions and lack of adherence to data protection laws.

As seen in Table 2, there are differences in principle coverage between the "What information we collect" and the "How we use your personal information" parts of the privacy policy.

Table 2. Mapping of the LinkedIn Privacy Policy "How we use your personal information" onto the privacy principles of the ISO 29100:2011

ISO 29100:2011 Privacy Principles

LinkedIn Policy Part	Consent and Choice	Purpose legitimacy and specification	Collection limitation	Data minimization	Use, retention and disclosure limitation	Accuracy and quality	Openness, transparency and notice	Individual participation and access	Accountability	Information security	Privacy compliance
PII	+	+	O	O	O	+	+	+	O	O	O
LinkedIn Communications	O	O	O	O	O	+	+	+	O	O	O
User Communications	O	+	+	+	+	+	+	O	O	O	O
Customized Content	O	O	O	O	O	+	+	O	O	O	O
Sharing info with Affiliates	+	+	O	O	O	+	O	O	O	O	O
Sharing info with Third Parties	+	+	O	+	+	+	+	+	O	O	O
Platform Services used by Third Parties	+	+	+	+	+	+	+	+	O	O	O
Polls and Surveys	+	+	+	+	+	+	+	+	+	O	O
Search	O	O	O	O	O	+	+	O	O	O	O
Groups	+	+	+	+	+	+	+	+	+	O	O
Testimonials & Ads through LinkedIn Ads	+	+	+	+	+	+	+	+	O	O	O
Talent Recruiting, Marketing & Sales solutions	+	+	+	+	+	+	+	+	O	O	O
Pages	+	O	O	O	+	+	+	+	O	O	O
Compliance with legal process	+	+	+	+	+	+	+	O	+	+	O
Disclosure to others	O	O	O	O	O	+	+	O	O	O	O
Service Providers	O	+	+	+	+	+	+	O	+	O	O

In the LinkedIn Privacy Policy certain references to "messages" have changed to "communications". The LinkedIn Team might communicate with the users through notices in their apps and send them updates about other Members that the users are connected to and about their actions.

There is also direct reference to the SlideShare settings page. This ensures the coverage of the principle "Openness, transparency and notice".

The content that the users share on LinkedIn is classified as either "Customized content", or "Sharing information with affiliates" or "Sharing information with third parties". The policy states that the aggregate information which the LinkedIn Team uses to customize content may come from other users, in addition to users in a LinkedIn member's network. "LinkedIn affiliates" are defined as entities controlled by, controlling or under common control with LinkedIn. Moreover, there is no reference to SlideShare' separate user agreement and privacy policy. The LinkedIn Team might use information from SlideShare and Pulse internally across different services even if a user has not tied her accounts on those services to LinkedIn by signing in to SlideShare or Pulse with her LinkedIn account. However, a user can limit the public visibility of her profiles on LinkedIn or SlideShare. Last but not least, a concern-raising addition to this part of the policy is the specific reference that LinkedIn Team may disclose information to protect Visitors. The "Accuracy and quality" principle is covered by the three classes of the LinkedIn sharing content.

The section "Talent recruiting, marketing and sales solutions" is meant to explicitly cover subscribers to LinkedIn's marketing solutions and sales solutions products, in addition to LinkedIn talent recruiting products. Personal information obtained independently of the LinkedIn services will not be added to users' LinkedIn profiles. This part covers almost all the principles to a large extent, with the exception of the three last principles i.e. "Accountability", "Information security" and "Privacy compliance".

The last paragraph of this policy part clearly states that the LinkedIn Team uses service providers to facilitate its services; further, LinkedIn service providers' access to and use of personal data are limited to this purpose. However, users are giving indirect consent for this usage and their access to their PII is not apparent by this part of the policy.

Comparing with the previous results, as shown in Table 3, the privacy principles are mostly covered to some extent by this part of the policy. The exception to the rule is the "Use retention and disclosure limitation" and "Accuracy and quality" principles that are applicable to all the features of this part.

As mentioned in the policy, if a user decides to close her account(s), her information will be removed from the Service within 24 hours. The LinkedIn team deletes closed account information and will de-personalize any logs or other backup information within 30 days of the account closure, specifying the exceptions of the users who have active SlideShare accounts. It is also specified by the policy that even if LinkedIn removes a user's data, her public data may be displayed in search engine results until the search engine refreshes its cache. The LinkedIn Privacy Policy also provides information on how a user can delete her information from SlideShare and how she can request a copy of the personal data to which she may be entitled.

LinkedIn's Customer Service keeps users' information for as long as your account is active or as needed. LinkedIn may retain users' personal data even after they have closed their accounts if the data retention complies with its legal obligations and meets the regulatory requirements. A very important obligation that LinkedIn members have

Table 3. Mapping of the LinkedIn Privacy Policy "Your choices and obligations" onto the privacy principles of the ISO 29100:2011

ISO 29100:2011 Privacy Principles

LinkedIn Policy Part	Consent and Choice	Purpose legitimacy and specification	Collection limitation	Data minimization	Use, retention and disclosure limitation	Accuracy and quality	Openness, transparency and notice	Individual participation and access	Accountability	Information security	Privacy compliance
Rights to Access, Correct, or Delete Your Info, and Closing Your Account	+	+	O	O	+	+	+	+	O	O	+
Data Retention	O	+	O	O	+	+	+	O	O	O	+
Your Obligations	O	O	O	O	+	+	O	O	O	O	O

when they register to the LinkedIn online community is to respect the terms of use, and its policies. This notice is highlighted so as to avoid cases where the sharing content is infringing. However, the same part specifies that users should give their consent to the LinkedIn team to administer their property rights that may also belong to third parties, such as trademarks or copyrights.

The aim of the last part of the policy is to provide some information to the data subjects before they start creating their account on LinkedIn. Such information is, for example, what is the minimum age to register to the LinkedIn platform. The PII principals are also informed about the partnership that LinkedIn has started with TRUSTe aiming to certify its members' privacy. Additionally, the LinkedIn policy specifies that it complies with the U.S.-E.U. and U.S.-Swiss Safe Harbor Frameworks. It is further noted that SlideShare.net has also been awarded the TRUSTe Privacy Seal of compliance.

A very important issue that has created concerns over the SNS users' privacy is the frequent changes to the privacy policies. As mentioned in the LinkedIn Privacy Policy, special notifications will be sent to the users following policy revisions. A special law for the residents of California known as "California's Shine the Light Law" has applied, aiming to protect any of the users' personal information with third parties from direct marketing. Last but not least, the HTTPS access and the corresponding SSL access over mobile devices to the LinkedIn platform have been enabled and cover the safeguarding requirement for Internet Security.

5 Conclusions

In this paper we examined the compliance of the LinkedIn Privacy Policy to the privacy principles of the ISO 29100:2011 standard. The study was based on the corresponding study that we have already done for the Facebook Data Use Policy. Similarly with our approach in [1] we used mapping techniques, which revealed that the principles are only partially covered by the majority of the policy parts.

The privacy framework as suggested by the ISO 29100:2011 standard provides guidelines, the effectiveness of which depends on SNSSP interpretation and expertise in implementing them in SNS platforms. The privacy principle coverage is necessary to be used in SNS communities primarily for evaluation of the existing SNS privacy, and subsequently for use and adaptation of the privacy controls according to the ISO 29100:2011 standard.

More user-understandable and effective privacy policies that adhere to the requirements of relevant ISO standards and those of national and international regulations should be embedded in the SNS infrastructure. Large-extent principle coverage will provide SNS with default data protection and privacy controls.

References

1. Michota, A., Katsikas, S.: The compliance of the facebook data use policy with the principles of the ISO 29100:2011. In: Proceedings of NTMS2014 – 6th International Conference on New Technologies, Mobility & Security, Dubai. IEEE (2014)
2. Krishnamurthy, B., Wills, C.E.: On the leakage of personally identifiable information via online social networks. In: WOSN 2009 Proceedings of the 2nd ACM Workshop on Online social networks, pp. 7–12
3. The ISO 27000 Directory, An Introduction to ISO 27001, 27002, 27008. http://www.27000.org/
4. ISO/IEC 29100. Information technology – Security techniques– Privacy framework. Technical report, ISO JTC 1/SC 27
5. Prabaker, M., Rao, J., Fette, I., Kelley, P., Cranor, L., Hongand, J., Sadeh, N.: Understanding and capturing people's privacy policies in a people under application. In: 2007 Ubicomp Workshop on Privacy
6. Reeder, R., Kelley, P., McDonald, A., Cranor, L.: A user study of the expandable grid applied to P3P privacy policy visualization. In: WPES (2008)
7. LinkedIn Privacy Policy. https://www.linkedin.com/legal/privacy-policy
8. Cutillo, L.A., Manulis, M., Strufe, T.: Security and privacy in online social networks. In: Furht, F. (ed.) Handbook of Social Network. Technologies and Applications. Springer, Heidelberg (2010)
9. SlideShare. www.slideshare.net
10. Pulse. www.pulse.me

The Use of Social Tagging in Social Business Process Management

Mohammad Ehson Rangiha(⊠) and Bill Karakostas(⊠)

School of Mathematics, Computer Science and Engineering,
City University London, London, UK
{Mohammad.Rangiha.2,Bill.Karakostas.1}@city.ac.uk

Abstract. Socially driven business process management is the latest paradigm in BPM research. Social elements present in social BPM from one hand and the rigid sequential workflows in traditional BPM systems from another hand had made it difficult to have a full understanding of what social BPM really means, until recently where goal-oriented approach was introduced to overcome this contradiction. One of the main characteristics of social business process management is its inherent collaborative nature during all of its phases starting from the design stage all the way to the execution and improvement phase. This paper aims to provide a model for social BPM in which the post execution tagging of business processes logs is utilised by a process management system to assist future process participants with recommendations for task execution and role assignment. It is believed that this approach will lead to a truly socially driven business process management system where there is transparent and continuous participation of the users.

Keywords: Social BPM · Tags · Social knowledge management

1 Introduction

Business Process Management (BPM) is a discipline where Information Technology and management intersect [14], to ensure the smooth running, monitoring, designing and improving of business processes.

Agility refers to BPM's ability to react quickly to internal and external events [1]. There has been significant attention to the area of flexible business processes over the past few years [2, 3]. One of the ways to achieve process agility is to introduce social elements into the BPM lifecycle. Social BPM (SBPM) is the congruence of social software and BPM, in the practice of actively involving all relevant stakeholders through the use of social software [15].

In recent years, a lot of research has been done regarding the underpinnings of SBPM. Some preliminary models have been produced [17], at a conceptual level to suggest possible mechanisms to implement SBPM. This paper expands on such previous work and proposes such a mechanism, derived from social software tools, namely tagging of business process execution traces (logs).

Social tagging has been proposed as a mechanism to support knowledge creation during the SBPM lifecycle. For example, social software in conjunction with model

© Springer International Publishing Switzerland 2015
B. Benatallah et al. (Eds.): WISE 2014, LNCS 9051, pp. 84–92, 2015.
DOI: 10.1007/978-3-319-20370-6_7

management approaches have been discussed in [18], where social networks are used to support process models by providing recommendations to people and supporting collaboration.

This paper focuses on the use of social tagging by the business process management system to support automatic task recommendations.

In order to achieve this, the paper covers the following sections: In Sect. 2, the related work in this area has been mentioned, in Sect. 3, a brief overview of social BPM is presented. Section 4 discusses the concept of tagging in the context of social media, while Sect. 5 discusses tagging in the context of social BPM and its application to task recommendation. Finally, Sect. 6 concludes with plans for future research and some final remarks.

2 Related Work

In order to overcome the limitations of traditional BPM model, authors [21–23] have proposed different approaches. For instance, [26] proposes process-oriented KM which uses process models for navigational and structural purposes [27]. Recently approaches using social software in conjunction with model management have emerged, [24] describes an approach using social networks to support process models by supporting collaboration and recommendation between and for the users. Using social tagging for finding models in a repository have also been suggested by authors [27–29]. Another approach explained in [25], suggests the idea of utilising tagging in the context of process models for the purpose of process management. Although these are great contributions in the field, however they do not have a solid design proposal illustrating how the mentioned ideas could be implemented. What could be learned from these approaches is that there is a great potential in the integration of social software and business process management, and it offers improvements to the BPM life-cycle.

The closest research to our approach which has also proposed a prototype for a given scenario is mentioned in [27]. The author argues that the support for creation and usage of processes models as well as for their dissemination are decisive factors in the improvement for business processes and then utilises social tagging to achieve this. As the author states this is not the only approach to the integration of social tagging and process models, our research differs in the proposed design of our model. Whilst [27] considers the structure of process models to consist of the following three levels: elements, groups of elements or sub-procedures and models, we have adapted a different architecture for the discovery of process knowledge in the SBPM as explained below.

3 Social BPM (SBPM)

Social Business Process Management is a collective effort from several users to ensure smooth and efficient execution of business processes. Benefits of SBPM has been discussed in [9]. There is consensus that by working together and creating a platform for social collaboration engagement, the social community can benefit from the 'wisdom of the crowd' i.e. the exploration of tacit knowledge amongst the participants [13]. This could eventually produce better quality processes and result in best practices.

Social BPM enables a large variety of users with varying degrees of training and background to contribute their domain knowledge into process performance [7]. This is achieved through creating an 'architecture of participation' [6] in which everyone feels part of the process execution. Of course, SBPM is not without its own limitations. For example, bias input from the users need to be avoided in order for the contribution to be a real reflection of the users' efforts [1].

4 Tagging

Social tagging assists in integrating models into knowledge management systems [1]. Tagging involves the assignment of unrestricted keywords to all kinds of content [8]. Tagging has several benefits, for instance, immediate feedback, and a sense of serendipity, in the sense that once users start creating tags, they end up clicking on similar tags which leads them to related information on a certain topic [4, 20]. Tagging, therefore, can help to make the content available for search to people using knowledge management systems.

Tagging in the context of business processes means that the users are able to assign tags to the various elements of the executed process so that they can refer to later on and be used by others. Furthermore, tags contextualize process related discussions and help users to mark the content with similar tags. Social tagging of content by multiple users also provides the opportunity for the content to be identified from different perspectives and to foster conversations between groups [5]. Business process management can therefore benefit from tagging for continuous improvement and dissemination of process specific knowledge purposes. This can help to bridge the gap between end users' informal/tacit knowledge and process [1]. The captured process knowledge can then be utilised in future process executions.

Research [8] has categorised social tagging based on their intention as follows:

- *Content-based*, which are tags that describe the content of items such as objects and living things that appear in a context, for example, "car", "cat"....
- *Context-based* which relate to tags that provide contextual information about the items, such as the geographical location where and when a photo was taken, e.g. "Winter", "October" ....
- Subjective, which are the tags which express opinions and qualities of the items, e.g. "sad", "old"....
- Organisational, in which tags define personal usage and tasks or indicate to a personal reference, e.g. "university documents".

5 Recommendation Mechanism for SBPM Through Tagging

5.1 Social Tagging in SBPM

Building on previous work on the use of tagging in a social context, we propose a model where social tagging can be used in the context of a social BPM system in order to add value to the future execution of the process through task recommendation.

In our proposed model of social BPM there are two main types of actors, the community user and the process owner. Users engage in discussion amongst themselves in order to perform tasks related to the fulfilment of process goals. The user interaction model in social BPM, during process execution has been discussed previously [10]. In this paper we focus on post-execution phase of the process. The main activities performed by the user, process owner and the SBPM system, are captured in the use case diagram of Fig. 1.

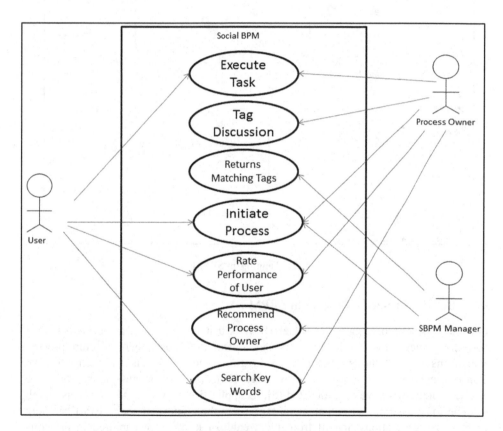

Fig. 1. Social BPM tagging use case

As shown in Fig. 1, one of the tasks carried out by the process owner, post-process execution is process tagging. The process owner visits the discussions carried out during the process and tags relevant parts of each discussion. Tagging involved adding free-form keywords – "Tags" – to the content [4]. The tags do not belong to any specific categories or taxonomies however, they must make sense to other participants that share understanding of the process and its context domain. Thus, the judgment of which parts of the discussion to tag and how is left to the process owner.

In Fig. 2, the proposed tagging mechanism is illustrated and the role of each actor in relation to the overall process and tasks is illustrated.

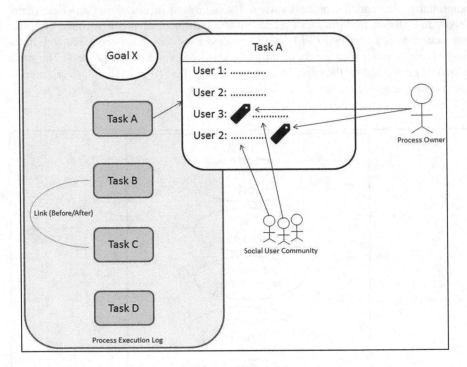

Fig. 2. Tagging in SBPM

5.2   Benefits of Social Tagging in SBPM

The main benefit of tagging in social BPM is that they provide a mechanism of a bottom-up integration of relevant users and content and utilises them in future process executions [11]. Although the idea of tagging process models for their effective management has been proposed previously [12], and the benefits it can bring to business processes have been debated [8], its application in an SBPM context is novel.

The main assumption is that social tagging in the context of social BPM can help users and organisations benefit from the wealth of knowledge captured in previous process execution logs. Through the effective use of tags, the wealth of tacit knowledge which has been captured through SBPM can be utilised for the improvement of process execution.

In this paper we also assume that the participants in an SBPM process will use one of the social tools available, such as wikis. Such tools allow the user inputs to the process performance to be captured (as hyperlinked text).

Automated business process management systems can utilise the accumulated tags in order to assist users with the execution of process. Users are able to use previously stored tags to retrieve process fragments (e.g. process tasks) tagged with these tags. Additionally, task sequences can be retrieved by following the links across retrieved tasks, which is an important part of process knowledge. Figure 3 illustrates this idea of using tags to facilitate task recommendations.

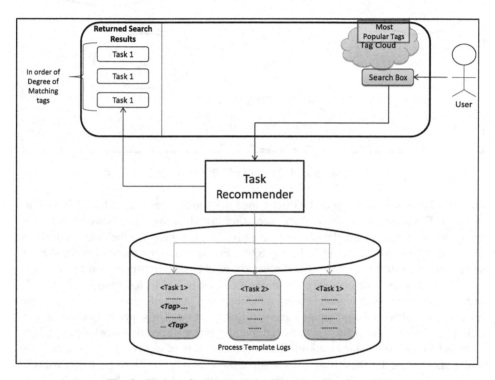

Fig. 3. Task retrieval approach using a tag based search

Figure 4 illustrates the key concepts involved in SBPM from the process tagging perspective. Although the main concepts such as process owner and process participant have been explained below, in the following section we illustrate through a scenario the remaining ones, such as *tag* and *tag cloud.*

5.3 A Social Tagging Scenario

As an example, consider the process of organising a summer camp. This process consists of tasks such as booking a site, finding suitable transportation, catering, and so on. After each of these tasks has been collectively accomplished, the process owner

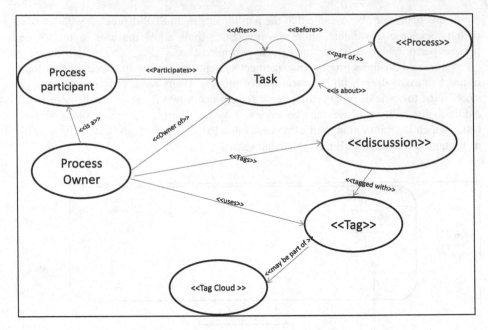

Fig. 4. Social tagging in SBPM meta-model

will revisit the wiki containing the discussions that took place to tag relevant fragments of them. For instance, if for the camp site, after investigating a number of camp sites, the team has decided on a cheap option, the process owner can tag the discussion about choice of venue with a tag like "Cheap Site". Furthermore, the discussion for the site selection task can be linked to the discussion of choosing transportation to the camp site. Thus, the task for choosing a site can be hyperlinked to the transportation task. Future process users that search using a "Cheap Site" tag will also be able to retrieve related tasks about transportation means to that location. Thus, not only domain specific knowledge ('cheap site') is retrieved but also process specific knowledge (i.e. how to travel to that particular location). The more instances of a process are executed and annotated, the higher the amount of knowledge that will be available for future users to utilise. For their more efficient utilisation, previously used tags can be stored in a 'Tag Cloud' [19] where the users can see what tags have been previously and their frequencies of use.

Figure 3 illustrates the overall mechanism for retrieval of relevant content searched by the user, using a cloud tag to find useful tags to include in her search.

6 Conclusions and Future Research

Over the past few years, research in the area of SBPM has increased. One of the models proposed for this concept has been the goal-oriented approach [16] which provides flexibility during the process runtime by providing what needs to be achieved, rather than specifying how it should be achieved. This led to further research on the main components of SBPM and a preliminary meta-model [9]. Process recommendation was identified as the core elements in this model, and this paper has focused on the process recommendation aspect of the model, discussing how can the steps, content and knowledge in a specific process model, be used in future process runs using social approaches such as wikis and tagging.

It was argued that by utilising the power of social tagging after the completion of the process, future users can benefit from wealth of process related ideas and approaches and reuse them as appropriate. The tagging of the tasks and discussions about them, adds to the whole process knowledge.

The next step in our research is to develop a proof of concept prototype of the proposed approach using a social software tool ('wiki') in order to validate it using a real case scenario. There also needs to be much more investigation with relation to producing a set of guidelines for defining process specific tags, and further investigation of the cloud tag idea to facilitate the searching for tags and to avoid mismatch errors that are common in tagging.

References

1. Bruno, G., Dengler, F., Jennings, B., Khalaf, R., Nurcan, S., Prilla, M., Sarini, M., Schmidt, R., Silva, R.: Key challenges for enabling agile BPM with social software. J. Softw. Maint. Evol. Res. Pract. **23**, 297–326 (2011). doi:10.1002/smr.523
2. Bessai, K., Claudepierre, B., Saidani, O., Nurcan, S.: Context-aware business process evaluation and redesign. In: Business Process Life-cycle: Design, Deployment, Operation & Evaluation (BPMDS 2008) (2008)
3. Ukor, R., Carpenter, A.: On modelled flexibility and service selection optimisation. In: The 9th Workshop on Business Process Modeling, Development and Support, Montpellier, France, June 2008
4. Prilla, M.: Semantic integration of process models into knowledge management: a social tagging approach. In: Proceedings of 11th International Conference on Business Information Systems, BIS 2008, Innsbruck, Austria, pp. 130–141 (2008)
5. Star, S.L.: The structure of ill-structured solutions: boundary objects and heterogeneous distributed problem solving. In: Gasser, L., Huhns, M.H. (eds.) Distributed Artificial Intelligence, vol. II, pp. 37–54. Morgan Kaufmann Publishers Inc., San Francisco (1989)
6. Erol, S., Granitzer, M., Happ, S., Jantunen, S., Jennings, B., Johannesson, P., Koschmider, A., Nurcan, S., Rossi, D., Schmidt, R.: Combining BPM and social software: contradiction or chance. J. Softw. Maint. Evol. Res. Pract. **22**(6–7), 449–476 (2010)
7. Pflanzl, N., Vossen, G.: : Human-oriented challenges of social BPM: an overview: In: Proceeding of 5th International Workshop on Enterprise Modelling and Information Systems Architectures, St. Gallen, Switzerland, EMISA 2013, pp. 163–176 (2013)
8. Cantador, I., Konstas, I., Jose, J.: Categorising social tags to improve folksonomy-based recommendations. J. Web Semant. Sci. Serv. Agents. World Wide Web **9**(1), 1–15 (2011)
9. Rangiha, M.E., Karakostas, B.: Process recommendation and role assignment in social business process management (pending publication). In: Proceeding of the Science and Information Organization, Science and Information (SAI) Conference, 27–29 August 2014
10. Rangiha, M.E., Karakostas, B.: A goal-oriented social business process management framework. In: The International Conference on Business Process Management (ICBPM 2014), London, UK, 26–27 September 2014

11. Grudin, J.: Enterprise knowledge management and emerging technologies. In: Proceedings of HICSS 2006 (2006)
12. Fengel, J., Rebstock, M., Nüttgens, M.: Modell-Tagging zur semantischen Verlinkung heterogener Modelle. In: Proceedings of EMISA 2008. Auswirkungen des Web 2.0 auf Dienste und Prozesse. EMISA Fachgruppentreffen (2008)
13. Surowiecki, J.: The Wisdom of Crowds, 1st edn. Abacus, London (2005)
14. Filipowska, A., Kaczmarek, M., Kowalkiewicz, M., Zhou, X., Born, M.: Procedure and guidelines for evaluation of BPM methodologies. Bus. Process Manag. J. 15(3), 336–357 (2009)
15. Pflanzl, N., Vossen, G.: Challenges of social business process management. In: 47th Hawaii International Conference on System Sciences, HICSS 2014, pp. 3868–3877 (2014)
16. Rangiha, M.E., Karakostas, B.: Towards a meta-model for goal-based social BPM. In: Lohmann, N., Song, M., Wohed, P. (eds.) BPM 2013 Workshops. LNBIP, vol. 171, pp. 104–112. Springer, Heidelberg (2014)
17. Rangiha, M.E., Karakostas, B.: A socially driven, goal-oriented approach to business process management. Int. J. Adv. Comput. Sci. Appl. (IJACSA) (2013). Special Issue on Extended Papers from Science and Information Conference. http://dx.doi.org/10.14569/SpecialIssue.2013.030402
18. Koschmider, A., Song, M., Reijers, H.A.: Social software for modelling business processes. In: First Workshop on Business Process Management and Social Software (2008)
19. Panke, S., Gaiser, B.: With my head up in the clouds: using social tagging to organize knowledge. J. Bus. Tech. Commun. 23(3), 318 (2009)
20. Quintarelli, E.: Folksonomies: power to the people. In: Proceedings of the 1st International Society for Knowledge Organization, Milan, Italy, June 2005
21. Shai, R.: BPM, and Agile Methodologies. http://www.oracle.com/technology/pub/articles/dev2arch/2008/05/kaizenbpm-agile.html. Accessed 23 December 2014
22. Scott, A.: Agile Modelling. http://www.agilemodeling.com/. Accessed 20 December 2014
23. Schmidt, D.C.: Model-driven engineering. IEEE Comput. 39(2), 25–31 (2006)
24. Koschmider, A., Song, M., Reijers, H.A.: Social software for modelling business processes. In: First Workshop on Business Process Management and Social Software (2008)
25. Fengel, J., Rebstock, M., Nüttgens, M.: Modell-Tagging zur semantischen Verlinkung heterogener Modelle. In: Proceedings of EMISA 2008. Auswirkungen des Web 2.0 auf Dienste und Prozesse. EMISA Fachgruppentreffen (2008)
26. Maier, R., Remus, U.: Towards a framework for knowledge management strategies: process orientation as strategic starting point. In: Proceedings of HICSS 2001
27. Prilla, M.: Models, social tagging and knowledge management? A fruitful combination for process improvement. In: Proceedings of 2nd Workshop on Business Process Management and Social Software in Conjunction with the Business Process Management Conference 2009 (2010)
28. Fengel, J., Rebstock, M., Nüttgens, M.: Modell-Tagging zur semantischen Verlinkung heterogener Modelle. In: EMISA 2008, Sankt Augustin, Germany, Gesellschaft für Informatik, September 2008
29. Vanderhaeghen, D., Fettke, P., Loos, P.: Organizational and technological options for business process management from the perspective of web 2.0. Bus. Inf. Syst. Eng. 2(1), 15–28 (2010)

SocIoS API: A Data Aggregator for Accessing User Generated Content from Online Social Networks

Magdalini Kardara[1], Vasilis Kalogirou[1],
Athanasios Papaoikonomou[1], Theodora Varvarigou[1],
and Konstantinos Tserpes[2(✉)]

[1] Dept of Electrical and Computer Engineering,
National Technical University of Athens, Athens, Greece
{nkardara, vaskalogirou, tpap, dora}@mail.ntua.gr
[2] Dept of Informatics and Telematics, Harokopio University of Athens,
Athens, Greece
tserpes@hua.gr

Abstract. Following the boost in popularity of online social networks, both enterprises and researchers looked for ways to access the social dynamics information and user generated content residing in these spaces. This endeavor, however, presented several challenges caused by the heterogeneity of data and the lack of a common way to access them. The SocIoS framework tries to address these challenges by providing tools that operate on top of multiple popular social networks allowing uniform access to their data. It provides a single access point for aggregating data and functionality from the networks, as well as a set of analytical tools for exploiting them. In this paper we present the SocIoS API, an abstraction layer on top of the social networks exposing operations that encapsulate the functionality of their APIs. Currently, the component provides support for seven social networks and is flexible enough to allow for the seamless addition of more.

Keywords: Social networks · Data aggregator · API · REST · SOAP

1 Introduction

Online communities, such as social networking and social media platforms, have experienced an outstanding boost in their popularity which in turn resulted to the existence of a large amount of online content created by the members of such communities. This content does not only refer to data, such as text posts, photos and videos, which are explicitly shared by the users online. It also involves a significant amount of social information related to users and implicitly derived by their actions, such as their interests and preferences as well as their relationships with other users.

Although some of this content remains private, a significant amount of it is made publicly available by its owners. More importantly, the social networks themselves, instead of limiting access and usage of their functionality and data, they have propagated them freely, making them part of their core offering to end users and at the same

B. Benatallah et al. (Eds.): WISE 2014, LNCS 9051, pp. 93–104, 2015.
DOI: 10.1007/978-3-319-20370-6_8

time allowing third parties to build applications on top of them. Currently the most popular social networks and media, such as Twitter [1], Facebook [2] and YouTube [3] expose all or part of their functionality through open RESTful APIs through which every user or third party application can gain access to their content and operations.

Both enterprises and researchers have long recognized the huge potential of the social graph information and user created content residing in social networks and looked for ways to harness them. For enterprises with appropriate tools for managing them, the data available in social network are potential sources of revenue, as they can be valuable assets in targeted advertising and viral marketing campaigns. In research, the popularity of social networks has brought new interest in various research domains, as the vast amount of user-generated content and the explicit connections between users allows the study of data analysis and social dynamics on an unprecedented scale.

Although the social networking content is ample and easily accessible, harnessing this content still presents several challenges. Despite the similarities in notions and basic functionality, data representation in social networks is highly heterogeneous. In addition to that, each social network offers its own API and due to the lack of a non commercial tool for accessing multiple APIs from a single API, a user looking to combine data from two or more social networks will have to invoke all the APIs and transform the data in a common format before processing them.

The SocIoS framework aims to address the abovementioned challenges. It is a software stack that operates on top of Social Networking Sites (SNS). SocIoS provides an abstraction layer for combining data and functionality from a multitude of underlying social media platforms as well as a set of analytical tools for leveraging that functionality.

At the core of the SocIoS project, lies the SocIoS API. It constitutes a single access point for a number of popular social networks exposing operations that encapsulate their functionality. For each supported SNS a respective adaptor has been developed. Currently, the component provides support for seven social networks: Facebook, Twitter, FlickR, Dailymotion, YouTube, Google + and Instagram. Support for additional social networks can be added by implementing the adaptor interface provided. SocIoS is a lightweight tool which fetches content from social networks in real time and does not perform any storage or caching of data. It deals mainly with public content with the exception of two methods which require authentication on behalf of the user.

SocIoS comprises both a definition of an object model and API and its respective implementation. While there are commercial products for uniformly accessing content from numerous social networks (for some examples see Sect. 2), to our knowledge there is no open source solution implementing such functionality. SocIoS is therefore a valuable asset for developers in need of a lightweight open source tool for aggregating and analyzing social content from a variety of online sources.

The remainder of this paper is structured as follows: Section 2 presents related work in the field of social network interoperability; Section 3 gives an overview of the SocIoS Framework; Section 4 describes the SocIoS object model; Section 5 focuses on the internal design of the SocioS API; Section 6 presents conclusions and future work.

2   Related Work

The diversity of SNS APIs and data object models necessitate a meta-API that will act as an aggregation point and provide seamless access to the whole spectrum of User Generated Content (UGC). In the market, there are commercial products that fulfill this need. First, GNIP [4] a company that was acquired by Twitter in April 2014, provides access to numerous social data sources, both in real-time and historical mode. Similar approaches are followed by HootSuit [5] and DataSift [6] which enable their users to manage multiple social networks and also offer various analytics services. In academia, a number of research projects have contributed tools with analogous capabilities, like +Spaces [7, 8] and the toolbox [9] developed by WeGov [10] which exploit social networking technologies for policy making, as well as SOCIETIES [11] which facilitates the creation of user communities with integrated social networking capability [12].

A popular approach when it comes to aggregating profiles in SNS, are the aggregator websites: one-stop shopping sites for SNSs that provide users with a common interface for accessing multiple social networks [13]. The main differentiation of these websites from API aggregators is the fact that they do not seek for a semantic aggregation of the main concepts in the SNSs but instead they wrap the APIs' outcome in a single interface without further analyzing them. Instead, the SocIoS platform, approaches the problem from an ontological point of view, by first attempting to identify the common notions in the underlying SNSs [14] and then wrapping the API calls in a single object model.

A relevant work towards the creation of a single SNS ontology has been conducted by Mika [15] in 2005. In Mika's work the starting point are not the existing SNSs but instead a theoretic structure of a social network. The adaptation of this for popular social media platforms should require significant effort since their concepts have been developed independently. In our approach we preferred the use of an object model deriving from the analysis of the operating online social networks. The OpenSocial specification [16] inspired the creation of a new object model which allowed the easy wrapping of underlying API calls to a new, single meta-API call. This approach is better analyzed in what follows.

3   SocIoS Framework and Approach

The SocIoS framework is a software stack that operates on top of SNSs with the purpose of:

- Aggregating data and functionality from a multitude of underlying social media platforms,
- Providing a tool for developers to build social analytics services on top of the supporting social media platforms,
- Accommodating newly created applications that use the abovementioned services and provide them through usable interfaces.

With the proper configuration and development of intermediate services, the framework can support any application that requires the harvesting of social media, filtering the content using sophisticated features while at the same time harnessing the scale issues of the endeavor (volume of data, number of users and platforms).

The objectives mentioned above are achieved through a layered Service-Oriented Architecture (SOA) which is depicted in Fig. 1. The SocIoS Framework consists of several main entities, such as the SocIoS API, the Auxiliary Services(i.e. Data Analysis and Added Value Services) and the Front-End. A short description of these components is given below.

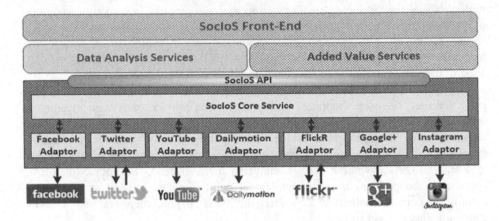

Fig. 1. SocIoS platform high level architecture

An important artifact of the SocIoS Framework, not depicted above, is the SocIoS Object model, an abstraction of the data models defined by the underlying social network APIs. This is used by all the SocIoS components for representing entities and the relations between them.

The SocIoS API is the core part of the framework, exposing a set of operations the higher service layers (SocIoS Auxiliary Services) and mapping them to collections of methods and objects of the social networking site APIs. It consists of a set of adaptors that perform the data transformation between the supported SNSs' APIs and the Object Model and a central component, the Core Service, responsible for coordinating the adaptors.

The Auxiliary Services are third party services that extend the functionality of the core services and use the same data models as the core services. Depending on their purpose, their operations may or may not be exposed as part of the SocIoS API in the sense that they can extend it. This differentiates them between integrated and non-integrated Auxiliary Services. The integrated services are data analysis services, providing analytics to the data delivered by the Core Services, while the non-integrated ones are added value applications that enhance the business potential of SocIoS. The Auxiliary Services are standalone components that can be re-used, they were, however, developed with the purpose to meet the requirements of a certain application. Some examples are:

- Media Item Ranking and Recommendation (Data Analysis): A service for assessing the subjective value of a media item to a specific user [17],
- Topic-Specific Community Detection (Data Analysis): A service for identifying social media user communities that are implicitly linked to each other [18],
- Event Detection (Data Analysis): A service for highlighting intense or unusual activity within a community [19],
- Social Filtering (Data Analysis): A service for managing social media user groups [20],
- The FlexiPrice service (Added Value): A service that enables two users (a buyer and a seller) to set a price of a content item [21],
- The Crowdsourcing Game (Added Value): A service that allows the posting of crowdsourcing tasks in the form of a game [22].

Finally, the SocIoS Front-End provides a user interface for interacting with the components as well as an authentication mechanism. It also deals with the user rights and privacy settings while in certain applications, it may also serve as a point of integration for the Core and Auxiliary Services.

In what follows, we emphasize on the definition of the SocIoS API, i.e. the part that is implemented by the core services.

4   SocIoS Object Model

Each social network has its own data model for representing entities (users, posts etc.) and the relationships between them. By examining the data models of some popular social networks, we come across objects that describe similar notions. For example, a photo uploaded in a social network and a video uploaded in another, can both be considered as "media items" and they both display similar properties, such as title, upload time, number of supportive manifestations etc. By identifying all the conceptually common objects, we can define a new data model and use it to capture data coming from any of the underlying social networks.

To this end, we introduce the Socios Object Model, a set of entities representing principal common notions in social networks. The Object Model consists of the following objects:

- **Person**: The Person object represents a user's profile on a social network. It contains the user's account and profile information.
- **MediaItem**: The MediaItem object represents a post published by a user in a social network. It can refer to a video, image or text post.
- **Activity**: The Activity object contains information about an action performed by a user in a social network.
- **Comment**: The Comment object represents a comment on a media item published in a social network.
- **SocialNetwork**: The SocialNetwork is an enumeration of the supported social networks, namely FLICKR, FACEBOOK, TWITTER, YOUTUBE, DAILYMOTION, GOOGLEP and INSTAGRAM

- **ObjectId**: The ObjectId is a wrapper that defines an object in a specific social network.
- **Address**: The Address object contains details about a location.
- **Name**: The Name object contains information about the user's full name.
- **License**: The License object contains basic information about the license attached to a media item.

SocIoS Main Objects				
Person	MediaItem	Activity	Comment	SocialNetwork
id	id	id	id	FLICKR
sn	sn	sn	sn	FACEBOOK
aboutMe	created	created	created	TWITTER
addresses	title	title	description	YOUTUBE
birthday	thumbnailUrl	description	userId	DAILYMOTION
currentLocation	description	location	username	GOOGLEP
username	duration	actorId	numPositiveVotes	INSTAGRAM
email	location	objectType		
gender	language	mediaItems		
name	license	persons		
photos	fileSize	activities		
profileUrl	rating			
memberSince	numRatings			
thumbnailUrl	numPositiveVotes			
utcOffset	numNegativeVotes			
numFriends	numComments			
inDegree	numViews			
outDegree	numResharings			
	numFavorites			
	tags			
	taggedPeople			
	type			
	url			
	userId			
	comments			

Fig. 2. SocIoS object model - main objects

The SocIoS Object Model was originally built based on the Opensocial Social API specification [16], which was intended for creating new applications that can run in the context of various social containers and therefore attempted to accommodate the potential requirements of such applications. This is different from the objective of SocIoS, which is to capture existing data residing in social networks, and it means that some of the concepts defined in the original specifications are redundant for our purposes. For example, the person-related fields defined by Opensocial cover numerous aspects of a person's data (e.g. body type, living arrangement, religious views), which are however rarely actually supported by the social networks themselves and even less so made available publicly through their APIs. Such fields have been removed from the SocIoS, object model, while at the same time several new fields have been added to include social information that can be retrieved through the social network APIs (e.g. number of comments or likes an item has received) and were not included in the Opensocial specification. The resulting object model, while maintaining the naming conventions and key concepts defined by Opensocial, has significant differences from the original specifications.

Figures 2 and 3 display the SocIoS objects and their fields. Each object defined in the model maps to one or more entities in each social network, while some objects are only present in a subset of the underlying networks (for example only Google + , Facebook, YouTube and Dailymotion have the equivalent of an Activity).

SocIoS Secondary Objects			
ObjectId	Address	Name	License
id socialNetwork	country extendedAddress latitude longitude postalCode region streetAddress	firstName lastName additionalName fullName	licenseType name url

Fig. 3. SocIoS object model - secondary objects

As can be seen, the objects can be conceptually divided to main and secondary, with the former representing core social network (which are also used as returned objects by the API methods) and the latter typically corresponding to complex fields belonging to the main objects. In addition to those, we have defined several filter objects, each one containing a set of conceptually related parameters that can be used for searches. These objects are typically used as input parameters in search related methods. The Filter Objects are depicted in Fig. 4.

SocIoS Filters						
PersonFilter	MediaItemFilter	ActivityFilter	AreaFilter	AddressFilter	LocationFilter	DateTimeFilter
keywords sns	created keywords location language licenseType sns	keywords language sns	latitude longitude radius	country postalCode region	addressFilter locationFilter	from to

Fig. 4. SocIoS object model – filters

5 SocIoS API

As mentioned above, the SocIoS API lies on top of several popular social networks and provides uniform access to their APIs. In terms of implementation, the SocIoS API is comprised of a central component acting as the single point of reference for the layers above, available both in SOAP and REST, and a set of adaptors. The component was developed in Java. The adaptors essentially act as wrappers on top of individual SNS APIs with which they communicate through REST.

As expected, the component is largely dependent on the APIs of the underlying social networks. This refers both to the functionality provided by each social network, as well as to their performance and limitations (e.g. number of calls per time frame). The component retrieves all information in real time, without storing or caching any user related data. Where necessary, authentication parameters are passed to the component by the layers above, as explained later on in the paper.

The following sections give an overview of the SocIoS Object model and an insight into the architecture design of the SocIoS API.

5.1   API Methods

As explained before, the SocIos API exposes a number of methods for interacting with the APIs of the underlying social networks. Some of these methods attempt to get data regarding specific objects whereas others retrieve objects that match certain criteria. Therefore, the input parameters either determine an identification of the objects we try to fetch, or act as filters for the search. The returned object contains the results of the queries that succeeded and detailed exceptions the ones that failed (if any). There is also a method for posting data.

The implementation of each method for each social network is subject to the limitations imposed by the SocIoS APIs themselves. For example Activity related methods are only implemented by social networks supporting the notion of an activity (i.e. Google + , Facebook, YouTube and Dailymotion, as stated above). Moreover, the functionality of each method may differ considerably from social network to social network based on the functionality provided by the respective network. For example, depending on the specific implementation of each network, the list of persons returned by the findPersonsByMediaItem method, may include just the owner of the media item or a full list of the people who have commented/liked/been tagged on it.

In order to avoid the need for the users to authenticate themselves for every single call, most of the SocIoS methods only deal with public information and do not require authentication. The only two exceptions are the myConnectedPersons and the post-Message methods, where user authentication is required by the underlying APIs. For these two methods, it is necessary to provide a valid authentication token for the user retrieved through the use of the OAuth protocol. Essentially what this means, is that the user allows SocIoS to gain access to their personal data or perform some action on behalf of them. The procedure for retrieving the OAuth tokens for each network is implemented by the SocIoS Front End, where the tokens for registered users are stored and kept updated.

Figures 5 and 6 present the SOAP and REST interfaces of the component respectively.

5.2   API Architecture

In terms of architecture, the SocIoS API consists of one central component, the Core Service, which acts as the single point of reference for the layers above, and a set of

SOAP API
GetPersons (List<ObjectId> personIds)
ConnectedPersons (ObjectId personId)
MyConnectedPersons (ObjectId personId)
FindPersons (PersonFilter personFilter, ObjectId mediaItemId, ObjectId activityId, ObjectId username)
GetMediaItems (List<ObjectId> mediaItemIds)
GetMediaItemsForUser (ObjectId personId, ObjectId username)
GetMediaItemsForPage (ObjectId pageId)
FindMediaItems (MediaItemFilter mediaFilter)
FindRelevantMediaItems (ObjectId mediaItemId)
GetActivities (List<ObjectId> activityIds)
GetActivitiesForUser (ObjectId personId)
FindActivities (ActivityFilter activityFilter)
GetComments (List<ObjectId> commentIds)
GetCommentsForMediaItem (ObjectId mediaItemId)
GetCommentsForActivity (ObjectId activityId)
PostMessage (ObjectId personId, String postText)

Fig. 5. SOAP API

REST API
getPerson - input params: {id, sn, format}
connectedPersons - input params: {id, sn, format}
myConnectedPersons - input params: {id, sn, format}
findPersonsByKeyword - input params: {keywords, sns, format}
findPersonsByUsername - input params: {username, sn, format}
findPersonsByMediaItem - input params: {id, sn, format}
findPersonsByActivity - input params: {id, sn, format}
getMediaItem - input params: {id, sn, format}
getMediaItemsForUser - input params: {id, sn, username, format}
getMediaItemsForPage - input params: {id, sn, format}
findMediaItems - input params: {from, to, keywords, country, lat, lon, rad, lang, lic, sns, format}
findRelevantMediaItems - input params: {id, sn, format}
getActivity - input params: {id, sn, format}
getActivitiesForUser - input params: {id, sn, format}
findActivities - input params: {keywords, lang, sns, format}
getComment - input params: {id, sn, format}
getCommentsForMediaItem - input params: {id, sn, format}
getCommentsForActivity - input params: {id, sn, format}
postMessage - input params: {id, sn, msg, format}

Fig. 6. REST API

adaptors. The Core Service is responsible for instantiating and coordinating the adaptors, as well as for gathering the results and returning them back to the client. The adaptors essentially act as wrappers on top of individual social network APIs with which they communicate through REST. Adaptors are part of the API (rather than deployed as standalone service) and are therefore Java objects instantiated and configured by the core services for each method invocation.

Each method implemented by the core service and exposed through the API maps to one or a combination of simpler methods implemented by the adaptors, with each adaptor providing an SNS specific implementation of each method. All adaptors (existing and new ones) must implement the ISnsAdaptor interface which defines all the methods that an adaptor must implement. Currently the SocIoS API contains adaptors for seven popular social networks, i.e. Twitter, Facebook, FlickR, Dailymotion, YouTube, Google + and Instagram. New adaptors can be easily added to the platform by creating a new implementation of the ISnsAdaptor interface and adding the name of the adaptor to the list of known social networks.

The SNS adaptors are instantiated and coordinated by the Core Services module. The Core Service is responsible for processing the parameter list and creating the input parameters that will be subsequently passed to each adaptor. For example, the Get-Persons method gets as input a list of ObjectId type parameters, each of which contains an id and a social network, and returns a list of Person object.

Upon receiving the request, the Core Service will process the list of ObjectId's received with the request and split it to a number of smaller lists, equal to the distinct number of social networks contained in the initial list. The list that will be passed to each adaptor will only contain the IDs belonging to the respective social network. After preparing the input parameters, the Core Service will instantiate the respective list of adaptors and invoke them in order to gather the results and get them back to the user. This process is depicted in Fig. 7.

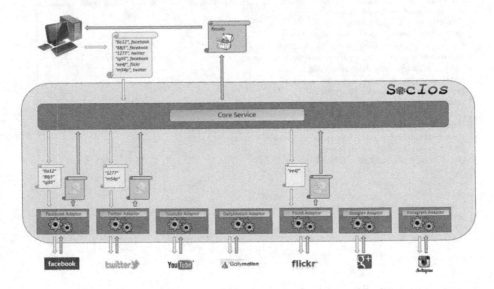

Fig. 7. Core Service and adaptors

The results returned by the adaptors are combined into a single return object, which also contains the errors that occurred during the execution and returned back to the end user. This means that errors occurring to one adaptor, will not significantly affect the functionality of the rest of the adaptors.

6 Conclusions and Future Work

In this paper we have presented SocIoS, a set of tools for aggregating and processing data from social networks. We described the SocIoS Object Model, a data model for representing social network entities and operations. We explained the functionality and implementation of the core component of the framework, i.e. the SocIoS API an abstraction layer on top of the social networks offering uniform access to their APIs. Currently the component supports seven popular social networks which can be easily extended to support more APIs with similar functionalities.

In the future we plan to extend the object model and API accordingly in order to accommodate more platforms that do not fall strictly under the social networking and media category, such as researchers' communities and location based communities. The SocIoS API is maintained as a live project in github, from where it can be downloaded [20].

Acknowledgements. This work has been supported by the RADICAL project (http://www. radical-project.eu) and partly funded by the European Union's Competitiveness and Innovation Framework Programme under grant agreement no 325138.

References

1. The Twitter REST API | Twitter Developers (2014). https://dev.twitter.com/docs/api. Accessed 18 July 2014
2. Graph API. https://developers.facebook.com/docs/graph-api. Accessed 18 July 2014
3. YouTube — Google Developers. https://developers.google.com/youtube/. Accessed 18 July 2014
4. The Source for Social Data - Gnip. http://gnip.com/. Accessed 18 July 2014
5. Social Media Management Dashboard - Hootsuite. https://hootsuite.com/. Accessed 18 July 2014
6. DataSift | Powering the Social Economy. http://datasift.com/. Accessed 18 July 2014
7. +Spaces-Policy Simulation in Virtual Spaces (FP7 EU Funded Research Project). http://www.positivespaces.eu/. Accessed 18 July 2014
8. Tserpes, K., Jacovi, M., Gardner, M., Triantafillou, A., Cohen, B.: +spaces: Intelligent virtual spaces for egovernment. In: 2010 Sixth International Conference on Intelligent Environments (IE), pp. 318–323 (2010)
9. Wandhöfer, T., Taylor, S., Alani, H., Joshi, S., Sizov, S., Walland, P., Thamm, M., Bleier, A., Mutschke, P.: Engaging politicians with citizens on social networking sites: the WeGov Toolbox. Int. J. Electron. Gov. Res. **8**(3), 22–32, 33 (2012)
10. WeGov-Where eGovernment meets the eSociety (FP7 EU Funded Research Project). http://www.wegov-project.eu/. Accessed 18 July 2014
11. SOCIETIES-Self Orchestrating Community Ambient Intelligence Spaces (FP7 EU Funded Research Project). http://www.ict-societies.eu/. Accessed 18 July 2014
12. Roussaki, I., Kalatzis, N., Liampotis, N., Jennings, E., Kosmides, P., Roddy, M., Lamorte, L., Anagnostou, M.: Enhancing social media with pervasive features. In: Meiselwitz, G. (ed.) SCSM 2014. LNCS, vol. 8531, pp. 265–276. Springer, Heidelberg (2014)

13. Benevenuto, F., Rodrigues, T., Cha, M., Almeida, V.: Characterizing user behavior in online social networks. In: Proceedings of the 9th ACM SIGCOMM Conference on Internet Measurement Conference, pp. 49–62. New York, NY, USA (2009)
14. Tserpes, K., Papadakis, G., Kardara, M., Papaoikonomou, A., Aisopos, F., Sardis, E., Varvarigou, T.: An ontology for social networking sites interoperability. In: 4th International Conference of Knowledge Engineering and Ontology Development (KEOD2012), pp. 245–250 (2012)
15. Mika, P.: Ontologies are us: a unified model of social networks and semantics. In: Gil, Y., Motta, E., Benjamins, V.R., Musen, M.A. (eds.) The Semantic Web – ISWC 2005, pp. 522–536. Springer, Heidelberg (2005)
16. OpenSocial Specification 2.5.1. http://opensocial.github.io/spec/trunk/OpenSocial-Specification.xml. Accessed 18 July 2014
17. Jacovi, M., Guy, I., Kremer-Davidson, S., Porat, S., Aizenbud-Reshef, N.: The perception of others: inferring reputation from social media in the enterprise. In: CSCW 2014 Computer Supported Cooperative Work, pp. 756–766. Baltimore, MD, USA, 15–19 February 2014
18. Kardara, M., Papadakis, G., Papaoikonomou, T., Tserpes, K., Varvarigou, T.: Influence patterns in topic communities of social media. In: Proceedings of the 2nd International Conference on Web Intelligence, Mining and Semantics, p. 10 (2012)
19. Papaoikonomou, A., Tserpes, K., Kardara, M., Varvarigou, T.: A similarity-based chinese restaurant process for social event detection. In: Working Notes Proceedings of the Mediaeval. 2013 Workshop Barcelona, Spain, October 18–19, CEUR-WS Org ISSN 1613-0073 (2013)
20. SocIoSEUProject/SocIoS, GitHub. https://github.com/SocIoSEUProject/SocIoS. Accessed 17 July 2014
21. Gonen, R., Raban, D., Brady, C., Mazor, M.: Increased efficiency through pricing in online labor markets. J. Electron. Commer. Res. 15(1), 58–76 (2014)
22. Raban, D., Richter, G., Corem, Y.: Harnessing the power of games to enhance organizational knowledge sharing system. In: ILAIS Conference, p. 73. Open University of Israel, 29 June 2011

Integrating Social Media and Open Data in a Cloud-Based Platform for Public Sector Advertising

Daniel Pop[1]($\boxtimes$), Alejandro Echeverria[2], and Juan Vicente Vidagany[3]

[1] Universitatea de Vest Din Timişoara, Bd. V. Pârvan 4,
300223 Timişoara, Românía
danielpop@info.uvt.ro
[2] Investigación y Desarrollo Informatico Eikon,
Parque Technologico Calle Benjamin Franklin, Valencia, Spain
aecheverria@idieikon.com
[3] TIE KINETIX, De Corridor 5, Breukelen, The Netherlands
juanvi.vidagany@tiekinetix.com

Abstract. Nowadays, Public Sector Advertising (PSA) is conveyed as unidirectional top-down stream of messages that clearly separates the content producers (governments usually) from content consumers (citizens). As social networks and Linked Open Government Data (LOGD) initiatives are moving forward e-Government towards connected government, PSA platforms need to embrace the modern paradigms of empowering citizens and communities to increasingly and actively participate in functioning of the society for their own benefits. In this position paper, firstly we present our findings related to the use of content from social networks as public ads and secondly, we propose an open and collaborative platform that supports semantically-enabled, participative PSA.

Keywords: Collaborative government · Semantic web · Public service advertising · Social networks · Web 2.0 · Public sector information

1 Introduction

Public sector information (PSI), sometimes referred to as government data, refers to all the information that public bodies produce, collect or pay for [11]. Examples are: geographical information, statistics, weather data, data from publicly funded research projects, and digitized books from libraries. Even though PSI is a large market in Europe, estimated around EUR 28 billion [10], less than 41 % of citizens, at average, are impacted by this [9]. Loads of pre-existing investments in e-Government back-offices, in platforms and services are available across Europe and they are deploying a wide set of services, but in most cases efforts are duplicated, there is little to no reuse of e-Government data, and obsolete technologies are still put in place [10].

Deploying advanced technologies to broaden communications channels, standardizing IT systems to reduce costs and complexity, or adopting more cost

© Springer International Publishing Switzerland 2015
B. Benatallah et al. (Eds.): WISE 2014, LNCS 9051, pp. 105–116, 2015.
DOI: 10.1007/978-3-319-20370-6_9

effective channels to deliver e-Government services are among most important strategies identified [25] to improve the operations in citizen-centric government. Besides improving operations, there are other side benefits resulting from utilization of innovative e-services and multi-channel communications, such as support for sustainability, fostering organizational change, better relationship with citizens or reducing costs.

Literature defines public service announcement (PSA), sometimes referred to as public service ad, as "messages in the public interest disseminated by the media without charge, with the objective of raising awareness, changing public attitudes and behaviour towards a social issue" [16]. Until nowadays, PSA in democratic government has been a form of communication intended to persuade citizens (viewers, readers or listeners) to take a certain action upon ideas, or services. PSA is still not adapted to 21st century technological and social environment. PSA is still predominantly built on the Weberian bureaucracy of which functional division, centralisation and hierarchy are key characteristics [14]. PSA is conveyed as unidirectional top-down stream of messages that clearly separates the content producers (governments usually) from content consumers (citizens), a characteristic of Web 1.0.

In the evolution of the World Wide Web technologies, Web 2.0 paradigm commonly refers to Web applications that removes the clear distinction between the'passive' content users/consumers and the'active' content producers, introducing the concept data'pro-sumers' (both consumers and providers of data). While this allows users to interact and collaborate with each other in a social media dialogue and helps the creation of virtual communities, current research on Web technology is geared towards Web 3.0, that is considered to be its next frontier, beholding the potential of intelligent information and Semantic Web [17]. Powered by Resource Description Framework (RDF) [12] and a rich ecosystem (vocabularies, languages, stores etc.), and integrating social networks platforms, the Web will become a tool that will support the efforts of governments and NGOs towards the deployment of citizen-centric systems. Open Data and Open Government Data (OGD) initiatives already support the migration towards Web 2.0, as recent literature [3,4,7] discusses about so called 2nd Generation of OGD Information Systems. In this context, public service announcements need to move forward from classical uni-directional, Web platforms or media channels towards collaborative Web 2.0 environments.

In the next section, we present a Web platform, deployed and validated in the framework of the SEED[1] project, that enables the transformation of social network content into public advertising; the validation phase in seven pilots across Europe proved that social media is a valuable resource for PA. Although the platform connects to social media channels, it doesn't enable collaboration and co-production, key elements of next generation Web platforms.

Driven by this finding, the remaining sections of this position paper address the main research topic of this study: the transition from Web 1.0 platform for PSA towards Web 2.0 platform for PSA. Thus, Sect. 3 will identify the key

---

[1] Speeding Every European Digital, http://www.seed-project.eu.

challenges in the roadmap towards PSA 2.0 and 3.0, while Sect. 4 discusses a multi-layer architecture of a PSA 3.0 platform and what'ingredients' are available to enable the implementation of such a platform. The proposed platform relies on Linked Open Data infrastructure and it is delivered using Cloud services. Last section concludes on the main achievements of this paper and it is looking into future research directions required to adapt public service advertising to the technological, social and economical context of nowadays.

2   Transforming Content from Social Networks into Public Advertising

Traditional PSA platforms allow little reuse of existing sources of information, thus content managers need to prepare the content for publication specifically for those platforms. Meanwhile, the social network implementations in public administrations is an environment that gathers valuable information for citizens and business. In order to asses whether social networks content is appealing for PSA, we conducted our experiments in the framework of SEED project, which provides a Web platform deployed using Software as a Service (SaaS) model that enables content managers to easily reuse the already available public sector information (PSI), from a wide range of sources, and transform it into public ads (PSA).

In a nutshell, the platform is able to adapt the content from social networks, such as Facebook, microblogging sites (Twitter), or video sharing platforms (YouTube, Vimeo), to advertisement purpose in public places. More details about the platform in [21]. The content manager, i.e. the person responsible for publishing digital content in an organization, initially creates an element in the platform that connects to a source of messages (e.g. a Twitter or Facebook account). In a second step, the element is included in one (ore more) structured playlist'playable' by any standard Web browser, on a variety of digital devices, from standard PCs or kiosks to Smart TVs, beamers or mobile devices. An element can be included in multiple playlists, and usually a playlist contains several elements, all together summing-up a'play time', usually, around ten minutes per playlist. In the last step, playlists are scheduled on different displays, such as one device can be scheduled to play several playlists at different hours of the day, and a playlist can be played simultaneously on multiple devices.

During the evaluation of the platform, performed for a period of 18 months by five municipalities (Pegeia in Cyprus, Rijeka in Croatia, Timişoara in Romania, Varna in Bulgaria and Ventspils in Latvia) and two regional authorities (Istria in Croatia and Pilsen in Czech Republic) in six European countries, we ran several surveys and interviews to evaluate six complementary dimensions: impact of i-PSA (interactive PSA) on effectiveness of administration services, cost savings, impact on raising citizens' awareness and digital inclusion, usability of the platform, interoperability with local infrastructures and lastly, scalability and affordability [21]. Related to the (re)use of content from social networks, we discovered that, except for one case, all pilots have used social network content for PSA. Interviews and surveys answered by both content producers (PA officers and content managers) and consumers (citizens, students) emphasized that whether is about tweets, Facebook wall messages or videos shared online, content on social environments conveys appropriate and useful messages. Figure 1 illustrates the usage of different sources of content – existing Web pages, Facebook profiles, static image libraries, RSS feeds, weather information services, videos, Twitter accounts and others – in the seven pilots. The number on each bar indicates the number of pilots (out of seven) using that specific source of content.

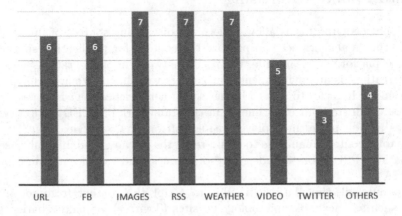

Fig. 1. Content usage vs. content source

The validation process not only proved the wider acceptance and usage of content from social networks, but also discovered other advantages of this approach, such as: easier access to public information, reusing as much as possible data and hardware enables PA to grow technologically and save money, or the fact that 60 % of content manager managed to easily integrate external PSI into their own deliveries using the platform.

Pilots surfaced the imperfections of the solution as well. If technical flaws were easily surpassed, those related to the human factor are demanding a higher attention, effort, skills and time: resources availability within PA to create, adapt or publish the content, end-users' (equally citizens and content providers) scepticism when facing new technologies, or winning decision makers' support. Our findings are inline with those produced by similar studies investigating the impact of social media content usage in government [2,20]. The real-life pilots support other ideas emerged in these studies, such as of improved communication between citizens and government, increased participation, more transparency, but also the importance of updating the legal framework on data management, privacy and security.

3   Moving Forward Towards a Novel Generation of PSA

Although advantages of reusing existing PSI for PSA were demonstrated by successful pilots, there are still gaps to be filled in the way towards connected semantic platforms, of which the removal of the clear distinction between the'passive' content users/consumers and the'active' content producers, plus the shift towards data'pro-sumers' (both consumers and providers of data) are outstanding milestones. We discuss below three key challenges: targeted public advertising, closing the feedback loop and organizational changes.

Targeted advertising defined as advertising methods that deliver individually catered advertisements based upon the content of the website, location of the user, browsing history, demographics, the user profile, or any other available information [15] is the state-of-the-art technique in online advertising, used by players such as Google AdWords, Bing Ads or Infolinks. Public service ads can and should benefit of targeted audience advertising. Imagine, for instance, a municipality operating five public displays scattered in different locations throughout the city (tax office, public library, hospital, police headquarter and a leisure centre). Audience in these spots is significantly different and even during one day the profile of visitors per location may change within different time intervals. Thus, the messages delivered need to automatically, transparently adapt to target audience with minimum effort from content managers.

Importance of closing the feedback loop in Open Government has been recently stressed out [1]. PSA makes no exception and the uni-directional stream of messages need to be enhanced with feedback mechanisms. This drives the need for building a framework where social mining techniques, such as sentiment analysis, will provide the tools that are missing, enabling traditional content providers (local/regional/national PA, NGO) to better measure the impact of their PSA and to guide behavioural change, performance improvement and engaging end-users in a more intelligent and participative interaction model.

According to Statista website [23], there are more than 1.6 billion social network users worldwide with more than 64 percent of internet users accessing social media services online. In Europe, the leader is Iceland with 70 % of internet users were monthly active social media users, logging on to social media services at least once per month; average EU value is 40 %, with 29 countries above the average and 11 below it. Due to large spread of social media in Europe and significant cultural differences in citizen-government interaction, a novel approach to PSA need to be flexible enough to support the integration of multiple social networks (Facebook, VKontakte), to be accessible from a variety of devices and to equally cover highly and less active countries.

Although the benefit of social media use for government response agencies was demonstrated emphatically through various cases, such as the Queensland disasters and the Haiti earthquake, a sustained success can only come when governments create new organizational units to manage newly created e-participation channels, and also to analyse the large quantities of both structured data (e.g. citizens rankings and ratings) and unstructured data (e.g. citizens postings in textual form) that will be created by them [18]. The personnel of these new units must have specialized skills concerning the new electronic modes of communication, but also be supported by modern information systems, such as high-performance Dynamic Semantic Publishing frameworks. A modern platform for PSA will enable the publication of automated metadata-driven information, requiring minimal content management, as it automatically aggregates and establishes links to existing content and services.

4   Open and Collaborative PSA Platform

In order to properly manage a modern provision of public services, moving towards creation of public value and citizens empowerment, a paradigm shift of today's modus operandi should be introduced into PSA strategies in order to enhance communication effectiveness and engagement among citizens, thus transforming traditional PSA into open and collaborative PSA. To meet these demands, we are proposing a novel PSA architecture, based on principles of collaboration, transparency and participation that is providing customised solutions for raising citizens awareness according to Open Government strategy, while reducing costs. The proposed system is leveraging on stocks of exiting PSI published as open data to deliver customised PSA messages.

We propose a Cloud-based framework integrated with semantic strategy for innovation in PSA, taking into account the different challenges in a multi-domain and multi-lingual context. The collaboration between citizens and PA is supported by collecting the feedback produced by citizens (end-users' in general) in interactive applications and social networks, on top of a semantically rich platform. Figure 2 sketches the main building blocks of the proposed system that will be briefly described in the remaining of this section.

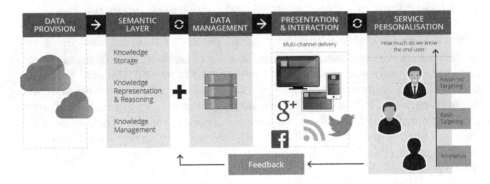

Fig. 2. Architecture overview of an open and collaborative PSA system

Data Provision Layer provides advanced data harvesting mechanisms in order to maximise the use of existing Public Sector Information (PSI) assets from digital repositories, cross-country Open Data portals and social media.

Examples of such sources are ENGAGE project[2], European Union Open Data Portal[3], national Open Data portals (data.gov.* portals), or public/enterprise social networks.

Semantic Layer transforms discovered data and services into a semantically linked database, creating an open, Cloud-based repository of existing, characterised services accessible as Open Data endpoints. As one needs to cater for different needs, this layer shall provide mechanisms to seek and map the relationships between discovered data sources using a Linked Data approach and provides an enhancement model to add value, enrich and extend the information with other components, such as multimedia resources, links to other related content, or multi-lingual translation.

Data Management Layer enables PSA content lifecycle management: curation, transformation, publication and distribution of PSA services into different and engaging formats (Atom, RSS, multimedia content, RDF aggregations), based on embedded Linked Data identifiers, ontologies and associated inference. It is also be responsible for monitoring and measuring all the information in the system.

Presentation and Interaction Layer implements the presentation layer across the different channels (digital screens, kiosks, projectors etc.), displaying the final transformation of the individual assets into attractive, engaging and interactive PSA services, through a multi-dimensional interactive points strategy, in order to maximize the reach of PSA.

Personalisation Layer ensures personalization of delivered messages. Knowing who we communicate with, where and when, its key to deliver an effective PSA aligned with the end user real needs. This layer is responsible for offering a different bundle of services depending on how much do we know about targeted audience and will follow a Life Event approach [24] (e.g. the start of a new business, the beginning of an unemployment period) to organise PSA delivery in an understandable and logical way, putting citizens in the centre for their own service delivery.

Feedback Measurement and Analysis Layer captures users behaviour, comments and reactions in social networks (re-tweets, sharing, likes) and processes the data to enrich the system itself and/or provide analytics for decision making. Business Intelligence and Social Mining advanced techniques shall be considered to provide different stakeholders configurable reports and various analysis on data consumption: PSA effectiveness, users engagement, or reputation analysis.

There are on-going initiatives and projects that can contribute with data or components to the implementation of proposed architecture. We are not claiming to make an exhaustive and complete overview here, rather highlighting some of the most promising candidates.

The ENGAGE[4] (FP7) project [8] builds an open data infrastructure incorporating diverse Open Data datasets (from data.gov.* portals) facilitating col-

---

[2] http://www.engagedata.eu.

[3] http://open-data.europa.eu.

[4] http://www.engage-project.eu.

laboration between scientists and empowers the deployment of open governmental data towards citizens. It combines the so-called classical functionalities of open data infrastructures (basic functionalities supported by most first generation open data platforms) and more novel Web 2.0 oriented functionalities. It may offer the basic functionalities of the Data Provision and Semantic Layer described previously, such as data publication and uploading , data modelling with flat metadata descriptions based on metadata standards, or visualization techniques (charts, plots, maps). The novel Web 2.0 capabilities aim to support open data'prosumers' and also extensive interaction and collaboration among them.

Similar to ENGAGE, Open Data Architectures and Infrastructures (Open DAI[5]), InGeoCloudS[6] or European Union Open Data Portal[7] initiatives build linked open data infrastructures, served from the Cloud, in order to open data and GeoData to a wider audience. Unique linked open data technology is provisioned for further information integration, exchanges and opens the path for cross-domains applications, such as PSA consumers.

The Semantic Layer is relying on knowledge modelling technologies to allow the representation of the internal semantic data model, but also to transform and link from various data providers to the internal data model. For this, an RDF vocabulary should be developed to represent PSA messages in the semantic web that will enable the link with similar vocabularies developed for public administration (e.g. e-Government Core Vocabularies in Europe [13]) or to support different aspects of the workflow coming from business managers, for example ONTORULE project [22]. It already exists good candidates to start from, such as RDF Site Summary[8] or SIOC ontology (Semantically-Interlinked Online Communities) [5] that can be adapted to internally represent the data model in a PSA system. Extensions of SIOC would be necessary to cope with geo location, for example or to link with vocabularies modelling applications and documents.

Special emphasis should be devoted to social networks because of their well-recognised role as valuable sources of information to be transformed into PSA messages. As they are data providers that publish data using non-structured models, their integration with the Semantic Layer data model requires adequate tools. Luckily, already nice efforts have been done. For example, Twarql[9], which is a service that enables annotations and management of streaming tweets in order to alleviate information overload. Twarql encodes information from Twitter posts as Linked Open Data in order to bring flexibility in processing and analysing of microblog data. Instead of requiring the use of keywords or custom software for filtering information, Twarql leverages SPARQL endpoints to query the data.

---

[5] http://open-dai.eu.
[6] http://www.ingeoclouds.eu.
[7] http://open-data.europa.eu.
[8] http://web.resource.org/rss/1.0/.
[9] http://wiki.knoesis.org/index.php/Twarql.

The SAM (Socialising Around Media) project[10] is developing an advanced media delivery platform based on 2nd Screen and content syndication within a social media context. It offers open and standardised ways of characterising, discovering and syndicating media assets interactively, thus it is creating richer experiences around media. Taking up the developments in this field and enhancing them to answer the needs of the 2nd generation PSA platform, it will contribute to the implementation of Presentation and Interaction and Personalisation layers.

As far as deployment of the platform concerns, we witness a wide diversity of Cloud computing services that challenges the application developers as nonstandard interfaces are provided for these services. Few middleware solutions were developed until now to support the design, deployment and execution of service-independent applications as well as the management of resources from multiple Clouds. Solutions fall into one of the two categories: hosted services (e.g. RightScale[11], Enstratius[12]) and deployable services (e.g. mOSAIC[13] [19]). For example, mOSAIC platform uses a multi-agent brokering system that will match end-users service requirements in order to find the best-fitting Cloud services to their actual needs and efficiently outsource computations. Hence, mOSAIC may provide us the Platform-as-a-Service (PaaS) that supports the integration and deployment of the entire system.

5   Conclusions

The rapid transformation of our society and the digital revolution along with budgetary pressures pose challenges for governments and the future of public services. The future of government is less and less in the hands of government alone. Technology has empowered citizens by offering them a way to make their voices heard and challenge government leaders about their ability and willingness to address public concerns and requests. The increased connectivity of citizens, the possibility for people to work together, perform tasks and distribute workload, regardless of distance and boundaries, as well as the opening of previously closed information and data mean that citizens are co-participants to the act of governing.

The proposed system enables Open Government approach and is proposing a new generation of Public Service Advertising platform embracing Semantic Web paradigm, facilitating cross-country collaboration, transparency and participation, reusing of open data and integration of the advent of social networks and ubiquitous connectivity. Although social media is already in use for marketing and communication activities in PA, its integration with IT infrastructure deployed at organizational level is poor. The proposed Cloud-based system will

---

[10] http://samproject.net.
[11] http://www.rightscale.com.
[12] http://www.enstratius.com.
[13] http://mosaic-cloud.eu.

integrate the social media channels and will automatically pull the information and adapt it to its function, which is advertise to public services.

Building the system proposed in this paper will raise several interesting research directions, not only at technical solutions, but also at socio-cultural and organizational levels. Open source libraries, largely adopted standards, multi-Cloud enabling platforms will be first-class candidates for building the system from the technological perspective. Research challenges ahead include: employing algorithms and tools for automatic meta-data extraction from open data, aggregating and querying meta-data repositories, automatic learning from collected feedback to name a few.

At social level, research will focus on best ways of capturing and analysing end-users' feedback (for example on social networks), how to address e-excluded groups, or what models are best suited for this modelling the feedback. Raising awareness on public value, as a total societal value, cannot be monopolised by individuals, rather will it be shared by all actors in society and will be an outcome of all resource allocation decisions.

The human-machine interaction facilitated by the platform need to address the widespread of mobile devices, but in the same time to keep the focus on e-excluded groups. For example, how end-users will be enabled to send their feedback with minimum effort (clicks) from a heterogeneous 'sea' of devices.

Nonetheless, all these technical barriers being surpasses, the challenge of a long-term policy for the interaction with citizens utilizing the new social channels still exists [18]. The implementation of the "Four R" approach (Review, Respond, Record and Redirect) [6] is key for updating and managing online content on these channels.

Acknowledgments. This work was partially funded by the European Commission FP7 and CIP Programmes grants no. 284595 HOST (High Performance Computing Service Centre) and no. 297192 SEED (Speeding Every European Digital), respectively. The authors wish to thank to reviewers for their valuable suggestions for improving the paper.

References

1. Alexopoulos, C., Zuiderwijk, A., Charalabidis, Y., Loukis, E.: Closing the open public data feedback loop: the ENGAGE platform. Share-PSI 2.0 Samos Workshop: Uses of Open Data Within Government for Innovation and Efficiency (2014). www.w3.org/2013/share-psi/workshop/samos/
2. Bertot, J.C., Jaeger, P.T., Hansen, D.: The impact of polices on government social media usage: Issues, challenges, and recommendations. Gov. Inf. Q. **29**(1), 30–40 (2012). http://www.sciencedirect.com/science/article/pii/S0740624X11000992
3. Bertot, J.C., Jaeger, P.T., Grimes, J.M.: Promoting transparency and accountability through ICTs, social media, and collaborative e-government. Transforming Gov. People Process Policy **6**(1), 78–91 (2012). Emerlad Insight
4. Bonsón, E., Torres, L., Royo, S., Flores, F.: Local e-government 2.0: social media and corporate transparency in municipalities. Gov. Inf. Q. **29**(2), 123–132 (2012). http://www.sciencedirect.com/science/article/pii/S0740624X1200010X

5. Breslin, J.G., Decker, S., Harth, A., Bojars, U.: Sioc: an approach to connect web-based communities. Int. J. Web Based Communities **2**(2), 133–142 (2006). http://dx.doi.org/10.1504/IJWBC.2006.010305
6. Brown, D.R.: Experiential Approach to Organization Development, 8th edn. Prentice Hall, Boston (2010)
7. Charalabidis, Y., Loukis, E., Alexopoulos, C.: Evaluating second generation open government data infrastructures using value models. In: 2014 47th Hawaii International Conference on System Sciences (HICSS), pp. 2114–2126 (January 2014)
8. Charalabidis, Y., Ntanos, E., Lampathaki, F.: An architectural framework for open governmental data for researchers and citizens. In: Janssen, M., Macintosh, A., Scholl, J., Tambouris, E., Wimmer, M., Bruijn, D., Tan, Y.H. (eds.) Electronic government and electronic participation joint proceedings of ongoing research and projects of IFIP EGOV and ePart 2011, pp. 77–85 (2011)
9. Commission, E.: Inside the five-year egovernment action plan (2011–2015) (2010)
10. Commission, E.: Amending Directive 2003/98/EC on re-use of public sector information (2011). http://eur-lex.europa.eu/LexUriServ/LexUriServ.do?uri=COM:2011:0877:FIN:EN:PDF
11. Commission, E.: Digital agenda for europe (2014). http://ec.europa.eu/digital-agenda/en/open-data-0
12. Cyganiak, R., Wood, D., Lanthaler, M.: Rdf 1.1 concepts and abstract syntax. Technical report, W3C (2014)
13. programme of the European Commission, I.: e-Government Core Vocabularies (2014). https://joinup.ec.europa.eu/asset/core_vocabularies/description
14. European Commission DG CNECT: A vision for public services (2013)
15. Farahat, A., Bailey, M.C.: How effective is targeted advertising? In: Proceedings of the 21st International Conference on World Wide Web, WWW 2012. ACM, New York, NY, USA, pp. 111–120 (2012). http://doi.acm.org/10.1145/2187836.2187852
16. Kerin, R., Hartley, S., Rudelius, W.: Marketing: The Core. McGraw-Hill/Irwin (2010). ISBN: 978-0078112065
17. Lassila, O., Hendler, J.: Embracing Web 3.0. IEEE Internet Comput. **11**(3), 90–93 (2007)
18. Magro, M.J.: A review of social media use in e-government. Adm. Sci. **2**(2), 148–161 (2012). http://www.mdpi.com/2076-3387/2/2/148
19. Petcu, D., Martino, B., Venticinque, S., Rak, M., Máhr, T., Lopez, G., Brito, F., Cossu, R., Stopar, M., Šperka, S., Stankovski, V.: Experiences in building a mosaic of clouds. J. Cloud Comput. **2**(1), 1–22 (2013). http://dx.doi.org/10.1186/2192-113X-2-12
20. Picazo-Vela, S., Gutirrez-Martnez, I., Luna-Reyes, L.F.: Understanding risks, benefits, and strategic alternatives of social media applications in the public sector. Gov. Inf. Q. **29**(4), 504–511 (2012). http://www.sciencedirect.com/science/article/pii/S0740624X12001025, social Media in Government - Selections from the 12th Annual International Conference on Digital Government Research (dg.o2011)
21. Pop, D., Moumtzi, V., Farinos, J.: The good, the bad and the beauty of advertisement for public sector services. In: Proceedings of the 14th European Conference on eGovernment, ECEG 2014. Academic Publishing (2014)
22. de Sainte Marie, C., Iglesias Escudero, M., Rosina, P.: The ONTORULE project : where ontology meets business rules. In: Rudolph, S., Gutierrez, C. (eds.) RR 2011. LNCS, vol. 6902, pp. 24–29. Springer, Heidelberg (2011)

23. Statista.com: Number of social network users worldwide from 2010 to 2017 (2014). http://www.statista.com/statistics/278414/number-of-worldwide-social-network-users/
24. Wauters, P., Declercq, K., van der Peijl, S., Davies, P.: Study on Cloud and Services Oriented Architectures (SOA) for e-Government SMART 2010–0074 (2011)
25. Zibret, B., Derka, M., Miklic, N.: How to become a citizen centric government. A.T. Kearney (2009). http://www.atkearney.com/documents/10192/6bc77242-149a-4515-b4c7-3295ca1ab594

A Survey on Approaches to Modeling Artifact-Centric Business Processes

Jyothi Kunchala[1(✉)], Jian Yu[1], and Sira Yongchareon[2]

[1] School of Computer and Mathematical Sciences,
Auckland University of Technology, Auckland, New Zealand
{kjyothi,jian.yu}@aut.ac.nz
[2] Department of Computing, Unitec Institute of Technology,
Auckland, New Zealand
sira@maxsira.com

Abstract. Business Process Modeling using artifact-centric approach has gained increasing interest over the past few years. The ability to put data and process aspects on an equal footing has made it a powerful tool for efficient business process modeling. The artifact-centric approach is based on key business-relevant entities called business artifacts, which are central for guiding business operations as they navigate through the business operations. The artifact-centric modeling approach can be laid in a four dimensional framework called BALSA for defining business processes, where the four dimensions include business artifacts, lifecycles, services and associations. Based on this data-centric paradigm, several artifact-centric meta-models have been emerged in the recent years. Although all the proposed models claim to support the artifact-centric approach, their support in specifying the BALSA elements of artifacts was not clearly described in the existing literature. This paper reviews all existing approaches to artifact-centric modeling and also discuss to what extent they align with the BALSA framework.

Keywords: Artifact-centric process modeling · Business artifacts · BALSA

1 Introduction

The business managers and analysts in organizations increasingly rely on business process modeling to document, understand and improve their business processes. Business Process Modeling [1] refers to the act of representing business operations with an objective to improve organizations current business processes. A business process model describes how the business operates to accomplish its objectives. Traditional activity-centric business process modeling is based on tasks and control-flow constructs, which only define how business processes operate, without revealing details about the data resulted from the business process execution. An "impedance mismatch problem" [2] arises with the separation of application, process, and control data by activity-centric process aware information systems while providing support to imperative procedural models, which eventually affect the flexibility of activity-centric business process modeling approaches.

© Springer International Publishing Switzerland 2015
B. Benatallah et al. (Eds.): WISE 2014, LNCS 9051, pp. 117–132, 2015.
DOI: 10.1007/978-3-319-20370-6_10

As opposed to the traditional activity-centric approaches to business process modeling, whose emphasis is completely on tasks and their control flows, a new data-centric approach for modeling business processes has been emerged, namely *artifact-centric* approach [3], which takes into account data and process aspects in a more comprehensive manner. The modeling approach is centrally based on business artifacts [4] i.e., core business-relevant entities that manage operations of the business, whose content changes in response to the business actions. The artifact-centric modeling becomes popular with its unique advantages such as: (1) it enables business managers to better understand and specify their business operations by providing a more intuitive framework [3]; (2) it provides more flexible and robust structure for business process specification [3]; and it has the potential to improve flexibility, compliance and reduce the complexity of traditional activity-centric business process approaches [5]; (4) it has the ability to help cut down the costs of business transformations [6].

The artifact-centric modeling approach can be laid in a four dimensional framework called BALSA- *Business Artifacts, Lifecycles, Services,* and *Associations* [1, 3]. *"By varying the model and constructs used in each of the four dimensions one can obtain different artifact-centric business process models with differing characteristics"* [3]. Currently there are many concrete artifact-centric modeling approaches such as GSM [7], ArtiNets [8], AXML [9], BPMN Extensions [10], and ACP-i [5]. Though all the proposed models claim to support the artifact-centric approach, their support in specifying BALSA framework was not clearly described in the existing literature.

In this paper, we aim to use BALSA as a reference framework or yardstick and see how each approach can be fit into this framework. To give the reader a concrete feel of each approach, we also use a common motivating scenario and demonstrate how to implement this scenario using each approach. This paper also help researchers and practitioners who have interests in the area of BPM to gain better understanding and knowledge of artifact-centric process modeling.

The remainder of this paper is organized as follows: Sect. 2 provides an introduction to the BALSA Framework with an example. Section 3 discusses artifact-centric modeling approaches and related work. Section 4 discusses and briefly evaluates all the modeling approaches studied against the framework. Finally, the conclusion and future work are given in Sect. 5.

2 BALSA Framework

2.1 BALSA Elements

With the focus on data aspects as its first-class citizens, the artifact-centric approach provides a four explicit, inter-related but separable "dimensions" in the specification of business processes [1, 3], where this four-dimensional framework is named as BALSA-Business Artifacts, Lifecycles, Services, and Associations. Each of these dimensions can be described as follows:

Business Artifacts: The term "artifact" has its own roots in the business domain. In general, we can describe an artifact as, a means to record business information needed to perform business operations. And in the business terminology, an artifact can be better described as a key business-relevant entity responsible for driving overall business operations to achieve business objectives [4]. An artifact serves as a basic building block for business process modeling by aggregating both the information aspects and process aspects in a more comprehensive way. An important aspect of artifact is its type, which can be characterized by its *data/information model* and *lifecycle model*, where the data model describes the business data that an artifact captures, and its lifecycle model specifies the possible stages that an artifact navigates through by responding to events and services that act on it. The data model can be specified in many forms, e.g., a name-value notation [4], an XML or ER model [1].

Lifecycle: The lifecycle of artifact can be described as key business-relevant stages, through which an artifact navigates from its initiation to the completion. Different artifacts may differ with their "life expectancies". In general, the lifecycle may be specified using flow charts, finite state machines, state charts or using declarative mechanisms [1].

Services: A service can be described as a business task or an action performed on the artifact to progress towards business objectives. Service invocation on artifact may result in a state change of the artifact, and/or update artifact's content. Services can be specified with pre-conditions and post-conditions [11–13].

Associations: Associations specify the association among services and artifacts and their constraints. Here the constraints correspond to the conditions under which services can be executed. The constraints may be specified procedurally [4] or declaratively [11–13], for e.g., using flowcharts or ECA (Event-Condition-Action) rules, respectively.

2.2 A Running Example

The figure shown below is adopted from [11], which presents a Customer Order processing scenario, and is used throughout this paper for illustrating the BALSA aspects of each concrete modeling approach. The process starts by receiving an order from the customer and ends with successful delivery. Here the Customer Order forms one of the key entities of the business and interacts with other entities of the business such as Delivery and Invoice to complete its processing (Fig. 1).

The information model of Customer Order artifact includes attributes such as *OrderID, OrderDate, CustID, CustAddr, CPhNum*. In the same way, the information model of Delivery artifact may include attributes such as *DeliveryID, DDate*, and *DStatus* and the information model of Invoice artifact may include *IVDate*, Total and *IVStatus* attributes. The lifecycle model of Customer Order artifact, specify the states as *Received, Scheduling, Ready, Delivery, Billing*, and *Completed*. In the same way other artifacts such as Delivery, Invoice also have their lifecycle states, where In *Transit* and *Delivered* states form lifecycle model of Delivery artifact and *Sent, Unpaid, Paid* states form the lifecycle model of Invoice artifact. Services in the above example include *Receive Order, Plan Schedule, Cancel Order, Prepare Order, Send Order, Send Invoice* and *Complete Order* are the services that act on Customer Order artifact to change its state. The Receive Order service instantiates a Customer Order instance and

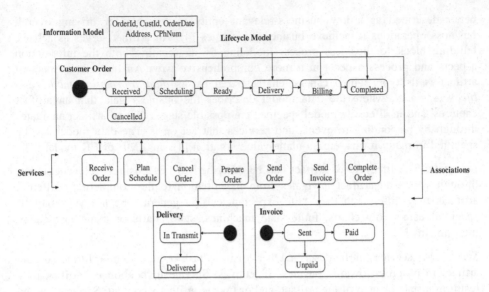

Fig. 1. Customer order processing scenario

puts it in the *Received* state. Similarly, Prepare Order service puts the artifact in *Ready* state. Similarly the Send Order and Send Invoice services act on multiple artifacts such as Customer Order and Delivery and Customer Order and Invoice. Association among artifacts and services are represented through arrows that specify which services are acting on which artifacts and when.

Though the example described above is simple, it does not lack of generality and can be used to demonstrate different modeling approaches. The following sections discuss each of the approaches studied in the paper in detail.

3   Artifact-Centric Modeling Approaches

With the emergence of artifact-centric approach, several artifact-centric modeling approaches have been proposed, of which have their own characteristics and provides different ways to specify business operations. Some of the promising modeling approaches are GSM [7], ArtiNets [8], AXML [9], BPMN Extensions [10], and ACP-i [5]. The following section provides details and discussions to those modeling approaches with the running example to demonstrate how each approach can be applied on.

3.1   Guard-Stage-Milestone

In recent years, a declarative style of meta-model for specifying artifact lifecycles, Guard-Stage-Milestone (abbreviated as GSM) [7] has been introduced by IBM. The key constructs of the GSM meta-model used in specifying artifact lifecycles include:

(1) *information model,* that holds all the data about an artifact instance; (2) *milestones,* specify business objectives that might be achieved by an artifact instance; (3) *Stages,* represents a set of activities performed by an artifact instance to achieve business objectives; and (4) *Guards,* simply act as sentries and represent a condition or triggering event to control stages and milestones.

GSM Modeling of BALSA Elements

GSM supports specification of BALSA elements. The following section describes how GSM meta-model represents each element of the BALSA framework.

Business Artifacts (Information Model): GSM specifies information model of artifact with attributes, where the artifact type can be a scalar, or a record type or a collection type. These attributes are categorized into 3 different types such as *Data attributes, Event attributes and Status attributes.* The Data attributes contain information about the artifacts. The Event attributes represent information about the triggering events. And, the Status attributes are intended to hold status information about the stages and milestones i.e., about the values associated to stages and milestones that change over time and are of type Boolean. The possible values of status attribute may be open/close (active/inactive) for stages and true/false for the milestones.

Lifecycle: The lifecycle of an artifact can be modeled using the constructs stages, milestones, guards. Here stages correspond to the states of the BALSA lifecycle. The stage structures the activities of an artifact instance and becomes true or said to be open when its associated guard becomes true. And the stage will be closed when its milestone is achieved or becomes true. The stage contains a stage body, guards, one or more milestones, and may contain multiple sub stages where stages at the same level can be executed in parallel.

Services: In GSM, the services are specified in the form of events, where event occurrence may result in a state change or modify the value of milestone. There are two types of event types such as external event types and status-change event types. GSM supports 4 kinds of status-change event types where first two are denoted in GSM-L syntax as S.opened() and S.closed() and the other two are denoted as m.achieved() and m.invalidated().

Associations: GSM uses Event-Condition-Action (ECA) rules in the specification of associations. The ECA rules take the form "take an action, when the event occurs under the specified condition". And in GSM, these ECA rules are formed from the sentries. The sentry here is expressed in the form 'on< event >if< condition >then< action >.

3.1.1   GSM Representation of the Running Example

The key constructs of the GSM meta-model are illustrated by using the sketch of Customer Order artifact type, described in the running example section. Different kind of nodes in the figure designate GSM constructs like, the rounded-corner rectangles represent stages, the guards are designated using diamonds and the small circles associated to each stage represent a milestone (Fig. 2).

For Customer Order artifact, the data attributes hold the values of attributes that include *customerId, orderId, orderDate, customerAddress, phNumber.* For the

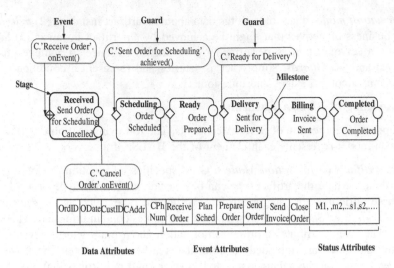

Fig. 2. GSM representation for customer order artifact

Delivery artifact the data attributes include *deliveryDate*, *status* and *invoiceId*, *total*, *status* are the data attributes of Invoice artifact. In the above figure, the upper portion represents a lifecycle model of Customer Order artifact that includes a set of stages with milestones, which the Customer Order artifact might achieve during its lifetime. The Customer Order artifact moves through its lifecycle with the result of event occurrences. For e.g., the *c.'ReceiveOrder'.onEvent()* event initiates the Customer Order artifact instance and puts it in *Received* stage. And in the same way the *'Cancel Order'* event triggers *Cancelled* milestone. In similar manner the result of event occurrences lead to the completion of Customer Order artifact. The status attribute of milestone, for example 'm' is initially initialized to FALSE and can become TRUE if the milestone is achieved. The status of stage such as 's' becomes open, if its associated guard becomes TRUE and will be closed if its milestone becomes TRUE. The Guard is simply a sentry, when the guard condition such as c.'Send Order for Scheduling' is achieved, the milestone becomes true, and the artifact instance enters next stage by triggering its guard value to true. Then the corresponding event can be invoked on the artifact instance. Here the variable 'c' is used to denote the artifact instance currently under consideration.

3.1.2 Interaction Between Artifacts

The GSM supports interaction among artifacts through conditions and events [14, 15]. The figure below illustrates the interaction between all the artifacts Customer Order, Delivery and Invoice. The dashed lines denote B-steps [14] that correspond to the incorporation of event into the GSM system, for example the 'Send Order' event allows interaction between Customer Order and Delivery artifacts, where its result changes the state of Customer Order artifact from *Ready* to *Delivery* and also initiates the Delivery artifact instance. Similarly the 'Send Invoice' event allows interaction between Customer Order and Invoice artifact (Fig. 3).

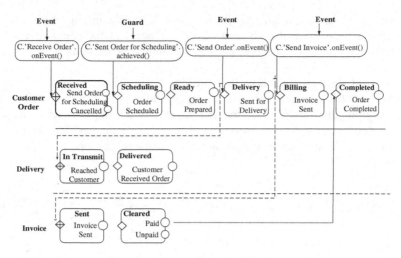

Fig. 3. Interaction between artifacts

3.2   ArtiNets

ArtiNets workflow model [8], a variant of artifact-centric workflow models introduced to support the specification of artifact lifecycles and their constraints. Inspired by DecSerFlow [16], a Declarative Service Flow Language, ArtiNets also allows declarative style in specifying constraints on artifact lifecycles. The key components of ArtiNet model are: *artifacts, services, places, and transitions.* ArtiNet framework is closely related to Petri nets [17], but only differs with two aspects: where artifacts form the key constructs of ArtiNet model instead of tokens, and the difference lies in the transition firing rule.

3.2.1   ArtiNet Modeling of BALSA Elements
Business Artifacts (Information Model): ArtiNet model primarily focuses on modeling the lifecycle aspects of artifacts, and their constraints. ArtiNet model may specify artifact's information model, but these details are not much addressed in its current literature.

Lifecycle: ArtiNet model uses four key constructs in the representation of BALSA Lifecycle such as *artifacts, places, services and transitions.* A place is a repository that stores artifacts, and transition correspond to the actions/events invoked on artifacts, that may change the location of artifact from one place to another. The transition firing may consume/generate only one artifact though it has multiple input/output places.

Services: A service in the ArtiNet model corresponds to a task performed on the artifacts, where the execution sequence of these tasks is defined by lifecycle constraints.

Associations: In ArtiNet model, the invocation of services on artifacts is limited by constraints (conditions). The constraints here may be the regular constraints, which are expressed using regular expressions [8] or counting constraints, which are expressed using semi-linear sets of Parikh map [8, 18]. Regular constraints specify a condition, under which a service can be invoked on the artifact, and the counting constraints specify how many number of times, the services should be executed.

3.2.2 ArtiNet Representation of the Running Example

An ArtiNet workflow representation of Customer Order artifact is given below, where the rounded rectangles represent the services (tasks) that act on Customer Order artifact and the circles represent the places (states) that the artifact exists. The arrows correspond to the transition of artifact from one place to the other place (Fig. 4).

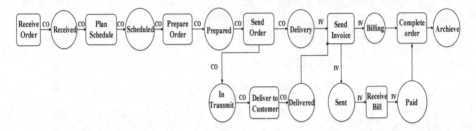

Fig. 4. ArtiNet representation for custer order scenario

The service invocation on artifact leads to a transition of artifact from one state to other state. In the above figure, 'Receive Order' service creates a CO instance and puts it in the '*Received*' state. Then with the invocation of 'Plan Schedule' service the artifact enters into the '*Scheduled*' state. In similar manner the artifact exist various other stages with response to service invocations, and can be archived when it finishes its completion. Association among the three artifacts is clearly illustrated in the above figure. And CO here is the Customer Order artifact instance which flows through the lifecycle, where the other artifacts may acquire it for processing, when required.

3.3 The AXML Artifact Model

The AXML artifact model [9] is a data-centric workflow approach that has been introduced to encapsulate data and workflow activities in a distributed environment. The AXML Artifact model is built based on Active XML [19], which is a declarative framework developed to tackle web services for distributed data management, and is designed to work in a peer-to-peer architecture. The AXML artifact model is designed to capture various aspects of artifacts such as their states, evolutions, interactions, and history [9, 20]. And the state of an artifact is represented with an AXML document, represented in a tree structure with XML data and some function calls.

3.3.1 AXML Modeling to BALSA Elements

Business Artifact (Information Model): AXML represents the artifact's data in the form of nodes in an artifact tree (AXML document). These nodes may be element nodes, content nodes. *Peer* act as a repository to store artifacts, supports interaction and provides computing resources for the artifacts they hold. The artifacts of one peer may exchange data (in the form of strings) with the artifacts of other peers, which can be reconstructed at the receiving peers.

Lifecycle: AXML supports modeling of artifact lifecycle, where the state of an artifact is represented with an AXML document that contains some nodes. These nodes may be element nodes, content nodes, function calls and sub artifacts.

Services: A service is a function call in AXML artifact model, which is specified with the function nodes in the AXML document. Here the services may be internal services or external services. Similar to GAXML, the function call in AXML has 4 components: *call guard*, which controls the activation of a function call, *argument query*, which computes call argument, *return guard*, that controls the result of the call, and *result query*, that computes the result of the call. The guards, arguments and return queries are specified using Boolean combinations of tree-patterns (BTPQ) [9] queries over the documents.

Associations: The association among services (function calls) and artifacts is restricted by constraints, which are expressed in the form (*event, precond, postcond*). The event here may correspond to a function call activated on the peer, the call received at some other peer, result sending and the reception of that result. Other events such as the artifact creation, state change or archiving may correspond to function calls. The precond and postcond are the conditions specified as formulas (BTPQ) over the artifacts states.

3.3.2   AXML Representation for Customer Order Artifact

An AXML document, which represents Customer Order artifact tree is shown below, that contains different kinds of nodes such as element nodes, content nodes, function nodes and some sub artifacts. The nodes such as cname, id, address, date are the element nodes, and the content nodes include Sam, 1001, 3214. The "creditCheck" element denotes a sub artifact, created by Customer Order artifact in order to check the details of the customer. And a function "warehouseCheck" is activated to check the availability of the order in the warehouse (Fig. 5).

3.4   BPMN Extensions

The BPMN (Business Process Modeling Notation) standard has been extended to support artifact-centric business process modeling. Various BPMN Extensions [10] proposed to model different aspects of artifact-centric approach include as artifacts, object lifecycles, location information, access control, goal states, and policies [21]. Artifacts form the key constructs of the model, lifecycle specifies the possible states of artifacts, location information specifies how the location of artifacts is changed, and access control specifies that the artifacts are accessed remotely. The extensions such as goal states and policies are mainly used in removing undesired behavior of artifact.

```
<customerorder artID="CO1">
<customer>
<cname> Sam </cname>
<id> 1001</id>
<address> Auckland</address>
<phno>2127378999</phno>
</customer>
<order>
<id>3214</id>
<date>20/03/2014</date>
<item1> LG Television</item1>
<item2>Samsung Mobile</item2>
</order>
<creditCheck artID="CO1-cc">
<number>xxxxxx1234</number>
<pin>xxxxxx</pin>
</creditCheck>
<fun funID="warehouseCheck"/>
</customerorder>
```

Fig. 5. AXML representation for customer order artifact

3.4.1   BPMN Modeling to BALSA Elements

Business Artifact (Information Model): BPMN uses a data objects representation for artifacts, where a placeholder symbol can be used to hold the data object and its name appears in the upper left corner of the place holder symbol. Representing information model of the artifact is out of scope of the current literature.

Lifecycle: The lifecycle of each artifact is modeled using the constructs like tasks, events and gateways, where the initial (start event) and final (end event) states of the artifact is denoted by standard BPMN symbols. The task here is simply a service, which changes the state of the artifact. And an event represents current state of the artifact. Goal states define desired final states of the data objects, and represented using parallel gateways which connect these states.

Services: The service corresponds to a task in BPMN, which is triggered by an agent. Here the agent can be a role or organization or location. Before executing a task on the artifact, the agents need to acquire it. The agent can acquire an artifact by knowing its location (e.g., URL) or by using any other addressing mechanisms.

Associations: BPMN supports associations among services and artifacts through policies, which restrict the execution sequence of tasks in different artifacts. Policies are also used in the specification of dependencies among tasks of one or two artifacts and are modeled using the constructs tasks and gateways.

3.4.2   BPMN Representation for Customer Order Processing Scenario

The figure below illustrates an artifact-centric BPMN model of the Customer Order processing scenario, where all the three artifacts are depicted using placeholder symbols with their names appear in the top left corner. The lifecycle of each artifact is modeled using the constructs like tasks, events and gateways, where the task is represented by rounded rectangle, which contain name of the task and the agent who triggers the tasks on artifacts, for e.g., Receive Order, Plan Schedule are the tasks with agents Customer and Employee (Fig. 6).

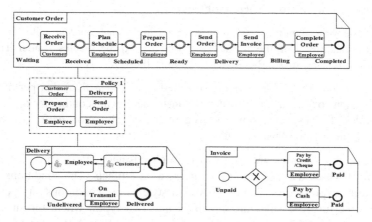

Fig. 6. Artifact-centric BPMN model of the customer order scenario

Events are represented in the model with double rounded circles, and denote current state of the artifacts like *Received, Scheduling* and *Completed* etc. The initial and final state of an artifact is represented by using BPMN symbols. Similar to the lifecycle representation, the location information is also included in the upper portion of the artifact with a stick figure, where each agent is assumed as a location, which specifies the current location of the artifact. Arrows between the agents represent message channels through which they exchange artifact instances.

The policy 1 in figure specifies the dependencies between the tasks of two artifacts Customer Order and Delivery, which can also be modeled using the constructs tasks and gateways. Here this policy describes that the "Prepare Order" task of Customer Order artifact should be executed before the "Send to Customer" task of Delivery artifact. We assume that an Invoice artifact has goal states as *"Pay by Credit/Cheque"* and *"Pay by Cash"* which are connected through a parallel gateway, to present two payment options for the customer. The customer can pay through any of the two modes, which completes processing of Invoice artifact.

3.5   ACP-i Model

The ACP-i model [5], an artifact-centric business process model is an extended version of ACP model presented in [22, 23], has been proposed to support inter organizational business process modeling. The core components of this approach include: *roles, artifacts, tasks* and *business rules*. The roles are the organization roles participate in the collaboration, an artifact here is a business entity or object that exists in the collaboration, a task is an operation (read/update) on artifacts performed by the organizations in the collaboration, and a business rule specifies a set of constraints on tasks in a Condition-Action style.

3.5.1 ACP-i Modeling to BALSA Elements

Business Artifacts (Information Model): The information model of an artifact is represented by using a name-value pair notation, where each attribute is of type scalar or by using an array list of nested attributes.

Lifecycle: Lifecycle of an artifact is represented using a state machine with set of states, where state transitions of the artifact is based on business rules. Label Transition System (LTS) is used in ACP-i model to capture these lifecycles.

Services: A service in ACP-i model is specified as a task (action) that performs read/update operations on the artifacts, which is constrained by the conditions, defined in the business rules. The organizations involved in the collaboration perform these tasks according to the defined business rules.

Associations: Associations are specified through business rules, which specify conditions, under which the task should be invoked on artifacts. The conditions here are the constraints expressed in Condition-Action style as pre-conditions and post-conditions. Here the business rules are classified into two types, where the first type of business rules are used to change the state of single artifacts, whereas the other type of business rules called synchronization rules can be used for expressing synchronization dependencies among artifacts and are used to change the states of multiple artifacts.

3.5.2 ACP-i Representation of the Running Example

The ACP-i model distinguishes artifacts into two types such as local artifacts, and shared artifacts. The local artifacts are the artifacts owned by the organizations and shared artifacts, correspond to the commonly agreed artifacts used for coordination among parties in the collaboration. To demonstrate ACP-i model let us assume the artifacts described so far are the shared artifacts such as Customer Order (CO), Delivery (D), Invoice (IV). We consider the other artifacts such as Stock Check (SC), Schedule Delivery (SD), Bill (B) in the figure as local artifacts whose details are kept private by the organizations, which own these artifacts and not revealed to the external parties in the collaboration (Fig. 7).

Once the order is received from the customer by executing the task receiveOrder (co), the employee interacts with the SC artifact to find the availability of the stock. If the stock is available, the employee prepares the order, where the SC artifact enters the *Order prepared* state to complete its processing. When the SC artifact enters the *Order prepared* state with the result of task prepareOrder(sc) task, which automatically triggers the state transition of CO from *Scheduling* to *Ready* state. The employee cancels the order if the stock is unavailable. When the order is ready, the employee interacts with Schedule Delivery (SD) artifact to schedule the delivery, this process ends when the DS artifact enters the state *Sent*, which consequently triggers the delivery state of CO artifact and initiates the artifact D.

For this scenario, the business rule can be expressed as (pre-condition : *instate(co, ready)^instate(sd,prepared)*; Task: *sendOrder(sd,co)*; post-condition: *instate(sd,sent) ^instate(co,delivery)^instate(d,init))*. Similarly the employee interacts with Bill artifact to prepare bill for the order, this process ends when the B artifact enters the state *Sent*, which consequently triggers the *Billing* state of CO artifact. The entire CO process ends

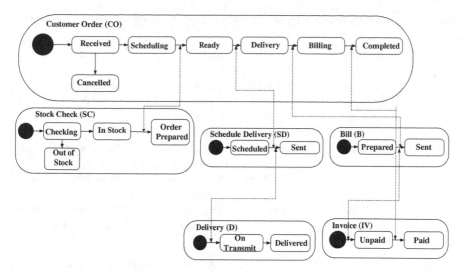

Fig. 7. ACP-i representation for customer order processing scenario

when it enters the *completed* state. The dashed lines represent the interactions among artifacts, which are specified through synchronization dependencies.

4 Discussion

The concept of business artifacts and the notion of modeling business processes in terms of artifact lifecycles were introduced in the literature by Nigam and Caswell [4]. This data-centric approach can be laid in a four dimensional framework called BALSA [1, 3] for defining business processes. This data-centric approach also formed foundation for various artifact-centric meta-models in recent years, where all the approaches support modeling of BALSA elements. The following table presents a quick overview of the above discussed approaches like, how each approach represents the four dimensional framework (Table 1).

GSM [7] has been introduced with the key motivation to aid business stakeholders in specifying and managing their business operations by using intuitive natural constructs that closely resembles the ideology of business stakeholders about their business operations. The GSM contrasts with procedural approaches such as BPMN by following a declarative approach, and supports parallelism within artifact instances and modularity through hierarchical constructs [15]. GSM supports modeling of BALSA framework, where programming data types are used in the specification of artifacts' data model and follows a declarative style in the specification of all the other aspects.

ArtiNets [8], also enables the declarative specification of constraints on artifact lifecycles in the spirit of DecSerFlow [16] language. ArtiNets, allow the integration of lifecycles in one model, where the coordination is acquired through transitions on multiple artifacts. But here the declarative style is followed only for specifying associations, and all the other aspects of the BALSA framework are specified procedurally.

Table 1. Comparison framework for all the artifact-centric modeling approaches studied in this paper

Approach	Information model	Lifecycle	Services	Associations
GSM	Programming data types	Declarative	Declarative (events)	Declarative (ECA-rules)
ArtiNet	Procedural	Procedural	Procedural (tasks)	Declarative (ECA-rules)
AXML	XML elements	Declarative	Declarative (function calls)	Declarative (ECA-rules)
BPMN	Procedural	Procedural	Procedural (tasks)	Procedural (policies)
ACP-i	Name-value pair notation	Declarative	Declarative (actions)	Declarative (condition action rules)

The AXML artifact model [9] also supports declarative lifecycles based on Active XML [19], by taking the hierarchical structure in data representation with XML elements and supports implementation of artifacts, which can be accessed among organizations in the collaboration. When compared to the GSM, that mainly focuses on managing data aspects, the AXML artifact model gives higher priority to structural aspects.

The standard BPMN [10] approach, has also been extended to support artifact-centric modeling, but follows a procedural style in representing all the aspects of BALSA framework and provides limited support to data aspects.

The other approach, ACP-i [5] also supports artifact-centric modeling, but mainly developed for modeling inter-organizational business processes. Similar to GSM and ArtiNets, the ACP-i model also focuses on behavior aspects, where Label Transition System (LTS) is used to capture these behavior aspects. Similar to GSM and AXML, the ACP-i also follows a declarative style in the specification of BALSA framework, but it uses a name-value pair notion to represent data model.

5 Conclusion and Future Work

In this paper, some key artifact-centric modeling approaches have been reviewed and discusses by using a four-dimensional framework called BALSA as a reference framework. A running example has been used to help illustrating each approach. We also present an initial evaluation and comparison of the approaches discussed in this paper. In the future, we plan to do more thorough evaluation of the approaches through both real-life case study and in-lab experiments.

References

1. Bhattacharya, K., Hull, R., Su, J.: A data-centric design methodology for business processes. In: Handbook of Research on Business Process Modeling. pp. 503–531 (2009)

2. Russo, A., et al.: Implementing and running data-centric dynamic systems. In: 2013 IEEE 6th International Conference on Service-Oriented Computing and Applications (SOCA). IEEE (2013)

3. Hull, R.: Artifact-centric business process models: brief survey of research results and challenges. In: Meersman, R., Tari, Z. (eds.) OTM 2008, Part II. LNCS, vol. 5332, pp. 1152–1163. Springer, Heidelberg (2008)

4. Nigam, A., Caswell, N.S.: Business artifacts: an approach to operational specification. IBM Syst. J. **42**(3), 428–445 (2003)

5. Yongchareon, S., Liu, C., Zhao, X.: An artifact-centric view-based approach to modeling inter-organizational business processes. In: Bouguettaya, A., Hauswirth, M., Liu, L. (eds.) WISE 2011. LNCS, vol. 6997, pp. 273–281. Springer, Heidelberg (2011)

6. Bhattacharya, K., et al.: Artifact-centered operational modeling: lessons from customer engagements. IBM Syst. J. **46**(4), 703–721 (2007)

7. Hull, R., Damaggio, E., Fournier, F., Gupta, M., Heath III, F., Hobson, S., Linehan, M., Maradugu, S., Nigam, A., Sukaviriya, P., Vaculin, R.: Introducing the guard-stage-milestone approach for specifying business entity lifecycles (invited talk). In: Bravetti, M. (ed.) WS-FM 2010. LNCS, vol. 6551, pp. 1–24. Springer, Heidelberg (2011)

8. Kucukoguz, E., Su, J.: On lifecycle constraints of artifact-centric workflows. In: Bravetti, M. (ed.) WS-FM 2010. LNCS, vol. 6551, pp. 71–85. Springer, Heidelberg (2011)

9. Abiteboul, S., et al.: The AXML artifact model. In: 2009 16th International Symposium on Temporal Representation and Reasoning, (TIME 2009). IEEE (2009)

10. Lohmann, N., Nyolt, M.: Artifact-centric modeling using BPMN. In: Pallis, G., Jmaiel, M., Charfi, A., Graupner, S., Karabulut, Y., Guinea, S., Rosenberg, F., Sheng, Q.Z., Pautasso, C., Ben Mokhtar, S. (eds.) ICSOC 2011 Workshops. LNCS, vol. 7221, pp. 54–65. Springer, Heidelberg (2012)

11. Bhattacharya, K., Gerede, C.E., Hull, R., Liu, R., Su, J.: Towards formal analysis of artifact-centric business process models. In: Alonso, G., Dadam, P., Rosemann, M. (eds.) BPM 2007. LNCS, vol. 4714, pp. 288–304. Springer, Heidelberg (2007)

12. Deutsch, A., et al.: Automatic verification of data-centric business processes. In: Proceedings of the 12th International Conference on Database Theory. ACM (2009)

13. Fritz, C., Hull, R., Su, J.: Automatic construction of simple artifact-based business processes. In: Proceedings of the 12th International Conference on Database Theory. ACM (2009)

14. Hull, R., et al.: Business artifacts with guard-stage-milestone lifecycles: managing artifact interactions with conditions and events. In: Proceedings of the 5th ACM international conference on Distributed event-based system. ACM (2011)

15. Damaggio, E., Hull, R., Vaculín, R.: On the equivalence of incremental and fixpoint semantics for business artifacts with guard–stage–milestone lifecycles. Inf. Syst. **38**(4), 561–584 (2013)

16. van der Aalst, W.M., Pesic, M.: DecSerFlow: Towards a truly declarative service flow language. In: Bravetti, M., Núñez, M., Zavattaro, G. (eds.) WS-FM 2006. LNCS, vol. 4184, pp. 1–23. Springer, Heidelberg (2006)

17. Murata, T.: Petri nets: properties, analysis and applications. Proc. IEEE **77**(4), 541–580 (1989)

18. Parikh, R.J.: On context-free languages. J. ACM (JACM) **13**(4), 570–581 (1966)

19. Abiteboul, S., Benjelloun, O., Milo, T.: The Active XML project: an overview. VLDB J. **17**(5), 1019–1040 (2008)

20. Abiteboul, S., Segoufin, L., Vianu, V.: Modeling and verifying active xml artifacts. IEEE Data Eng. Bull. **32**(3), 10–15 (2009)

21. Lohmann, N., Wolf, K.: Artifact-centric choreographies. In: Maglio, P.P., Weske, M., Yang, J., Fantinato, M. (eds.) ICSOC 2010. LNCS, vol. 6470, pp. 32–46. Springer, Heidelberg (2010)

22. Yongchareon, S., Liu, C.: A process view framework for artifact-centric business processes. In: Meersman, R., Dillon, T.S., Herrero, P. (eds.) OTM 2010. LNCS, vol. 6426, pp. 26–43. Springer, Heidelberg (2010)

23. Yongchareon, S., Liu, C., Zhao, X.: An artifact-centric view-based approach to modeling inter-organizational business processes. In: Bouguettaya, A., Hauswirth, M., Liu, L. (eds.) WISE 2011. LNCS, vol. 6997, pp. 273–281. Springer, Heidelberg (2011)

A Connectivity Based Recommendation Approach for Data Service Mashups

Sai Zhang[1], Guiling Wang[1(✉)], Zhongmei Zhang[2], and Yanbo Han[1]

[1] Research Center for Cloud Computing, North China University of Technology,
Beijing, People's Republic of China
qingqingbixue@163.com, {wangguiling,yhan}@ict.ac.cn
[2] Tianjin University, Tianjin, China
gloria_z@126.com

Abstract. Data service mashup provides a development fashion that integrates heterogeneous data from multiple data sources into a single Web application. This paper focuses on the problem of recommending useful suggestions for developing data service mashups based on the association relationship of data services. Firstly the data service association relationship is analyzed from three angles: the data dependence, inheritance and the potential association between data services. Based on the analysis, a measure of the data service association relationship called connectivity is proposed to assess the relationship of any two data services. Then a recommendation method is proposed to suggest the next useful data services based on the connectivity. The experimental evaluation demonstrates the utility of our method.

Keywords: Data service · Data service mashup · Data service recommendation

1 Introduction

Now mashup is a kind of popular interactive Web application that combines data with and/or functionality from one or more data source. There are a variety of categories of mashups, such as data mashup, process mashup, the presentation mashup and so on [1]. Data mashup is a kind of particular mashup, which allows users to access, process and combine data from various data sources and solve a certain type of data integration problems [2, 3, 8]. For instance, Lisa is a HR employee and she is assigned the task of building a Web application that enables other employees to quickly find the nearby businesses point such as restaurants, gas stations, banks, etc. Different from the traditional data integration, its requirements cannot be completely defined in advance. Aimed at this problem, a feasible method is to encapsulate all kinds of heterogeneous data resources as data service [6–8] and enable users to access, process and combine the underlying data sources in data services by graphical mashup programming environment. Such kind of development fashion is called data service mashup in this paper.

Though the data service mashup tools usually are visual and graphic, it's still challenging to solve the data integration problems for non-professional users due to the following reasons: (1)The mashup operations are still complicated for users. Taking the mashup platform like Yahoo! Pipes as an example, there are more than 40 kinds of

© Springer International Publishing Switzerland 2015
B. Benatallah et al. (Eds.): WISE 2014, LNCS 9051, pp. 133–147, 2015.
DOI: 10.1007/978-3-319-20370-6_11

operations and their usage are unpleasant. It's not easy for users to understand and use them smoothly. (2)There are plenty of data services. Just on Yahoo! Pipes, there exists more than 20,000 data services that encapsulate all kinds of data sources. Each of them owns particular characteristic and parameters. Choosing a proper data service for personalized requirement is always a tedious work. (3)Users are not absolutely clear about their demand. In the process of building data services mashup, users only have vague cognizance for what they need. For instance, the user wants to know the specific location according to a certain longitude and latitude value. So "Map", "Satellite!Map", "Mul-Dimension!Map" all conform to the user's need. But they are different, "Map" show the space in 2-Dimension image, "Satellite!Map" show the space in the form of a satellite image, "Mul-Dimension!Map" show the space in 3-Dimension image. User needs to consider which is the best. These factors all make it inconvenient for users to build data service mashup. If we can put forward a kind of effective method to recommend data services for users in the process of building data service, it will greatly alleviate the pressure of the users.

The contributions of this paper are two-fold. First, a new concept called "connectivity" is proposed to assess the strength of the association relationship of data services, it both considers the direct association relationship such as dependencies, inheritance and considering the potential association. Second, an effective data service recommendation method based on connectivity of data services is proposed.

The paper is organized as follows: in order to better illustrate the problems, Sect. 2 gives a motivating scenario. Section 3 presents the preliminary definitions and work. Section 4 introduces the association relationship of data services and Sect. 5 gives a detailed calculation of connectivity based the analysis in Sect. 4. Section 6 introduces the recommendation method. Section 7 introduces the experiment results and related work is presented in Sect. 8. Finally, we make a conclusion and discuss some possible future work in Sect. 9.

2   Motivating Scenario

In order to illustrate how the recommendation approach can be used to meet the challenge that non-professional users can't build the data service mashup conveniently, we take a scenario in the domain of criminal investigation as an example. It is about how to find out and catch the escaped criminal suspect after a criminal case is reported.

The police came to the crime scene and confirmed the victim's identity. The police also found out that the place where the crime occurred was not the place where the crime item was found, and what's more, the two places are far apart from each other.

In order to find the criminal suspect, the traditional approach is looking up files or base on intuitive experience to find the connection between events and information, it is a tedious work for the police. With the gradual improvement of information systems of various departments in modern society, the police can search for clues from a variety of information systems and video surveillance systems, etc. For example, when the police confirm the victim and the murder place, they need to extract the victim's ID, the victim's social relationship (the victim's recent call, the victim's relatives, the victim's QQ, the victim's microblog, the victim's purchase record, etc.) and the vehicle information of recent contacts. The police find some vehicle information of recent contacts is the same with the vehicle information of murder place, the recent contact is murderer and the case is resolved. But it's difficult for users to find these suitable data services based on these requirement. By comparison again and again, the data services that police used are GetVictim, GetContacts, GetRelatives, MonitorVehicles and GetVehicles according to the requirement. The complete process of building data service mashup with these data services is shown as Fig. 1.

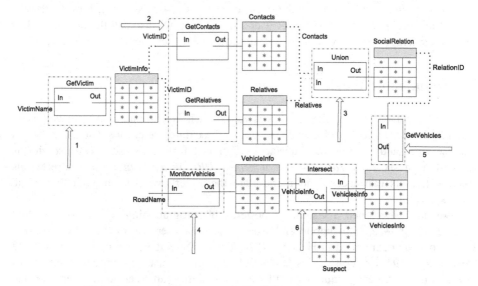

Fig. 1. The complete process of building data service mashup

At the beginning, the police only know the victim's name. How to choose the next data service depends on the police's work experiences or repeated lookups. With the help of recommendation, there are some step are changed. At the second step, the mashup environment recommends a set of data services including GetContacts and GetRelatives which are most related with GetVictim. The police select GetContants and GetRelatives and go on. At the fifth step, the mashup environment recommends a set of data services including GetVehicles which are most related with GetVictim. The police select GetVehicles and go on.

This paper focuses on how to recommend the most appropriate data service for users to meet their requirements. With the help of recommendation, in the process of building data service mashup, users could drag and drop the data services from the recommendation list to meet their need. Therefore, the police can build the data service mashup by themselves and don't depend on the expert's experience and IT professionals' programming skill any more.

The key benefits of our recommendation approach are: (1) Shorter development time. With the help of our recommendation approach, the police can choose data services without the help of the IT professionals and expert's experience. (2) Discovery of the potential data association relationship. With the help of our approach, the potential association relationship of data sources such as the data dependency relationship and the similarity relationship help user think problems more comprehensively and select the proper data service. (3) Reuse of professional experiences. With the help of our approach, the professional experiences in criminal investigation can be transformed into knowledge and be recommended to other users during the development of the mashups.

The recommendation problem in our work is: In the process of building data service mashup, given a known data service(precursor data service), how to recommend the subsequent data service for users. In the next, we also call the precursor data service as source data service, and the subsequent data service as target data service.

3   Preliminary Work

The way that data stored in the network is varied, such as relational database, web page, excel table, etc. In order to facilitate the use of these data, we encapsulate these data as data services and provide the interfaces of unified format to users. Data service is defined as a six tuple: $ds = <id, name, desc, URI, params, out >$ in our previous work [4], users can access and manipulate the underlying data through the public interface of ds.

We have developed a visualized nested table programming environment (called "Data Service Space") to support end users to build data service mashup. We can use it to encapsulate data stored in HTML, XML and JSON as data service and provide the interface of data service to users and build data service mashup through a variety of operations of different granularity until the output of mashup meets to the user's need at last. We are working towards supporting recommendation method based on Data Service Space.

Analyzing the data service mashup history built by users on Data Service Space, the result can be divided into four parts: KB_{ds}, KB_{inh}, KB_{dep} and KB_{ms}. They consist of the knowledge base KB. $KB_{ds} = \{\langle MID_i, srcds_j^i, targetds_j^i \rangle | i = 1, 2, \ldots, n_m; j = 1, 2, \ldots, n_{mi}\}$ records the predecessor and successor of data services and MID is the unique identification of every mushup. $KB_{inh} = \{\langle ds_j, inhset(ds_j) | j = 1, 2, \ldots, n_{inh} \rangle\}$, every two-tuple records one data service ds and the set consists of data services that inherit from ds. $KB_{dep} = \{\langle ds_k, depset(ds_k) | k = 1, 2, \ldots, n_{dep} \rangle\}$, every two-tuple records one data service ds and the set consist of data services that are dependent with ds on input/output. $KB_{ms} = \{m_i, copyset(m_i) | i = 1, 2, \ldots, n_m\}$, every two-tuple records one mashup m and the set consist of mashups that copy m.

According to the knowledge base KB, for each data service ds in KB, we can know all the mashups which ds exists in, the data service set consists of the precursor of ds, the data service set consists of the subsequent of ds, the set consists of data services that are dependent with ds on input/output and the set consist of data service that are inherited from ds. For each mashup m in KB, we know all mashups that copy m.

4 The Association Relationship of Data Services

We think there exists direct or indirect association relationship among data service. For data service ds_a and ds_b in KB, the output of ds_a can be the input of data service ds_b or the input of ds_a can be the subset of the input of ds_b or user are always using ds_b as the subsequent of ds_a. Such association relationships of data services provide theoretical basis for recommendation method in this paper. For a candidate data service, the stronger its relationship with the source data service, the more likely it will be recommended as the target data service. First, let us analyze the association relationship of data services as follows.

4.1 Direct Association Relationship

The direct Association Relationship of data services can be divided into two classes: data dependence relationship and inheritance relationship through the analysis of the input and output of data services. In order to show the relationship more clearly, we illustrate it with data service ds_a and ds_b as an example. Suppose that $ds_a, ds_b \in KB$, the input of ds_a is $ds_{ain} = \{att_{a\_i1}, att_{a\_i2}, \ldots, att_{a\_in_a}\}$, and the output of ds_a is $ds_{aout} = \{att_{a\_o1}, att_{a\_o2}, \ldots, att_{a\_o_a}\}$. The input of ds_b is $ds_{bin} = \{att_{b\_i1}, att_{b\_i2}, \ldots, att_{b\_in_b}\}$, and the output of ds_b is $ds_{bout} = \{att_{b\_o1}, att_{b\_o2}, \ldots, att_{b\_on_b}\}$, the data dependence relationship and inheritance relationship can be defined as the following:

- If there exists data dependence between the input/output of two data services, for example, the input of ds_b is from all or a port output of ds_a, that is, $ds'_{aout} \subseteq ds_{bin}(ds'_{aout} \subseteq ds_{aout})$, then there exists data dependence relationship between ds_a and ds_b, ds_b depends on ds_a.
- If the input of ds_a is the non-empty subset of the input of ds_b and the output of ds_a is the non-empty subset of the output of ds_b, that is $(ds_{ain} \subset ds_{bin}) \cap (ds_{aout} \subset ds_{bout})$, then ds_b inherits from ds_a.

4.2 Potential Relationship

In the process of building data service mashup, different users may choose the same target data service in the next step when they have chosen the same source data service and have the same requirements in the next step. For example, Lisa are building data service mashup and she has chosen the data service named Map and she need data service about weather, then we traverse the KB and find there are n (more than the threshold value we set) mashups appear that Map is the precursor of data service named Weather (that is, Map $\rightarrow$ Weather), then we think that there exists some association relationship between Map and Weather. In this paper, we call the association relationship of data services that derived from the collective wisdom of users as the potential relationship. For this kind of association relationship, users' experience of building mashups are analyzed and reused as knowledge for later development.

5 Connectivity

The key of our paper is recommending data service according to the association relationship of data services, in order to define the relationship in a quantitative way, we introduce "connectivity" to measure the strength of association relationship. The connectivity of ds_i and ds_j is represented as $C(ds_i, ds_j)$. It's calculated as Eq. (1), in which $Dep(ds_i, ds_j)$ is the data dependence of data services and it measures the strength of data dependence relationship between ds_i and ds_j. $Inh(ds_i, ds_j)$ is the inheritance degree and it measures the strength of inheritance relationship between ds_i and ds_j. $Pot(ds_i, ds_j)$ is the potential relationship degree and it measures the strength of potential association relationship. We use parameters, α, β, γ, with $\alpha + \beta + \gamma = 1$, as the weight of the three facets: data dependence relationship, inheritance relationship and potential relationship.

$$C(ds_i, ds_j) = \alpha Dep(ds_i, ds_j) + \beta Inh(ds_i, ds_j) + \gamma Pot(ds_i, ds_j) \qquad (1)$$

5.1 Data Dependence of Data Services

We can learn from Sect. 4, that if all or a part of the output of a data service can be the input of the other data service, there exists data dependence relationship between them. We use $Dep(ds_i, ds_j)$ to measure the strength of the data dependence relationship between two data services. We represent the source data service as ds_{src}, its output is $ds_{src-out} = \{att_{src-out1}, att_{src-out2}, \ldots, att_{src-outn}\}$, n is the number of attributes of the output. The input of any candidate target data service is $ds_{target-in} = \{att_{target-in1}, att_{target-in2}, \ldots, att_{target-outn'}\}$, n' is the number of attributes of input parameters of the candidate data service. We divide the data dependence into three classes according to the output of source data service and the input of target data service as follows:

- If $ds_{target-in} \subseteq ds_{src-out}$, that is, the attributes of all the input parameters of the candidate target data service is the subset of the output attributes of source data service, $Dep(ds_{src}, ds_{target}) = 1$.
- If $ds_{src-out} \subset ds_{target-in}$, that is, the output attributes of source data service is the subset of the input parameters of the candidate target data service, then the calculation formula is as follows, $Dep(ds_{src}, ds_{target}) = 1/num_{src}$, in which num_{src} is the number of data service which the input of target data service comes from.
- If $ds_{target-in}$ is unrelated with $ds_{source-out}$, that is, the input of candidate target data service has no association relationship with the output of source data service as above, then $Dep(ds_{src}, ds_{target}) = 0$.

5.2 Inheritance Degree

The inheritance degree called $Inh(ds_i, ds_j)$ measures the strength of inheritance relationship of data services. We know if ds_i is important in KB, then data service that inherits from ds_i is important too. The data service importance is represented as $Imp(ds_j)$. In this paper we think about three factors when we calculate the data service importance, that is, the basic importance of data service, inheritance relationship of data services, and the importance of mashup. We use three parameters, h, j, k, with $h + j + k = 1$, to weigh the impacts of the three facets.

We can get the basic importance $base(ds)$ according to the times that ds appears in KB_{ds}. The more times data service appears, the higher basic importance it has. For all the data services, their total importance $\sum base(ds) = 1$. Besides, we think the data service can gain the importance from the mashups that it exists in and the data service that it inherits from. For example, data service ds_a exist in the mashup m and ds_a inherits from ds_b, so if m and ds_b have high importance, the importance of ds_a also has high importance.

In order to get the importance of ds affected by importance of mashup, we need to traversing KB_{ds} and find the mashups which ds exists in. Here the mashup importance is measured by the times that copied by others in the KB, it is likely to calculate the basic importance of data service. We use the letter m represents a data service mashup and $c(m)$ represents the data services of m. We think the mashup gives its importance to each data service in it equally, that is, $imp(ds) = imp(m)/num(c)$, in which $ds \in c(m)$ and $num(c)$ is the number of data service in $c(m)$.

When we calculate the importance of data service according to inheritance relationship, we should construct a directed graph according the inheritance relationship. Data service is the node in the graph. If there exists inheritance relationship between data services, there exists an edge and the edge points to the data service which is new born. All the data services in KB construct the whole graph G according to the inheritance relationship. If any data service ds is important, the data services which inhert from it could get a boost in their importance. We consider each data service mashup as a webpage and its data services as the links in the webpage, so we can use PageRank to calculate the data service importance affected by the mashup and inheritance relationship.

We initialize $Imp_0(ds) = base(ds)$ and then recursively calculate the value $Imp_1(ds), \ldots, Imp_{i-1}(ds), Imp_i(ds)(i > 1)$ until $|(ds) - Imp_iImp_{i-1}(ds)|$ reaches the threshold value we set, it's calculated as algorithm 1.

```
Algorithm 1. Data Service Importance
Input:
    a weighed directed graph G; weight variable h, j, k;
importance difference threshold t_imp;
1:  Init two temporary collection,C1 for mashup, C2 for
inheritance;
2:  temporaty variable lable,imp, inhImp, tempInhImp ;
3:  for each ds_i ∈G.node do
4:  ds_i.imp_n =ds_i.base
5:  end for
```

```
6:   lable== true;
7:   while(lable)
8:   {
9:     for each dsi ∈G.node do
10:      findBelongmashup(dsi,C1);
11:      for each m∈C1 do
12:        tempMasImp= m.imp/m.comNum;
13:        masImp+= tempMasImp;
14:      end for
15:      findConnectedNodes(dsi,G,C2);
16:      for each dsinh ∈C do
17:        numsim= findSimNumBeginWithDs(dsinh,G);
18:        tempInhImp= dsinh.imp_n/numinh;
19:        inhImp+= tempInhImp;
20:      end for
21:      imp= h*dsi.base+j*inhImp+k*masImp;
22:      dsi.imp_p= dsi.imp_n;
23:      dsi.imp_n= imp;
24:    end for
25:    lable= false;
26:    for each dsi ∈G.node do
27:      If(|dsi.imp_n- dsi.imp_p|>timp)
28:      {
29:        lable= true;
30:        break;
31:      }
32: end for
33: }
34: Output G;
```

Given source data service ds_i, we can get the importance of data services that inherit from it through the method above. The higher importance it has, the more likely it will be recommended firstly as the target data service.

5.3 Potential Relationship Degree

We use the potential relationship degree to measure the strength of potential relationship that derived from the collective wisdom and represented as $Pot(ds_i, ds_j)$. According to the description about the potential relationship in Sect. 3, in order to calculate $Pot(ds_i, ds_j)$, firstly, we need to find the data service sets frequently coexisted within the same mashup. We call the data service sets as the frequent subset if its coexistence number is more than the threshold that we set. Our paper uses gSpan to find all the frequent subset because it's widely recognized as the best algorithm for searching frequent subset [11]. It uses a pattern-growth strategy and Depth First Search to traverse search space, it can output all the frequent subset through a single pass search.

We should transform each data service mashup into a graph structure before we collect the frequent subset with gSpan algorithm. It's the same with the inheritance relationship graph introduced in Sect. 5.2, the node is data service in the graph. The difference is that there is an edge between data services if one data service is the precursor or successor of another, and the edge points to successor. The following two points should be noticed when we construct the graph:

- When there exists an aggregator operation (union, join, cart, except, intersect) [10] between two data services ds_i and ds_j, we set the edge as undirected because each of them can be the precursor or the successor another.
- If the output of an aggregator operation on two data service ds_i and ds_j flows into the input of data service ds_k, we consider that the output of ds_i and ds_j are both the input of ds_k, so ds_k is the successor data service of ds_i and ds_j.

After transform all the data service mashup to mix graphs, we take them as the input of gSpan algorithm and set the maximum number of the frequent subset and the minimum support degree. The output of the algorithm is the frequent subset abbreviated as FS. Because of the limitation of length, the detailed introduction of the algorithm will be introduced in our other paper.

When we get the frequent subset, the potential relationship between ds_i, ds_j(ds_i is precursor)can be divided into two classes as follows:

- If ds_i, ds_j coexist in the same frequent subset, then $Pot(ds_i, ds_j) = 1$.
- If there is not ds_i in the frequent subset, we need to traverse the KB and find the data service connected directly with ds_i. For every data service, the more times connected with ds_i in KB, the stronger potential relationship with ds_i.

Take the data service mashup in Sect. 2 as an example, we apply these rules above to the data service mashup built by police and get its graph structure as shown in Fig. 2. For data service GetContacts and GetRelatives, the undirected edge connected them shows police do aggregator operation and their output is the input of GetVehicles.

Finally, we get the connectivity of data services through the three modules: data dependence of data services, the inheritance degree of data service, and the potential relationship degree. We will represent the recommendation algorithm in the Sect. 6 according to the connectivity of data services.

6   The Recommendation Method

In Sect. 5, we have defined the connectivity to measure the association relationship of data services. This section will introduce how to recommend the target data services given a source data service with connectivity.

The process of recommendation is divided into three steps: (1)traversing KB according to the source data service and choosing the set that consists of candidate target data services; (2)calculating the connectivity of any candidate target data service

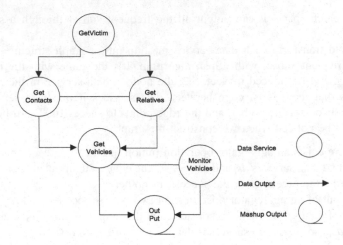

Fig. 2. Comparision of the connectivity-based and FRPT-based recommendation method

and source data service and sorting candidate target data service by the connectivity; (3)modifying the KB after user choose the target data service.

In order to choose the candidate data service, the method respectively search for the data service which its data dependence with source data service reaches the threshold value t_{dep}, the data service which its importance reaches the threshold value t_{imp} and the data services which its potential relationship degree with source data service reaches the threshold value t_{pot}. They make up the set of candidate target data services set_{ca}. When user selects a data service ds, the method recommend the set_{ca} of ds immediately.

The recommendation mechanism chooses data service ds_{tar} from set_{ca} in turn and calculates its connectivity with source data service with the formula $C(ds_{src}, ds_{tar}) = \alpha Dep(ds_{src}, ds_{tar}) + \beta Inh(ds_{src}, ds_{tar}) + \gamma Pot(ds_{src}, ds_{tar})$. We currently assign the weights, α, β and γ as 1/3, and they could be tuned according to the user requirements. Since recommending data service for user is a time-critical function, we sort these data services in set_{ca} according to their connectivity with source data service by quick sort, the result is set_{tar}. But it's not realistic to recommend all the candidate target data services to users, so we set a k value and recommend the top-k candidate target data services of set_{tar}.

Then the recommendation mechanism modifies the existing knowledge base KB after user choose the target data service ds_{tar}. Firstly, adding the record of precursor and successor of new mashup in KB_{ds}. Secondly, traversing KB_{inh}, if ds_{tar} has inheritance relationship with some data services, the recommendation mechanism modifies two-tuples of these data services and the same modification in KB_{dep}. Thirdly, when users finish the data service mashup, the recommendation mechanism judge whether it copies any mashup in KB. If it does, the recommendation mechanism will modify the records in KB_{ms}. These modification all provide data basis for the next recommendation.

7 Experiments

This section introduces experiment to evaluate the recommendation accuracy and performance.

7.1 Data Sets

To evaluate the effectiveness of our approach in real life environment, we choose the data on Yahoo! Pipes, a popular data mashup platform because Yahoo! Pipes was launched in 2007, over 90,000 developers have created mashups on it and these mashups are executed over 5,000,000 times each day. Yahoo! Pipes currently contains over 16 thousand data mashups (called pipes), the large number of data services can prove the result effectively. What's more, most of the operators in the pipes can be transformed into operators in Data Service Space. For example, the Sources module defined in Yahoo! Pipes can be implemented with the "importable" operator in Data Service Space; the Filter, Tail, Rename, Sort modules are equivalent with the column operators RowFilter, ColumnRename, RowSort defined in Data Service Space, etc. In a word, the experiment results evaluated on the data set from Yahoo! Pipes have the same significance for our mashup environment Data Service Space.

We crawl 16177 pipes from Yahoo! Pipes and wipe off the incomplete and useless ones, the surplus 14269 pipes is the effective experiment data. Then we randomly selected 100 pipes as the test data set (i.e. objects to accept the data service recommendation) and 1200 pipes from the other pipes as sample data set (i.e. the knowledge base to support the recommendation algorithm).

7.2 Accuracy of Recommendation Algorithm

Assume the number of recommended candidate data services is k, the number of data service mashups required to be recommended is n, where the data service for i-th data service mashup required by user is ranked as $R_i(0 \leq R_i \leq k)$. We use $score(i)$ to represent the score of target data service recommendation for the i-th data service mashup. The full mark is k. If the required data service is not in the recommendation list, the score is zero. The score is calculated as formula:

$$score(i) = \begin{cases} k - R_i, & (0 < R_i < k) \\ 0, & (R_i = 0) \end{cases} \qquad (2)$$

The accuracy of the recommendation algorithm can be evaluated by the ratio of the sum of the scores of n data service mashups and the full score of $(k*n)$, as the formula (3) shows:

$$\tau = \frac{\sum_{i=1}^{n} score(i)}{k * n} \qquad (3)$$

7.3   Evaluation Results

We learn that the recommendation accuracy became higher with the increase of the k. However, it does not conform to the principle of recommendation if the candidate list is too long. Here we select $k = 7$. For the sample data set, we select 300, 400, 500, ..., 1200 data service mashups and compute the average recommendation accuracy for three groups of sample data set. The results are shown in Fig. 3.

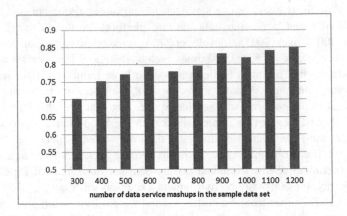

Fig. 3. Recommendation accuracy with different sample data set

The experiment results above show the effectiveness of our recommendation method and we can observe from Fig. 3 that most of the accuracy of our recommendation method is increasing with the increasing of the number of data service mashups in the sample data set. We also conducted an experiment according to "forward recommendation probability theorem, FRPT" published in our previous work [13], in which the connectivity are not taken into consideration. Figure 4 also shows that the accuracy of our recommendation method is higher than the algorithm based on "forward recommendation probability theorem" proposed in our previous work.

8   Relatated Work

In order to help the non-professional developers to develop data service mashups, some research work focus on effective mashup recommendation include mashup Advisor [14], MatchUp [15], sMash [16], MashStudio [17], Soudip Roy Chowdhury's work [18], imashupAdvisor [19], etc. Chowdbury et al. [13] classified the related work on mashup recommendation into three types: goal-oriented approach [14] aim to assist end users by automatically deriving compositions that satisfy specific goals; pattern-based approach [15 ~ 19] aims to recommend composition patterns in response to modeling actions, e.g., to auto-complete partial mashup models; and the hybrid approach [20] jointly use the goal-based and pattern-based approaches together.MatchUp [15] computes top-k recommendations out of a graph-structured knowledge base containing components and glue patterns and their relationships. The approach is based on the

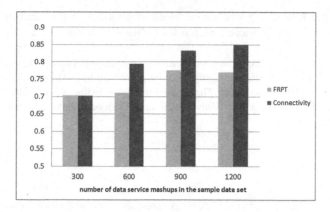

Fig. 4. Comparision of the connectivity-based and FRPT-based recommendation method

assumption that the inheritance relationship among components or component composition patterns is given. MashStudio [17] is also based on a graph-structured repository with collected mashup processes. Given the current partial mashup, the approach recommends a list of ordered mashup fragments (cliques) leveraging on the conditional probability calculation.

The knowledge base in Chowdhury's work [18] and imashupAdvisor [19] both are composed by structured mashup patterns. The approach decomposes patterns into their constituent elements and transforms them into a structure directly mapped to the recommendations. Chowdhury et al. considered five types of patterns: parameter value, component connector, component data mapping, component co-occurrence and complex pattern. The mashup patterns considered in imashupAdvisor include data mapping and parameter similarity between components, component co-occurrence, component download times, etc.

Different from other's work, the approach proposed in this paper is recommending data service according to the connectivity of data services we propose. It synthesizes three factors: data dependence relationship, inheritance relationship and potential relationship. However, our approach can be combined with Chowdhury's work [18] and imashupAdvisor in the same mashup platform to accommodate the needs of different users.

9 Conclusion and Future Work

It is challenging for those mashup developers with no or little programming skills to develop data service mashups. This paper focuses on the problem of recommending the target data services given a source data service during the development of data service mashup. Different from the existing recommendation approach for mashups, we recommend data services according to the connectivity that we define. It's calculated according to the data dependence relationship, inheritance relationship and potential relationship of data services. We also experimentally demonstrate the accuracy of our approach. In the future, we will make an effort to improve the performance of our approach so that it can be more suitable for online recommendation.

Acknowledgment. This work is supported in part by Beijing Natural Science Foundation (No.4131001), Scientific Research Common Program of Beijing Municipal Commission of Education (KM201310009003), and The Project of Construction of Innovative Teams and Teacher Career Development for Universities and Colleges Under Beijing Municipality (IDHT20130502).

References

1. Hoang, D.D., Paik, H.-y., Benatallah, B.: An analysis of spreadsheet-based services mashup, ADC 2010. In: Proceedings of the Twenty-First Australasian Conference on Database Technologies, pp. 141–150, (2010)
2. Jhingran, A.: Enterprise information mashups: integrating information, simply. In: Proceedings of the 32nd International Conference on Very Large Databases, Seoul, Korea, pp 3–4, (2006)
3. Altinel, M., Brown, P., Cline, S., Kartha, R., Louie, E., Markl, V., Mau, L.,Ng, Y. H., Simmen, D.,Singh, A.: Damia: a data mashup fabric for intranet applications. In: Proceedings of the 33rd International Conference on Very Large Databases, Vienna, pp 1370–1373, (2007)
4. Guiling, W., Feng, Z., Yanbo, H.: An Approach to Situational Data Integration Based on Data Service Hyperlink [J]. Telecommun. Sci. **30**(2), 51–59 (2014)
5. Yahoo Pipes, http://pipes.yahoo.com/pipes/
6. Liu, X., Huang, G., Mei, H.: Discovering homogeneous web service community in the user-centric web environment. IEEE Trans. Serv. Comput. **2**(2), 167–181 (2009)
7. Wang, G., Yang, S., Han, Y.: Mashroom: end-user mashup programming using nested tables. WWW 2009: 861–870
8. Han, Y., Wang, G., Ji, G., Zhang, P.: Situational data integration with data services and nested table. SOCA **7**(2), 129–150 (2013)
9. Heß, A., Johnston, E., Kushmerick, N.: ASSAM: A Tool for Semi-automatically Annotating Semantic Web Services. In: McIlraith, S.A., Plexousakis, D., van Harmelen, F. (eds.) ISWC 2004. LNCS, vol. 3298, pp. 320–334. Springer, Heidelberg (2004)
10. Wang, G., Zhang, S., Liu, C., Han, Y.: A Dataflow-Pattern-Based Recommendation Approach for Data Service Mashups.In: IEEE International Conference on Services Computing, (2014, in press)
11. Han J, Kamber M.: Data Mining, Southeast Asia Edition: Concepts and Techniques[M]. Morgan kaufmann (2006)
12. Zijian, Z., Kohavi, R., Mason, L.: Real world performance of association rule algorithms. In: Proceedings of the seventh ACM SIGKDD International Conference on Knowledge discovery and data mining. ACM (2001)
13. Wang, G., Fang, J., Han, Y.: Interactive Recommendation of Composition Operators for Situational Data Integration. CSC, pp. 120–127 (2013)
14. Elmeleegy, H., Ivan, A., Akkiraju, R., Goodwin, R.: Mashup advisor: a recommendation tool for mashup development. In: ICWS 2008, IEEE Computer Society, pp. 337–344 (2008)
15. Greenshpan, O., Milo, T., Polyzotis, N.: Autocompletion for mashups. VLDB 2009, pp. 538–549 (2009)

16. Chen, H., Lu, B., Ni, Y., Xie, G., Zhou, C., Mi, J., Wu, Z.: Mashup by surng a web of data APIs. VLDB 2009, pp. 1602–1605 (2009)
17. Yang, J., Han, J., Wang, X., Sun, H.: MashStudio: An On-the-fly Environment for Rapid Mashup Development. In: Xiang, Y., Pathan, M., Tao, X., Wang, H. (eds.) IDCS 2012. LNCS, vol. 7646, pp. 160–173. Springer, Heidelberg (2012)
18. Roy Chowdhury, S., Daniel, F., Casati, F.: Efficient, Interactive Recommendation of Mashup Composition Knowledge. In: Kappel, G., Maamar, Z., Motahari-Nezhad, H.R. (eds.) Service Oriented Computing. LNCS, vol. 7084, pp. 374–388. Springer, Heidelberg (2011)
19. Ma, Y., Lu, X., Liu, X.Z., Wang, X.D., Blake, M.B.: Data-driven synthesis of multiple recommendation patterns to create situational web mashups. Sci. China Inf. Sci. **56**(8), 1–16 (2013)
20. Roy Chowdhury, S., et al.: Complementary assistance mechanisms for end user mashup composition. In: Proceedings of the 22nd International Conference on World Wide Web companion. International World Wide Web Conferences Steering Committee (2013)

Using Incentives to Analyze
Social Web Services' Behaviors

Zakaria Maamar[1]([⊠]), Gianpiero Costantino[2], Marinella Petrocchi[2],
and Fabio Martinelli[2]

[1] Zayed University, Dubai, UAE
zakaria.maamar@zu.ac.ae
[2] Istituto di Informatica E Telematica, CNR, Pisa, Italy
{gianpiero.costantino,marinella.petrocchi,fabio.martinelli}@iit.cnr.it

Abstract. This paper discusses how incentives allow social networks to
attract more members and reward those that are honest by retaining
them. These members referred to as social Web services process users'
requests in return for a certain usage fee and also expose certain behaviors in return of the incentives they receive. The usage fee is linked to
a performance level that the social Web service needs to maintain at
run time. In the case of any discrepancy between the usage fee and performance level the social Web service is expected to compensate users.
However the compensation might not always take place. Simulation
results illustrate why honesty is rewarding for social Web services, which
has a positive impact on both their performance and the performance of
the networks to which they belong.

Keywords: Honesty · Incentive · Social network · Social web service

1 Introduction

On different occasions, e.g., [12,14], we discussed the outcome of blending social
computing (exemplified by Social Networks (SNs)) with service-oriented computing (exemplified by Web services technology). We refer to this outcome as
Social Web Services (SWSs). Compared to regular (i.e., no-social) Web services,
SWSs establish and maintain networks of contacts; count on their ("privileged")
contacts when needed; form with their contacts strong and long lasting collaborative groups; and know with whom to partner so that efforts to reconciliate
ontology and policy disparities are minimized [12].

To support SWSs perform the aforementioned operations three types of SNs
are developed [12]: collaboration, substitution, and competition. A SWS uses (*i*) a
collaboration SN to recommend peers that it "prefers" working with in the
case of putting together compositions, (*ii*) a substitution SN to recommend
peers that can replace it in the case it fails in its ongoing composition, and

---

Composition (*aka* composite Web service) means putting Web services together in
response to users' complex needs.

© Springer International Publishing Switzerland 2015
B. Benatallah et al. (Eds.): WISE 2014, LNCS 9051, pp. 148–160, 2015.
DOI: 10.1007/978-3-319-20370-6_12

(*iii*) a competition SN to be aware of the peers that compete against it in the case of selection. In the first two networks the recommended peers (whether collaborators or substitutes) can reject a SWS's demands to participate in an ongoing composition. Different reasons can be behind the rejection: risk of over-load due to existing commitments or limited rewards such as financial. However, a rejection can delay a composition completion, which is not "appreciated" when this composition' implements a critical business process.

In real life, people are motivated to accomplish their duties efficiently and timely through rewards *aka* incentives [20]. Students are given extra points for additional work and employees are given bonuses for completing deals, for exam-ple. In the IT field, incentives are used in different areas such as multiagent systems [18], mobile ad hoc networks [5], and peer-to-peer systems [20]. In [17], Obreiter and Nimis develop a complete taxonomy of incentive patterns. They use an elementary cooperation model, based on offering and remunerating ser-vices, to illustrate how incentives help provision more services. Due to the nature of SWSs (as stated above) we deem appropriate defining new forms of incentives that would help answer the following two questions: why did a WS, after sign-ing up in a specific SN and thus becoming a SWS, decide to be either honest or dishonest? And what are the consequences of such a decision on its reputation? The rest of this paper is organized as follows. Section 2 is an overview of SWSs and suggests an example of network of SWSs. Section 3 discusses the approach for offering incentives to SWSs in terms of parameter definition and simulation results. Section 4 concludes the paper and highlights some future research work.

2   Background

This section consists of an overview of social Web services and then an example of network of social Web services.

2.1   Social Web Services in Brief

A good number of researchers have recently shown interest in blending social com-puting with service-oriented computing[1]. Three communities analyze this specific blend. A first community deploys SNs of persons using Web services as a develop-ment technology of these SNs. A second community deploys SNs of SWSs to address issues like Web services discovery. Last but not least a third community mixes SNs of users and SNs of SWSs to develop composite Web services.

In the first community, we cite different initiatives reported in [1,2,15,16,19, 21]. In [1], Al-Sharawneh and Williams mix semantic Web, SNs, and recommender systems to help users select Web services with respect to their functional and non-functional requirements. In [2], Bansal et al. examine trust for Web services discovery. Users' trust in the providers of Web services is the social element in

---

[1] Other disciplines that are subject to this blend include healthcare [7] and commerce [9].

this discovery. In [15], Maaradji et al. propose a social composer known as *SoCo* to advise users on the next actions to take in response to specific events like selecting specific Web services. Last but not least, Wu et al. rank Web services based on their popularity among users [19].

In the second community, we cite other initiatives reported in [3,10,13,22]. In [3], Chen and Paik build a global social service network to improve service discovery. They link services together using specific data correlations. In [10], Maamar et al. develop a method to engineer SWSs. Questions that the method addresses include what relationships exist between Web services, what SNs correspond to these relationships, how to build SNs of SWSs, and what social behaviors can SWSs exhibit. Last but not least, Maamar et al. use SNs of SWSs to tackle the "thorny" problem of Web services discovery [13]. Web services run into various situations at run time like competing against similar peers during selection, collaborating with peers during composition, and replacing similar peers during failure despite the competition. These situations help build the privileged contacts of a SWS.

In the last community that mixes SNs of users and SNs of SWSs, Maamar et al. intertwine these networks to compose, execute, and monitor composite Web services [11]. To achieve this intertwine three components namely composer, executor, and monitor are developed. The social composer develops composite Web services considering social relations between users and between Web services. The social executor assesses the impact of these relations on these composite Web services execution progress. Finally, the social monitor replaces failing Web services to guarantee the execution continuity of these composite Web services.

2.2   Example of Network of Social Web Services

In previous work [10,13,22], we developed different SNs to address issues like discovering Web services for composition needs and assigning social qualities to Web services based on their performance. In the following we summarize substitution SN.

Figure 1 shows a substitution social network. Since all the SWSs in this network have the same functionality, any member is a potential candidate to replace a failing peer. To evaluate the weight of a substitution edge, referred to as *Substitution Level* ($\mathcal{L}_{Sub}$, Eq. 1) between sws_i and sws_j, Functionality Similarity Level ($\mathcal{L}_{\mathcal{FS}}$), No-Functionality Similarity Level ($\mathcal{L}_{\mathcal{NFS}}$), and Reliability Level ($\mathcal{L}_{\mathcal{R}}$) are used. More details on this equation are given in [22].

$$\mathcal{L}_{Sub}(sws_i, sws_j) = \mathcal{L}_{\mathcal{FS}}(sws_i, sws_j) \times \mathcal{L}_{\mathcal{R}}(sws_i, sws_j)$$
$$\times (1 - \mathcal{L}_{\mathcal{NFS}}(sws_i, sws_j)) \qquad (1)$$

where:

- $\mathcal{L}_{\mathcal{FS}}(sws_i, sws_j)$ corresponds to the similarity level between the respective functionalities of sws_i and sws_j. Functionality similarity assessment requires ontologies; more details are given in [6].

- $\mathcal{L}_{\mathcal{NFS}}(sws_i, sws_j) = \omega_1 \times (|\mathcal{P}(sws_{i,1}) - \mathcal{P}(sws_{j,1})|) + \cdots + \omega_n \times (|\mathcal{P}(sws_{i,n}) - \mathcal{P}(sws_{j,n})|)$ with $\mathcal{P}(sws_{i,k})$ is the value of the kth non-functional property of the ith SWS (assumed to be between 0 and 1), ω_k is a weighting factor representing the importance of a non-functional property, and $\sum_{k=1}^{n} \omega_k = 1$.
- $\mathcal{L}_{\mathcal{R}}(sws_i, sws_j) = \frac{\mathcal{SR}(sws_i, sws_j)}{\mathcal{TR}(sws_i, sws_j)}$, with $\mathcal{SR}(sws_i, sws_j)$ as the total number of successful replacements that sws_i made for sws_j (i.e., no failure) and $\mathcal{TR}(sws_i, sws_j)$ as the total number of requests that sws_i received to replace sws_j. $\mathcal{L}_{\mathcal{R}}(sws_i, sws_j)$ shows how successful sws_i is when it replaces sws_j.

3 Approach to Incentivize SNs and SWSs

Making SWSs sign up in (private) SNs and participate in ongoing compositions for either collaboration or substitution needs are examples of scenarios that require incentives. The objective is to ensure the successful completion of these scenarios. For instance, a SWS signs up in a SN when it sees a value in its action (e.g., more participation in users' compositions), although the SWS can remain independent from any network. The same applies to a SN that accepts a membership demand from a SWS when it sees a value in its action too (e.g., marketshare increase with respect to competition). In the following, we assume that a SN is led by an authority component (SN_{auth}) that connects SWSs to existing members in the network, broadcasts messages to SWSs, etc. More details on a SN_{auth}'s duties are given in [14].

3.1 Parameter Definition

To analyze how to incentivize both SN_{auth}s (representing networks) and SWSs, we set different parameters for each. In addition to these two parties, users as a third party are included in this analysis as they impact the behaviors of SNs and SWSs and thus, their incentives. It is worth mentioning that the SN_{auth}s

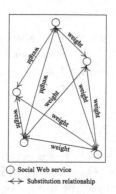

○ Social Web service
⟷ Substitution relationship

Fig. 1. Illustration of a substitution SN of SWSs

act as brokers when they assist users identify appropriate SWSs with respect to their requests.

Parameters associated with a SN_{auth} include:

1. SN_{auth}-membership fee (mf): a SN_{auth} establishes a membership fee for those SWSs that wish to sign up in its network. The membership fee is an income for the SN_{auth} and thus, needs to be maximized. This could be done by accepting a maximum number of SWSs' membership demands to the network while considering the computing capacities (e.g., performance and storage) of the IT infrastructure upon which this network is deployed.

2. SN_{auth}-quality level (ql): a SN_{auth} establishes a quality level for its network based on the feedback that it receives from users who interact with the SWSs in this network. We recall that the SN_{auth} recommends SWSs to process users' requests. Thus the SN_{auth} would like to maintain a high quality-level (compared to a certain threshold) by retaining the "good" SWSs that comply with their non-functional properties (QoS) at run-time (also satisfy users' requests) and ejecting those that perform poorly (below a certain threshold, say SN_{auth}-minql$_{SWS}$). Retention and ejection are part of network management but do not fall into this paper's scope. A user's feedback on a SWS is sent directly to the SN_{auth}. This latter analyzes how long the SWS has been performing at a certain level so that it detects any serious QoS inconsistencies. Intermittent drops in this level does not always reflect the "real" performance of the SWS.

   To compute SN_{auth}-ql, we adopt concepts from reputation systems (e.g., [8]), where past transactions of actors are taken into account to estimate the probability of acting well in the next transaction, and we use the well assessed Beta reputation model [4]. This model takes as input the sum of all positive feedback on SWSs (indicated as α) that the network authority has received up to the current moment and divides them by the total number of received feedback (indicated as $\alpha + \beta$, where β is the sum of all negative feedback). The SN_{auth}-ql is established as per Eq. 2:

$$SN_{auth}-ql = \frac{\alpha_{SWS_{i=1,\cdots}}}{\alpha_{SWS_{i=1,\cdots}} + \beta_{SWS_{i=1,\cdots}}} \tag{2}$$

3. SN_{auth}-maintenance cost (mc): a SN_{auth} bears a cost when managing its network due to payment related to IT infrastructure upgrade, for example. The maintenance cost is an expense for the SN_{auth} and thus, needs to be minimized. This could be done by restricting the membership in the network to "good" SWSs as described earlier.

Parameters associated with a SWS include:

1. SWS-performance level (pl): a SWS has a performance level that reflects how it is doing with respect to its QoS. For the sake of simplicity, we relate this performance level to the number of users' requests (nbr) that a SWS handles simultaneously according to a certain threshold ($thresh$) without any

performance-level degradation (Eq. 3).

$$SWS - pl = \begin{cases} 1 & \text{if } nbr \leq thresh \\ \frac{1}{nbr-thresh} & \text{otherwise} \end{cases} \tag{3}$$

2. SWS-quality level (ql): it is established by considering the positive and negative feedback that users submit to the SN on a specific SWS. Like with the SN_{auth}-ql, the SWS-ql is established as per Eq. 4:

$$SWS\text{-}ql = \frac{\alpha_{SWS}}{\alpha_{SWS} + \beta_{SWS}} \tag{4}$$

3. SWS-usage fee (uf): a SWS establishes a usage fee when processing users' requests related to ongoing compositions. The usage fee is an income for the SWS and thus, needs to be maximized. This could be done by accepting the maximum number of users' requests without impacting negatively the SWS's performance level. We propose two options to establish a usage fee: the network's SN_{auth} imposes it on a SWS (one reason is to ensure equilibrium among all the members and, hence, extreme low usage-fee by some SWSs is avoided) or the SWS self-defines it (this setting is adopted in the experiments shown in Sect. 3.2). In either way, a portion of the usage fee is assigned to the SN_{auth} in return of facilitating the connection between the user and SWS. Thus, SWS-uf = SWS-uf$_{SN_{auth}}$ + SWS-uf$_{SWS}$. Depending on the performance level (Eq. 3), a usage fee is defined as per Eq. 5[2]:

$$SWS - uf = \begin{cases} val_i & \text{if } pl \in [v_1, v_2[\\ val_j & \text{if } pl \in [v_2, v_3[\\ \vdots & \vdots \\ val_k & \text{otherwise} \end{cases} \tag{5}$$

As per the aforementioned parameters, the profits for a SN_{auth} and SWS are established as per Eqs. 6 and 7, respectively:

$$SN_{auth}\text{-}profit = SN_{auth}\text{-}mf + SWS - uf_{SN_{auth}} - SN_{auth}\text{-}mc \tag{6}$$

$$SWS - profit = SWS - uf_{SWS} - SN_{auth}\text{-}mf \tag{7}$$

Parameters associated with a User (U) include:

1. U-budget request (br): a user has a monthly budget that she spends on the demands of asking SWSs to take part in her ongoing compositions. The budget is reset at the beginning of each month.
2. U-service cost (sc): a user selects a service cost for the SWS that she would like to use depending on its performance level (Eq. 5). For the sake of simplicity we substitute cost service with usage fee.

---

[2] The usage-fee structure is similar to the practices in the airline industry where three fares on a flight are suggested: first, business, and economy. These fares can even differ in the same travel class.

The following discusses the behaviors of SWSs when the SN_{auth}, acting as a broker, recommends them to process users' requests. The recommendations are associated with incentives in term of guaranteeing better profit for SWSs and SN_{auth} and are dependent on the usage fee that users pay with respect to a certain performance level. A SWS may not perform as expected by accepting, for instance, more users' requests than its performance level handles (Eq. 3). Thus, a user who notices a degradation in the level performance associated with a certain usage fee (e.g., response time above 10s), she will judge negatively the SWS performance.

3.2   Experiments

We describe the experiments for analyzing the SWSs' behaviors after signing up in SNs and receiving users' requests for processing. A JAVA-based simulator was developed and deployed on a 1.7 GHZ Intel Core I5 and 4 GB RAM laptop. Every chart has been plotted using a single line, which represents the mean value of all simulations with a confidence interval of 95 %[3].

Scenarios - To analyze SWSs, SNs, and Us, we set-up two scenarios:

1. **Scenario A.** SWSs always accept users' requests independently of the current number of requests (nbr) that are under processing. If this number exceeds the threshold, i.e., $nbr > thresh$ then the performance level of SWS will decrease and the user will be refunded in a probabilistic way.
2. **Scenario B.** When the current number of requests (nbr) that are under processing exceeds the threshold, a SWS accepts a user's request with a probability of 50 %. Like in **Scenario A**, the user will be refunded in a probabilistic way.

After some primary tests, we decided to use the following probabilistic refund function: the user is not refunded with a probability of 60 % when $0.75 \leq SWS - pl < 1$; the user is not refunded with a probability of 70 % when $0.5 \leq SWS - pl < 0.75$; and the user is not refunded with a probability of 80 % when $0 \leq SWS - pl < 0.5$.

We deployed 3 social networks, SN_0, SN_1, and SN_2, having 20 SWSs each, for a total of 60. We decided that each SN contains SWSs with the following usage fee: SWSs $\in SN_0$ have a usage fee equal to 5; SWSs $\in SN_1$ have a usage fee equal to 10; and SWSs $\in SN_2$ have a usage fee equal to 15.

Each simulation lasts 360 days. Every 30 days the profits of both SN and SWS, quality level of SN, and number of SWSs per SN, are logged. We inform readers that, during simulation, the SWSs are kicked out by a SN when their SWS-ql drops below the SN_{auth}-minql$_{SWS}$. Finally, we established that a SN pays the maintenance cost every 100 days and receives the membership fee every 100 days from each SWS.

---

[3] http://tinyurl.com/7crgf for more details on the confidence interval.

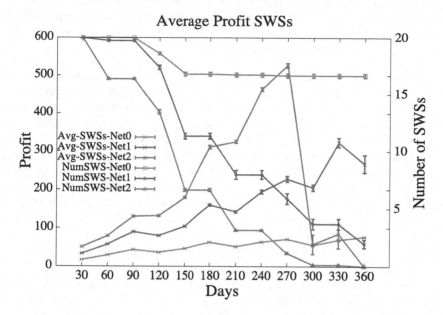

Fig. 2. Representation of average profit *vs.* number of SWSs - Scenario A

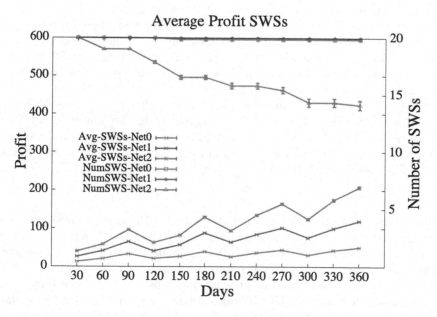

Fig. 3. Representation of average profit *vs.* number of SWSs - Scenario B

Analysis. The analysis of the different simulations revolves around four parameters: SWS-profit (averages all the profits of the SWSs that are in a SN), SN_{auth}-profit, SN_{auth}-ql, and number of SWSs. The analysis of the last parameter is embedded into the other parameters.

1. SWS-profit. Figures 2 and 3 contain three different lines (starting at the top) that show the number of SWSs in their corresponding SN. These SWSs could be kicked out from a network as stated earlier. When comparing Figs. 2 and 3 ("Avg-SWSs-Net2" lines), the SWSs in Scenario B adopt a conservative behavior. They accept users' requests in a probabilistic way, since they know this could affect their performance levels. This behavior allows SWSs to remain in the network. In Fig. 2 we report that SWSs are kicked out from SN_2 since their quality level becomes below the SN_{auth}-minql$_{SWS}$. Same situation affects SWSs that are part of SN_1. Only a few SWSs are kicked out from SN_0. We recall that thresholds are different for SNs, in fact the lowest threshold is in SN_2, then SN_1, and finally SN_0. Always in Fig. 2, the line that collapses ("Avg-SWSs-Net2") is provoked by the exclusion of SWSs that do not produce profit anymore.

   The chart in Fig. 3 reports that SWSs are pretty stable in their SNs, and the result is that SN_2 leads the average profit of all SWSs that are within the network, followed by SN_1 and then SN_0.

2. SN_{auth}-profit. Both Figs. 4 and 5 highlight that the profit of all SNs is high due to the income made through the membership fees and portions of the usage fees associated with SWSs. In Scenario A, all the SNs have a lower profit compared to those in Scenario B. Moreover, they are kicked out from the SNs that stop receiving their shares from the SWSs' offered services. This situation is more evident in SN_2 in which the profit line increases just a bit after 270 days. In Scenario B the situation is different since more SWSs remain in their network and this helps achieve a higher profit justifying the fact that a honest behavior provides a higher income.

3. SN_{auth}-ql. The social networks' quality levels are lower in Scenario A (Fig. 6) because the SWSs accept every single request which for sure will affect their performance levels. In Scenario B (Fig. 7) the networks' quality levels are higher because the SWSs accept additional requests only in a probabilistic way. This helps maintain a higher quality level.

Discussions. The simulations aimed at examining the consequences of accepting additional users' requests by SWSs, since this could affect their performances and qualities as well. In Scenario A, we configured the SWSs to embrace a "dishonest" behavior, since all the requests are accepted. In Scenario B, SWSs adopted a "honest" behavior (or, at least, less "dishonest"), since they accept extra requests but in a probabilistic way. Comparing both scenarios, the findings reveal that the profit, in particular for SN_1 and SN_2, is higher in Scenario B than in Scenario A confirming that honesty pays off with a higher profit. Moreover, dishonest behaviors are strongly discouraged since they increase the probability

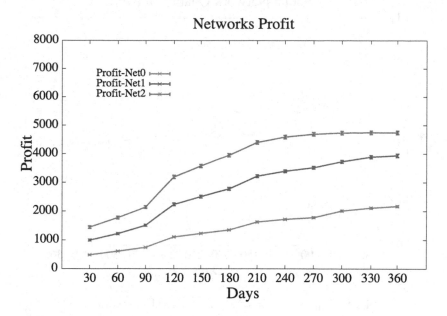

Fig. 4. Representation of SN profit - Scenario A

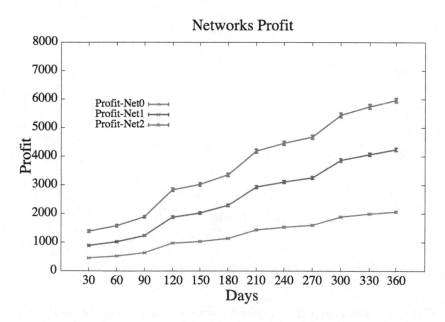

Fig. 5. Representation of SN profit - Scenario B

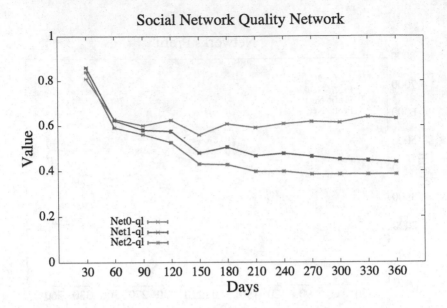

Fig. 6. Representation of SN quality-level - Scenario A

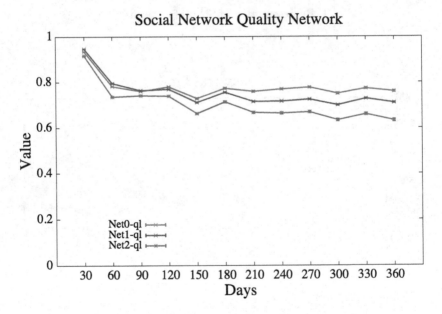

Fig. 7. Representation of SN quality-level - Scenario B

for SWSs to be kicked out from networks, with a de-population of the latter (this should lead to lower profits, after a certain time) and with the consequence of restricting the interactions with the SWSs. Finally, dishonesty has the negative aspect to reduce a network's quality level of SNs in Scenario A compared to SNs in Scenario B.

4   Conclusion

This paper analyzed social Web services' behaviors using incentives as a means to reward those that are honest. In the scenario under investigation, SWSs are incentivized to remain in a network, which will increase their profits. Also, for the same profit-based motivations, SN_{auth}s are incentivized to attract and retain more SWSs in their networks. Different parameters were defined including membership fee, quality level, and maintenance cost for social networks, performance level, quality level, and usage fee for social Web services, and finally budget request and service cost for users. A set of simulations were carried out supporting the honest behavior that some social Web services embrace. In term of future work, we would like to examine how the rewards can boost the competitiveness of networks.

References

1. Al-Sharawneh, J., Williams, M.A.: A social network approach in semantic web services selection using follow the leader behavior. In: Proceedings of the 13th Enterprise Distributed Object Computing Conference Workshops (EDOCW 2009), Auckland, New Zealand (2009)
2. Bansal, S., Bansal, A., Blake, M.B.: Trust-based dynamic web service composition using social network analysis. In: Proceedings of the International Workshop on Business Applications for Social Network Analysis (BASNA 2010), Bangalore, India (2010)
3. Chen, W., Paik, I.: Improving efficiency of service discovery using linked data-based service publication. Inf. Syst. Front. **15**(4), 613–625 (2013)
4. Commerce, B.E., Jøsang, A., Ismail, R.: The beta reputation system. In: Proceedings of the 15th Bled Electronic Commerce Conference, Bled, Slovenia (2002)
5. Crowcroft, J., Gibbens, R.J., Kelly, F.P., Ötring, S.: Modelling Incentives for Collaboration in Mobile Ad-Hoc Networks. Performanc Evaluation **57**(4), 427–439 (2004)
6. Di Martino, B.: Semantic web services discovery based on structural ontology matching. Int. J. Web Grid Serv. **5**(1), 46–65 (2009)
7. Domingo, M.C.: Managing healthcare through social networks. Computer **43**(7), 20–25 (2010)
8. Jøsang, A., Ismail, R.: A survey of trust and reputation systems for online service provision. Decis. Support Syst. **43**(2), 618–644 (2007)
9. Maamar, Z., Faci, N., Kouadri Mostéfaoui, S., Akhter, F.: Towards a framework for weaving social networks into mobile commerce. Int. J. Syst. Serv.-Oriented Eng. **2**(3), 32–46 (2011)
10. Maamar, Z., Faci, N., Krug Wives, L., Yahyaoui, H., Hacid, H.: Towards a method for engineering social web services. In: Ralyté, J., Mirbel, I., Deneckère, R. (eds.) ME 2011. IFIP AICT, vol. 351, pp. 153–167. Springer, Heidelberg (2011)

11. Maamar, Z., Faci, N., Sheng, Q.Z., Yao, L.: Towards a user-centric social approach to web services composition, execution, and monitoring. In: Wang, X.S., Cruz, I., Delis, A., Huang, G. (eds.) WISE 2012. LNCS, vol. 7651, pp. 72–86. Springer, Heidelberg (2012)

12. Maamar, Z., Hacid, H., Huhns, M.N.: Why web services need social networks. IEEE Internet Comput. **15**(2), 90–94 (2011)

13. Maamar, Z., Krug Wives, L., Badr, Y., Elnaffar, S., Boukadi, K., Faci, N.: LinkedWS: a novel web services discovery model based on the metaphor of "social networks". Simulation Modelling Practice and Theory, vol. 19(10). Elsevier Science Publisher (2011)

14. Maamar, Z., Faci, N., Boukadi, K., sheng, Q.Z.: Commitments to regulate social web services operation. IEEE Trans. Serv. Comput. **7**(2), 154–167 (2014)

15. Maaradji, A., Hacid, H., Daigremont, J., Crespi, N.: Towards a social network based approach for services composition. In: Proceedings of the 2010 IEEE International Conference on Communications (ICC 2010), Cap Town, South Africa (2010)

16. Nam Ko, M., Cheek, G.P., Shehab, M., Sandhu, R.: Social-Networks Connect Services. IEEE Comput. **43**(8), 37–43 (2010)

17. Obreiter, P., Nimis, J.: A taxonomy of incentive patterns - the design space of incentives for cooperation. In: Proceedings of Second International Workshop on Agents and Peer-to-Peer Computing (AP2PC 2003), Melbourne, Australia (2003)

18. Shoham, Y., Tanaka, K.: A dynamic theory of incentives in multi-agent systems. In: Proceedings of the Fifteenth International Joint Conference on Artificial Intelligence (IJCAI 1997), Nagoya, Japan (1997)

19. Wu, Q., Iyengar, A., Subramanian, R., Rouvellou, I., Silva-Lepe, I., Mikalsen, T.: Combining quality of service and social information for ranking services. In: Baresi, L., Chi, C.-H., Suzuki, J. (eds.) ICSOC-ServiceWave 2009. LNCS, vol. 5900, pp. 561–575. Springer, Heidelberg (2009)

20. Xiao, X., Zhang, Q., Shi, Y., Gao, Y.: How much to share: a repeated game model for peer-to-peer streaming under service differentiation incentives. IEEE Trans. Parallel Distrib. Syst. **23**(2), 288–295 (2012)

21. Xie, X., Du, B., Zhang, Z.: Semantic service composition based on social network. In: Proceedings of the 17th International World Wide Web Conference (WWW 2008), Beijing, China (2008)

22. Yahyaoui, H., Maamar, Z., Lim, E., Thiran, P.: Towards a community-based, social network-driven framework for web services management. Future Gener. Comput. Syst. **29**(6), 1363–1377 (2013)

Creating and Modelling Personal Socio-Economic Networks in On-Line Banking

Beatriz San Miguel(✉), Jose M. del Alamo, and Juan C. Yelmo

Center for Open Middleware (COM), Universidad Politécnica de Madrid,
Campus de Montegancedo, 28223 Pozuelo de Alarcón, Madrid, Spain
{beatriz.sanmiguel,jose.delalamo,juancarlos.yelmo}
@centeropenmiddleware.com

Abstract. The banking industry is observing how new competitors threaten its millennial business model by targeting unbanked people, offering new financial services to their customer base, and even enabling new channels for existing services and customers. The knowledge on users, their behaviour, and expectations become a key asset in this new context. Well aware of this situation, the Center for Open Middleware, a joint technology center created by Santander Bank and Universidad Politécnica de Madrid, has launched a set of initiatives to allow the experimental analysis and management of socio-economic information. PosdataP2P service is one of them, which seeks to model the economic ties between the holders of university smart cards, leveraging on the social networks the holders are subscribed to. In this paper we describe the design principles guiding the development of the system, its architecture and some implementation details.

Keywords: Social networks · On-line banking · User modelling · Ontology

1 Introduction

Detailed information about customers and users has become a critical asset for most organizations. Context and personal data give them *"the ability to understand and even predict where humans focus their attention and activity at the individual, group and global level"* [1]. Companies, governments and other organizations can leverage on these data to improve their products, boost their users' experience, personalize their services, develop and deliver new products tailored to their customers' needs and expectations, fidelize existing customers and attract new ones, etc. On-line banking is not an exception and, for some time now, banks have been collecting and processing information about their customers to improve their traditional services.

However, new entrants in the domain threaten traditional retail and commercial online banking business models, by leveraging on their proficiency in technology and knowledge generation. Inevitably, *"...banks that are not prepared for such new competitors face certain death"* [2]. Furthermore, some studies call for a business model switch towards user-centricity that consistently puts the customer at the heart of all activities [3]. This is especially important in some regions were unbanked people (those adults who do not use traditional financial services) reach an astonishing 65 % of the population [4].

© Springer International Publishing Switzerland 2015
B. Benatallah et al. (Eds.): WISE 2014, LNCS 9051, pp. 161–175, 2015.
DOI: 10.1007/978-3-319-20370-6_13

Well aware of this situation, the Center for Open Middleware (COM), a joint technology center created in 2011 by Santander Bank and Universidad Politécnica de Madrid, has launched some initiatives aimed at meeting the aforementioned challenges. COM is the incubator of an open software ecosystem developing middleware solutions and experimenting with new software approaches. Specifically, the POSDATA (Personal and Social Data Analysis) project provides a conceptual framework and technology support to allow the experimental analysis and management of personal and social data of university students with the goal of personalizing, and thus improving, the services provided by universities and Santander Bank.

In this paper we introduce an innovative service developed within the POSDATA framework, namely PosdataP2P (Person-to-Person), which enables issuing payments to and demanding money from the student's social relationships. With the goal of gaining knowledge on this users' base, we characterize the PosdataP2P users, by proposing a model that includes raw personal data generated by our service as well as other data available at the user's social networks.

The structure of this paper is organized as follows. The next section briefly introduces the POSDATA project and the PosdataP2P service. Then, Sect. 3 provides a background regarding personal data and its associated terminology, and Sect. 4 discusses the current challenges in the user modelling process and the most relevant issues regarding the POSDATA framework. After that, we present the system architecture of our solution, describing its components and relevant processes in Sect. 5, and we give some implementation details in Sect. 6. Finally, Sect. 7 analyses the related work, and Sect. 8 concludes the paper and also points out directions for future work.

2 The POSDATA Project

The POSDATA project provides a conceptual framework and technology support to allow the experimental analysis and management of personal and social data of the Santander University Smart Card (USC) holders [5].

The USC is a smart card issued by different universities in collaboration with Santander Bank. It can be used as a personal identification enabling services such as the electronic signature, access control to restricted areas, library loans, request of academic files, discounts in different associated businesses, and many other services. The USC holders can top-up their cards, so that they are able to use services such as vending machines or photocopiers. Optionally, the USC can be enabled to gain access to Santander Bank financial services, working as a credit/debit card linked to the holder's saving account. The USC is currently used by almost 6,3 million people in over 262 universities worldwide.

Leveraged by the POSDATA goals of gaining knowledge on these students in a banking context, an experimental service (currently a prototype), called PosdataP2P, has been developed. PosdataP2P service allows USC holders to make payments to or demand money from their friends using alternative social channels such as texting systems e.g. Telegram, or online social networks e.g. Facebook or Twitter.

To use PosdataP2P service, USC holders have to activate the service first, providing their USC information. Then, they choose the social channels that they want to use to carry out financial transactions. The PosdataP2P website supports USC holders in these steps, and additionally provides them with the terms of service and privacy policy, details on their current balance and recent activities, information on the social channels they have enabled, and so on.

Once PosdataP2P service is activated and configured, its users can start making financial transactions by simply posting messages to their friends within their enabled social channels. The only restrictions imposed by PosdataP2P are that (1) the user issuing a payment must have a balance equal or greater than the amount being transferred; and, (2) the texts used to trigger the transactions must follow a predefined pattern to be understood by the service. This pattern includes four basic elements:

- the identification of the terminator of the transaction i.e. the friend who receives the money or from whom the money is demanded;
- the amount of money to be transferred;
- the verb that identifies the financial transaction (either "*send*" or "*demand*"); and
- the identification of PosdataP2P service at the social channel.

Figure 1 shows an example of the three text messages required to carry out a payment using the Facebook channel. First, Bob sends a post to make a payment of 4.5€ to his friend Alice. Then, the PosdataP2P service requires Bob to confirm the transaction and authorize it by using a second authentication factor and channel. Finally, the service notifies Bob (and Alice, not shown in Fig. 1) when the transaction is completed.

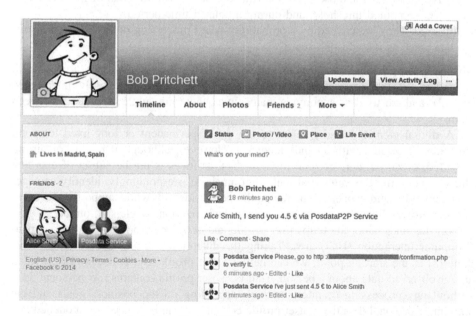

Fig. 1. Screenshot of the PosdataP2P service using Facebook as a channel.

Interestingly, the use of the PosdataP2P service generates financial data regarding USC holders, which properly combined with social information from the holder's online social network can be used to build a model intended to improve and personalize USC-based services. However, gathering information from disparate sources and integrating it to produce knowledge about users entails a set of challenges, which are discussed in the following sections.

3 From Personal Data to User Models

Personal data can be defined as the digital data created by and about one person [1]. There are many taxonomies of personal data, but we will consider the proposed by the Organization for Economic Co-operation and Development (OCDE) in [6], which categorizes data according to the manner in which they were originated:

- Provided: The data are originated from direct actions taken by the data subject, whereby they are fully aware of the actions that lead to data origination. For example, as a USC holder fills in the PosdataP2P service registration form, he is willingly giving demographic data and expressing some of his preferences.
- Observed: The data are captured by others and recorded in a digital format. For example, data regarding the payments among USC holders are captured by the PosdataP2P service.
- Derived: The data are generated from other data, and are not based on probabilistic reasoning. Examples of these data are classifications based on existing data such as active customer for those users that transfer or request amounts of money over a given, computed threshold, and during a defined time period.
- Inferred: They are created by a probability-based processing of any of the previous data, such as a credit risk score.

All this set of personal data are denoted as *"identity"*, *"user profile"*, or *"user model"* depending on the application area. Although these terms are closely interrelated (Fig. 2), and are used as synonyms many times, there are subtle differences between them.

A digital *identity* broadly refers to the set of permanent or long-lived temporal attributes associated with an individual [7]. However, although it might contain all provided, observed, derived, and inferred data, its focus is on the subset of data that allows identifying the individual within a domain. Correspondingly, identity management functions and capacities guarantee the person identity while supporting business and security applications, e.g. authentication, authorization, single sign-on, etc.

On the other hand, the terms *user profile* and *user model* originate in the Human-Computer Interaction (HCI) area. Taking the differentiation that many authors have done [8] as the starting point, we can define a user profile as a collection of provided and/or observed data about a person. That is, a user profile contains raw personal data, without any processing or interpretation. Depending on the business goals and the amount of personal data that a user profile contains, it can be processed, modelled and interpreted to obtain a user model. This process is called user modelling.

As a result, a user model is understood as the interpretation of a person in a specific context for an organization. It includes what the organization thinks the user is, prefers,

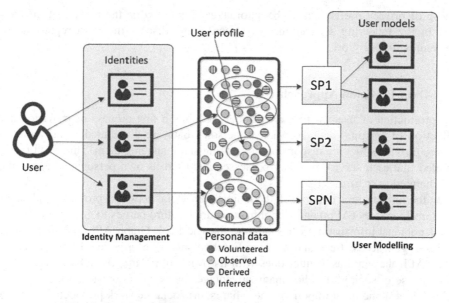

Fig. 2. Relationships between user identity, profile, and model.

wants, or is going to do, and comprises mainly derived and inferred data but can also include volunteered or observed data. The user model can be used to predict user behaviour, recommend new contents or services, or personalize user interaction, among others. In the end, it represents a core business element: improving user experience and engaging users; therefore, organizations can provide better services. These improvements may turn into competitive advantages and economic benefits.

User modelling process covers different stages that can take place cyclically [9]. First, a data collection stage analyses what, how, and where the personal data is obtained. Then, a processing stage creates relevant knowledge with the previous data and produces a user model. Finally, the user model is applied to some business process, sometimes generating new personal data as a result, which may feedback the first stage closing the loop.

4   Challenges in the User Modelling Process

Traditionally, user modelling is a one-sided process where service providers autonomously collect personal data and then generate user models that satisfy their business objectives in a specific domain. As time passed, it emerged the need of sharing, interchanging, and eventually reusing personal data and user models (or parts of them) between service providers. This process entails a set of challenges such as the means to retrieve and share information from different sources, how to build a user model from raw data, and how to represent it. Moreover, given that it involves the use of sensitive information, users have to be included in the user modelling process. They need tools and mechanisms to manage and control their flows of personal data, and to support the setting of privacy preferences to be automatically enforced at the request of information. In the following subsections, we describe and discuss the most representative challenges for our work.

4.1   Data Provision Approach

The production of user profiles and models requires a first process of provision and collection of personal data. Nowadays, personal data are distributed across different service providers that are responsible for storing and managing them. This traditionally entailed that each service provider possessed and used its own personal data, but this has changed over time.

In the online social context, all the mainstream social networks provide Application Program Interfaces (APIs) and web infrastructure for third parties to gather and modify users' personal information. For example, the Facebook Graph API [10] allows third parties to gain access (read and write) to Facebook users' information through a HTTP-based API, the same as Twitter does with its own proprietary REST-based API [11].

The use of social APIs has many advantages but some drawbacks too, being the lack of control the most important one. That is, the social network providers decide the terms of use and service, imposing protocols, rate limits or prices, modifying them depending on their business requirements. This can be translated into constant updates and changes for systems. One of the most recent examples is the change introduced by Facebook where the whole list of friends is no longer available for third parties.

To cope with the heterogeneity of personal and social information sharing on the Web some initiatives have come about such as OpenSocial [12]. It includes a set of open APIs that developers can use to gain access to users' personal resources hosted by different providers that have implemented them, for example, Google or LinkedIn.

4.2   Personal Data Representation

One of the most problematic issues related to the use, sharing and interchanging of personal data is to identify what elements are needed and how they are represented from a syntactic and semantic perspective.

The variety of personal data types is huge, probably as big as service providers, business needs and application domains. On the other hand, there are too many proposals of standards and proprietary solutions to represent each personal data category. For example, as regards social information about users, different standards have been proposed such as XHTML Friends Network (XFN), Family Tree Markup Language (FTML) or Friend of a Friend (FOAF) [13], in addition to the proprietary solutions used by different social networks providers.

As a result, the diversity of personal data representations raises the challenge of choosing the representation technique that better fits the organization needs. There are a lot of techniques that have been used over the time such as a feature-based pairs (or vector-space solutions), history-based models, user-rating matrixes, etc. One of the most beneficial possibilities has been the use of ontologies, as they provide formal semantics, facilitation of reuse and portability, and allows the automation and use of inference engines to obtain user models [14]. It is important to note that when there is a description of a domain, represented by an ontology, an individual user model can be represented as a partial graph of the concepts [15].

4.3   Identity and Privacy Management

Other issues related to sharing personal data between different administrative domains is the proper authentication of the users in each domain, the management of the authorizations to gain access to protected resources, and the protection of the users' privacy rights.

Identity management is the discipline that deals with these issues as it refers to the processes involved with the management and selective disclosure of user-related information either within an institution or between several of them, while preserving and enforcing privacy and security requirements [16]. Identity management on the Web has empowered users to gain control of the personal information that is exchanged between the parties involved, by considering user-centric architectural and usability aspects [17].

Nowadays, the delegation of the authorization model proposed by OAuth 2.0 [18] has become the cornerstone supporting identity management on the Web: All the Facebook, Twitter and other social-based APIs for personal information sharing rely on OAuth 2.0 to manage access to users' social information. The OAuth 2.0 framework introduces a third role to the traditional client-server authentication/authorization model: the resource owner. Following this model, the client (which is not the resource owner, but is acting on his/her behalf) requests access to resources controlled by the resource owner, but hosted by a container i.e. the online social network. OAuth 2.0 allows the social network provider to verify the identity of the client making the request, as well as ensuring that the resource owner has authorized the transaction without revealing their credentials.

Regarding privacy aspects, data protection laws of most countries as well as international privacy guidelines or directives [19], such as the OECD Privacy guidelines and the European Union Data Protection Directive, require basic privacy principles to be guaranteed when personal data (be it identity, user profile or user model) are collected or processed. Among others, these principles include: minimizing the routine collection and use of personally identifiable information; implementing user-centric approaches where users have the maximum control over their data; and providing privacy as the default option.

5   The Personal Socio-Economic Network

The PosdataP2P service provides users with new on-line banking channels (texting systems and popular social networks) that fit university students' habits. It processes texts from different social channels that are transformed into financial orders if applicable. This information can be collected and modelled to obtain a Personal Socio-Economic Network (PSEN) that represents the interchange of money between people.

In the following section, we present an overview of the PosdataP2P service architecture, detailing just those modules and processes required for the PSEN modelling process.

5.1   General Architecture

Figure 3 represents the PosdataP2P architecture and its relations with the different social channels, Santander Bank infrastructure, and the user. We can distinguish seven main modules within PosdataP2P architecture: User Manager, Registrar, Listeners, Dispatchers, Analyser, and User Data Store.

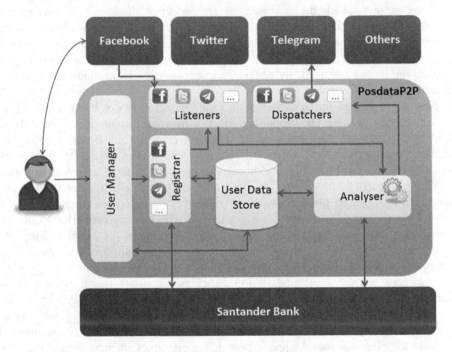

Fig. 3. PosdataP2P service architecture.

The User Manager allows users to interact with the PosdataP2P service to sign in, activate their social channels, and check and manage their data and user accounts. The User Data Store is the central entity where all the personal socio-economic information is stored. The Registrar is the module in charge of identity management interactions, enabling the communications with the user social channels and Santander Bank infrastructure.

The Listener comprises a set of components (one for each social channel) that are waiting for user texts that fit a predefined pattern where the PosdataP2P service is identified. Once a listener detects a user request it is redirected to the Analyser, which checks the validity of the user order, interacting with Santander Bank infrastructure to make payments if applicable. The Analyser is also in charge of communicating with the Dispatcher, which notifies users of the result of their orders or asks for extra information. Moreover, the Analyser processes and models the results of the transactions and stores them in the User Data Store.

User Model Feeding. The first process that we have considered in the production of the PSEN is the provision of personal data. This information can be obtained from three sources in the PosdataP2P service: the users themselves, their activation of social channels, and their use of the service.

Users provide volunteered information when they sign in to the PosdataP2P service through the User Manager. It contains several web pages and a main form that users fill in to provide personal data. Specifically, the service asks for user's first name, last name, gender, date of birth, email and USC number. Some of this information is redirected to the Registrar to certify, together with Santander Bank, the user identity.

Next, users can choose and activate their different social channels to make financial transactions. This step requires a dialog with the social channel provider, including an authentication process to confirm the user identity at the provider and an authorization mechanism to access, share and exchange personal data. At the end of the process, the PosdataP2P service only collects the user identifier of each social channel and the associated authorization tokens.

Finally, the use of the PosdataP2P service generates relevant information. In our case, the Analyser receives all the user requests for money transfers and demands.

All the information collected in the previous processes (sign in, social channels activation, and service use) are modelled and stored in the User Data Store module, making up the PSEN.

PSEN Representation. We have defined an ontology to model the PSEN, following the ontology development methodology proposed by [20]. It abstracts the main concepts from our PosdataP2P scenario. Furthermore, we have considered the reusing of existing ontologies, which is a must to allow semantic and syntactic interoperability. Thus, we have identified the FOAF ontology as the best alternative for representing people in a social network context and therefore, we have extended it to include the economic concepts.

FOAF is a Semantic Web vocabulary or specific-domain ontology of the area of social networks, managed by the FOAF project [21]. It includes the main terms to describe people, the links between them and the things they create and do. Among its concepts, it includes the *Agent* class to represent a person, organization, or a group. We have focused our definition of the PSEN on the *Person* class of FOAF, given the current functionalities of the PosdataP2P service.

A *Person* in FOAF includes a set of properties that allows us to model a user of the PosdataP2P service. Specifically, we have used the corresponding FOAF properties to describe the user's demographic information: *firstName, lastName, gender, age, birthday,* and *mbox.*

The *mbox* property represents an email address, and is usually used to identify a person. However, we identify a user in PosdataP2P by his USC number. On the other hand, given that each user has associated a set of social channels, we have modelled his identifiers in these channels. In this sense, we have made use of the *OnlineAccount* class of FOAF that allows the modelling of different web identities or online accounts of a person.

An online account includes two main properties in FOAF: *accountName* and *accountServiceHomepage*. The former is a textual representation of a unique identifier associated with the user account, while the *accountServiceHomepage* indicates the homepage of the service provider for this online account. We have related a person to different instances of the *OnlineAccount* class to represent the USC identification and each of the social channels activated by the user.

As regards the economic concepts that the PosdataP2P service manages, we have defined a main class called *EconomicActivity*. It represents the different economic transactions that can take place between people. To date, we have identified two main economic activities that have been defined as subclasses of the *EconomicActivity* class: *Payment* and *Demand*. The former indicates that a person has carried out a payment to another person; while the second one indicates that a person is asking for money to another person.

Each economic activity has associated two principal properties: *initiator* and *terminator*. They associate an economic activity with two persons, representing who starts the activity and who is the objective of it, respectively. Thus, two persons are related by an *EconomicActivity* and a person can have several economic activities.

In addition to the previous one, the *EconomicActivity* class includes other three properties:

- *money:* relates the economic activity with a *Money* class to represent how much is being paid or demanded. The *Money* class includes the amount and type of the money, using Dbpedia information [22]
- *timestamp:* indicates when the activity took place via a combination of date and time of day via a xsd:dataTime
- *channel:* indicates what social channel was used to carry out the economic activity such as Facebook, Twitter, etc.

It is important to point out that FOAF, and specifically the *Person* class, includes a *knows* property to relate a person to another person. It takes the broadest view of "knows", meaning a reciprocal interaction between them but it does not imply a friendship or endorsement. In this sense, the PosdataP2P service creates knows relations when an economic activity between two persons is detected.

Figure 4 symbolizes the definition of the *EconomicActivity* class and its relation to the *Person* class of FOAF. We have omitted the details of the *Person* properties to represent demographic user information but we include the new concepts defined in the PSEN.

Identity and Privacy Management. The PosdataP2P service requires an identity management infrastructure to manage the different users' identities associated with the USC holder and each of his activated social channels. As we have seen before, OAuth 2.0 has become the standard to manage digital identities on the Web and thus, we have based our infrastructure in this standard, developing it in the Registrar.

The process begins when the user chooses a social channel to be activated. The user is then redirected to the social channel provider site to grant our service the required

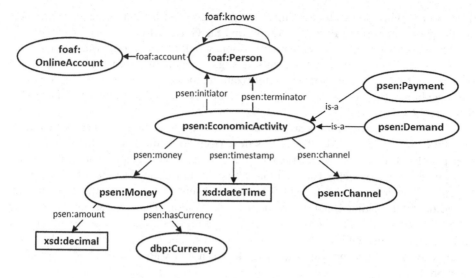

Fig. 4. Definition of an economic activity.

level of authorization. If successful, the social channel provider delivers an authorization token that allows subsequent access to the user profile and information.

The PosdataP2P service has been designed to observe privacy-by-design principles [23] and therefore, to guarantee explicit and conscious user governance of their personal information in a safe and easy way. In particular, the service reduces the personal information retrieved from external sources to the minimum necessary: Users' identification at the social channels, the credentials required by OAuth 2.0, and their posts to enable the PostdataP2P service. Furthermore, the PosdataP2P service allows its users to manage the sources of personal data comprehensibly from a central control point working as a digital identity dashboard. From there, users are able to manage their associated channels and carry out their access, object and cancel rights for the information stored.

6   Implementation Details

We have developed the infrastructure necessary to produce and manage the PSEN, within the PosdataP2P service prototype. First, web components have been developed to give shape to the PosdataP2P service and Santander Bank infrastructure including its main features: user registration, activation of social channels, and checking and management of user balance and PSEN information. Moreover, we have simulated Santander Bank functionalities to communicate with PosdataP2P service in the registration process and the carrying out of payments.

Additionally, we have implemented the Facebook channel to allow users to issue money transfers through simple text messages (specifically, posting predefined texts, see Fig. 1). Facebook provides developers with different products and APIs that allows building different functionalities and applications, and getting information from their users and pushing notifications to them. In this sense, we have developed a Facebook application that uses the Facebook Login and the Graph API.

The Facebook Login allows our application to link the Facebook user account with the PosdataP2P service. It implements a slight variant of OAuth 2.0 protocol for carrying out the authentication and authorization processes. We have used it to gather the Facebook user identifier and authorization token, and to activate a Facebook listener.

The Facebook listener is part of our Facebook application and has been implemented using the Graph API that allows developers to read and write to the Facebook user profiles. It includes a special feature called Real Time Updates that notifies about changes in a specific field. The data that an application can subscribe to is limited by Facebook policies, and with the notification that is sent, it is only possible to know that a field has been modified, but not the actual modification. This last part has been made by REST requests to Facebook's servers. The information that can be asked for and collected is mainly delimited by the user. It uses specific permissions in the login process to assure that the user knows what, when and who can read and manipulate their profile.

As regards the PSEN modelling and storage, we have used Protégé [24] to define the ontology and Jena [25] to manage the population and storage of the PSEN instances. The former is a free, open-source ontology editor and a framework written in Java that supports Resource Description Framework (RDF) specifications and the latest Web Ontology Language (OWL 2) from the W3C. Protégé provides two main environments, a desktop tool and a web-based implementation, to create, upload, modify and share ontologies. We have used the desktop solution that is quite intuitive and allows us to import FOAF and create our PSEN ontology easily.

On the other hand, the PSEN development environment has been implemented with Jena. It is also a free, open-source Java framework that provides all the necessary components for creating and reading Resource Description Framework (RDF) graphs, working with models based on RDF Schema and Web Ontology Language (OWL), querying RDF through SPARQL, and reasoning over the stored data to expand and check the content.

7   Related Work

As we have seen above, user model creation involves four main stages: data collection, modelling and application, in addition to user involvement to manage and control their flows of personal data. These ones have been widely studied and analysed over the time and we can find related literature, either addressing one of them in depth or proposing particular solutions for some of them in different application domains. For example, [26] describes the evolution of specialised systems, namely Generic User Modelling Systems, that tackle the different user modelling stages; [15] presents the user modelling techniques, its challenges and the state-of-the-art research, focusing on ubiquitous environments; and [27] gives an overview of user modelling in connection with the semantic technologies.

Considering the social network context, there are many efforts that cover the user modelling stages, either focusing on a single social network or integrating information from some of them. For example, [28] obtains Facebook data for recommendation processes; [29] retrieves user interactions from Facebook to produce behavioural patterns; [30] proposes a model to capture social relationships and status from different social media contexts; or [31] describes how to aggregate different user profiles from several social networks. The study presented in [32] includes an in depth comparison of the user modelling strategies in a multi-social context.

Our work is aligned with these last solutions, fitting and contributing to user modelling in a multi-social network context. Unlike the other proposals, we have focused our efforts on creating a relation to the personal financial sector. To the best of our knowledge, this is the first effort to integrate social and economic data aiming at modelling users.

8   Conclusions and Future Work

In this paper we have presented our approaches and contributions to modelling a personal socio-economic network that includes the economic activities carried out between people in social contexts. Our work has been focused on the collection of personal data from several sources, and the modelling (including the representation) of this information. For that, we have leveraged on an innovative service, namely PosdataP2P, developed in the context of a Santander Bank research initiative.

The PosdataP2P service allows users to make or demand payments to their friends through simple text messages, using different social channels such as Facebook, Twitter and Telegram. It produces a set of relevant information that we have collected and stored ontologically to model the personal socio-economic network. This advanced approach tackles a set of ambitious tasks of integrating data from diverse sources, identity management, and representation of new knowledge, which we have described.

Our future work includes exploring and designing the elements required by the PosdataP2P service to allow third parties to retrieve custom-made user models from the personal socio-economic network, to better fit the business needs of the requesting parties. These models will comprise personalized social-economic networks or inferred values for a person such as all of his payments or debts, the total amount of money exchanged, or the friends' list that he interacts more with. Moreover, we will continue to advance on user-centric approaches to identity management that allow users to choose and control how, when and by whom are their personal data being used.

Acknowledgments. This work is part of the Center for Open Middleware (COM), a joint technology center created by Universidad Politécnica de Madrid, Banco Santander and its technological divisions ISBAN and PRODUBAN.

References

1. Schwab, K., Marcus, A., Oyola, J. R., Hoffman, W.: Personal Data: The Emergence of a New Asset Class. An Initiative of the World Economic Forum (in Collaboration with Bain & Company, Inc.) (2011). http://www3.weforum.org/docs/WEF_ITTC_PersonalDataNew Asset_Report_2011.pdf
2. Gonzalez, F.: Banks need to take on Amazon and Google or die. Financial Times (2013). http://www.ft.com/intl/cms/s/0/bc70c9fe-4e1d-11e3-8fa5-00144feabdc0.html
3. Auerbach, P., Argimon, R.F., Hieronimus, F., Roland, C., Teschke, B.: Banking on Customer Centricity - Transforming Banks into Customer-Centric Organizations. McKinsey & Company, EMEA Banking Practice (2012)
4. Chaia, A., Dalal, A., Goland, T., Gonzalez, M.J., Morduch, J., Schiff, R.: Half the World is Unbanked. Financial Access Initiative Framming Note (2009). http://www.gsma.com/mobilefordevelopment/wp-content/uploads/2012/06/110109halfunbanked_0_4.pdf
5. Observatorio TUI, International University Smart Card Research Centre. http://en.observatoriotui.com/home
6. Working Party on Security and Privacy in the Digital Economy: Protecting Privacy in a Data-driven Economy: Taking Stock of Current Thinking. Organisation for Economic Co-operation and Development (2014)
7. Windley, P.: Digital Identity. O'Reilly Media Inc., Sebastopol (2005)
8. Fröschl, C.: User Modeling and User Profiling in Adaptive E-learning Systems. Master's thesis, Graz University of Technology (2005)
9. Barla, M.: Towards Social-based User Modeling and Personalization. Dissertation thesis, Slovak University of Technology in Bratislava (2014)
10. Facebook Developers, The Graph API. https://developers.facebook.com/docs/graph-api
11. Twitter Developers. https://dev.twitter.com/
12. OpenSocial. http://opensocial.org/
13. Nabeth, T.: D2.3: Models. Deliverable. In: Future of Identity in the Information Society Consortium (2005)
14. Sosnovsky, S.: Ontological Technologies for User Modeling. Committee of the School of Information Sciences, University of Pittsburgh (2008)
15. Kuflik, T., Kay, J., Kummerfeld, B.: Challenges and solutions of ubiquitous user modeling. In: Krüger, A., Kuflik, T. (eds.) Ubiquitous Display Environments, pp. 7–30. Springer, Heidelberg (2012)
16. Álamo, J.M., Fernández, A.M., Trapero, R., Yelmo, J.C., Monjas, M.A.: A Privacy-Considerate Framework for Identity Management in Mobile Services. Journal Mob. Netw. Appl. **16**(4), 446–459 (2011)
17. Bhargav-Spantzely, A., Camenisch, J., Gross, T., Sommer, D.: User centricity: A taxonomy and open issues. J. Comput. Secur. - Second ACM Workshop Digit. Identity Manag. **15**(5), 493–527 (2007)
18. The OAuth 2.0 Authorization Framework. https://tools.ietf.org/html/rfc6749
19. Wright, D., Raabb, C.: Privacy principles, risks and harms. Int. Rev. Law, Comput. Technol. **28**(3), 277–298 (2014)
20. Noy, N.F., McGuinness, D.L.: Ontology Development 101: A Guide to Creating Your First Ontology. Technical report, Stanford Knowledge Systems Laboratory (2001)
21. Foaf project. http://www.foaf-project.org/
22. DBpedia. http://dbpedia.org/About

23. Notario, N., Crespo, A., Kung, A., Kroener, I., Le Métayer, D., Troncoso, C., del Alamo, J. M., Martín, Y.S.: PRIPARE: a new visión on engineering privacy and security by design. In: Cleary, F., Felici, M. (eds.) CSP Forum 2014, CCIS, vol. 470, pp. 65–76. Springer, Heidelberg (2014)
24. Protégé. http://protege.stanford.edu/
25. Apache Jena. https://jena.apache.org/
26. Kobsa, A.: Generic user modeling systems. In: Brusilovsky, P., Kobsa, A., Nejdl, W. (eds.) Adaptive Web 2007. LNCS, vol. 4321, pp. 136–154. Springer, Heidelberg (2007)
27. Aroyo, L., Houben, G.J.: User modeling and the adaptive semantic web. J. Semant. Web 1, 1–6 (2010)
28. Shapira, B., Rokach, L., Freilikhman, S.: Facebook single and cross domain data for recommendation systems. J. User Model. User-Adap. Inter. 23(2–3), 211–247 (2013)
29. Ortigosa, A., Quiroga, J.I., Carro, R.M.: Inferring user personality in social networks: A case study in Facebook. In: 11th International Conference on Intelligent Systems Design and Applications, pp. 563–568. IEEE, New York (2011)
30. Kabir, M.A., Han, J., Yu, J.: Alan Colman User-centric social context information management: an ontology-based approach and platform. Pers. Ubiquit. Comput. 18(5), 1061–1083 (2014)
31. Orlandi, F., Breslin, J., Passant, A.: Aggregated, interoperable and multi-domain user profiles for the social web. In: 8th International Conference on Semantic Systems, pp. 41–48. ACM, New York (2012)
32. Abel, F., Herder, E., Houben, G.J., Henze, N., Krause, D.: Cross-system user modeling and personalization on the Social Web. User Model. User-Adap. Inter. 23(2–3), 169–209 (2013)

Cloud-Based Video Monitoring Framework: An Approach Based on Software-Defined Networking for Addressing Scalability Problems

Nay Myo Sandar[1], Sivadon Chaisiri[1], Sira Yongchareon[2]([✉]), and Veronica Liesaputra[2]

[1] School of Information Technology, Shinawatra University, Chiang Mai, Thailand
`55401002-5@st.siu.ac.th`, `sivadon@ieee.org`
[2] Department of Computing, Unitec Institute of Technology, Auckland, New Zealand
`sira@maxsira.com`, `vliesaputra@unitec.ac.nz`

Abstract. Closed-circuit television (CCTV) and Internet protocol (IP) cameras have been applied to a surveillance or monitoring system, from which users can remotely monitor video streams. The system has been employed for many applications such as home surveillance, traffic monitoring, and crime prevention. Currently, cloud computing has been integrated with the video monitoring system for achieving value-added services such as video adjustment, encoding, image/video recognition, and backup services. One of the challenges in this integration is due to the size and geographical scalability problems when video streams are transferred to and retrieved from the cloud services by numerous cameras and users, respectively. Unreliable network connectivity is a major factor that causes the problems. To deal with the scalability problems, this paper proposes a framework designed for a cloud-based video monitoring (CVM) system. In particular, this framework applies two major approaches, namely stream aggregation (SA) and software-defined networking (SDN). The SA approach can reduce the network latency between cameras and cloud services. The SDN approach can achieve the adaptive routing control which improves the network performance. With the SA and SDN approaches applied by the framework, the total latency for transferring video streams can be minimized and the scalability of the CVM system can be significantly enhanced.

Keywords: Cloud computing · Video monitoring · Video surveillance · Software-defined networking

1 Introduction

A video monitoring or surveillance system has been applied for over a half-century [1] and employed for many applications such as home surveillance, traffic monitoring, transport safety, anomaly identification, and crime prevention. Video monitoring cameras deployed in the system have grown from the analog

© Springer International Publishing Switzerland 2015
B. Benatallah et al. (Eds.): WISE 2014, LNCS 9051, pp. 176–189, 2015.
DOI: 10.1007/978-3-319-20370-6_14

closed-circuit television (CCTV) to the Internet protocol (IP) cameras. In addition, a dashcam (or dashboard camera) which is used in the vehicle and smart glasses (e.g., Google Glass) which is a wearable display device with a built-in tiny camera and network connectivity can be potentially applied to the video monitoring system as well [2,3].

Recently, cloud computing has been applied to a video monitoring system for providing value-added services [4]. In a cloud-based video monitoring (CVM) system, value-added services associated with on-demand storage capacity and scalable processing power are available for video distribution, video backup, video database management system, video encoding, and image/video recognition, for example. In practice, video data streamed from analog CCTV, webcams, and IP cameras can be transferred to the cloud services. Then, the video data processed or stored by the cloud services can be remotely monitored and managed by the users from their Internet-connected devices such as surveillance monitors, personal computers, smartphones, tablets, and set-top boxes. The CVM system can serve a large number of cameras and users. Dropcam [5], Smartvue [6], and Ivideon [7] are, for example, CVM providers.

In terms of client/server architecture, both cameras and users are *clients* of the cloud services. When numerous clients are simultaneously connected to the cloud services for sending and receiving video streams, scalability problems could incur although the CVM system provides a large pool of resources and network bandwidth to the server-side cloud services. Since the network for the clients is usually shared by multiple devices and users, a serious network bottleneck could easily incur in such an access network. When multiple clients operate in a congestive network with the small amount of Internet bandwidth (especially, bandwidth for home users or small enterprises), video streams from cameras or cloud services will cause a size scalability problem. The small amount of buffer memory allocated for a camera is another issue that increases jitter in streaming video. In addition, a large number of active clients located in different physical locations could increase the delay to transfer video streams, and then could cause a geographical scalability problem due to network delays.

To address the aforementioned scalability problems, this paper proposes a CVM framework. The framework applies two major approaches, namely *stream aggregation* (SA) and *software-defined networking* (SDN). The SA approach provides *aggregators* which are buffering servers with high speed network connectivity bridging clients and cloud services. In a specific physical area, an aggregator can be allocated close to a set of clients and can connect these clients together. Thus, the network delay can be significantly reduced by the aggregator. The scalability can be improved by the aggregator, since numerous traffic from the clients can be preprocessed, buffered, and cached to offload the network bandwidth and the cloud services. The aggregators can be offered to the CVM provider by Internet service providers (ISPs) or cloudlet providers [8].

The SDN approach offers programmability for network management in which network performance can be improved [9]. With the SDN approach, the CVM provider can flexibly manage a virtual network (consisting of virtual routers and links), and also allocate the appropriate amount of network bandwidth from

ISPs to the aggregators and the cloud services. With the virtual network management, the CVM provider can design the optimal control of traffic scheduling, congestion, and routing. As a result, by applying both SA and SDN approaches together, the network latency can be minimized and the scalability of the CVM system can be significantly improved.

The rest of this paper is organized as follows. Related work is reviewed in Sect. 2. Section 3 describes the proposed CVM framework. Next, usage scenarios of the proposed CVM framework are demonstrated in Sect. 4. Finally, the paper is summarized in Sect. 5.

2   Related Work

Recently, video streaming services including video monitoring systems are trending to be deployed in a cloud infrastructure or platform since cloud computing offers a large pool of resources. Most resources can be provisioned on demand and charged on a pay-per-use basis. Cloud-based video monitoring systems have been designed and developed. For example, a video monitoring system proposed in [10] applied the Hadoop framework for storing and processing video streams in a large scale cloud computing infrastructure. In [11], the SmartHub system was proposed to process video streams from cameras in order to overcome limitations of the cameras. An algorithm was proposed in [12] to choose appropriate cloud providers for improving the quality of service (QoS) of video streaming and reducing the cost to utilize the cloud resources. In [13], the Scalable Video Coding proxy based on cloud computing was proposed that can deliver high-quality video streams. An integer programming model was formulated in [4] to allocate virtual machines (VMs) provided by a cloud provider for operating a video surveillance platform. The model minimizes the number of VMs, while QoS requirements of the platform can be fulfilled.

Although cloud computing provides a scalable computing environment for video streaming services, there are scalability problems when a large number of cameras in different locations simultaneously transfer video streams to cloud services via unreliable networks. The concept of aggregators or concentrators is introduced to deal with the problems. Aggregators have been applied in a smart (electrical) grid to achieve scalable connectivity that interconnects a large number of smart meters which simultaneously transfer data, related to metered power usage, to the same target [14]. In a video streaming system, the work in [15] applied multiple aggregators for the distribution of live multimedia content over wireless Internet connections in which the quality of video streaming can be improved.

Delivery of bulk video data from the growing number of cameras to cloud computing requires a large amount of network bandwidth and can incur a geographical scalability problem. To address such issues, the software-defined networking (SDN) approach can be applied to achieve better network performance. In [16], the OpenQoS controller design based on the SDN approach was proposed to enable the quality of service for multimedia delivery.

Unlike previous works, this paper proposes the cloud-based video monitoring framework that applies particularly both aggregators and SDN approaches to gain the benefits of the two approaches. That is, the aggregator approach can greatly lessen the network latency over the clients' network, while the SDN approach which provides the flexible network management can minimize the network latency in the network connectivity of both aggregators and public cloud providers. As a result, the size and geographical scalability of the cloud-based video monitoring system based on this framework can be significantly enhanced.

3   Proposed Framework

This section presents the proposed CVM framework primarily designed for a CVM provider. Figure 1 depicts the architectural layers of the framework. The framework consists of five layers, i.e., client, stream aggregation (SA), software-defined networking (SDN), cloud services, and cloud resource layers. In particular, this paper introduces both SA and SDN layers that offer intermediate

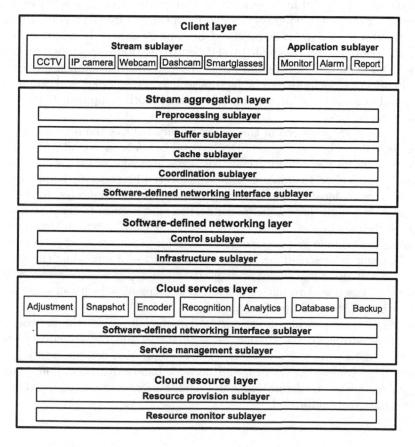

Fig. 1. Architectural layers of the proposed framework.

services for enhancing the size and geographical scalability of the CVM system. Without applying the SA and SDN services, the total delay in a traditional CVM system (denoted by d_{total}) for transferring a piece of video streams to or from the client is mathematically expressed as follows:

$$d_{total} = d_{client} + d_{service} + d_{network} \tag{1}$$

where client delay (d_{client}), service delay ($d_{service}$), and network delay ($d_{network}$) accumulate to render the total delay. For the camera, the client delay may include processing, buffering, and streaming delays in the camera. For the user who accesses an application of the CVM system, the client delay involves the time needed to load and execute the application and other related processes, and the time needed to render the video streams on the user's terminal screen, for example. The service delay includes the time needed to process functions of cloud services and access cloud resources. The client delay could be difficult to be reduced without upgrading the hardware of the client's terminal (e.g., cameras or the user's access device), while the service delay could be mitigated by software-engineering and high performance computing techniques. For example, programming code of a cloud service can be optimized by a compiler, tuned by a better software design, or parallelized by a programmer. In addition, a load balancing technique can be applied to efficiently distribute requests from clients to servers for gaining faster response time or greater throughputs of the services. The network delay includes several factors such as transmission and propagation delays, and queueing and processing delays in network equipment (e.g., routers and switches) [17].

The framework proposed in this paper mainly reduces the network delay by the services offered by the SA and SDN layers. The SA layer provides aggregators located in different physical locations. An aggregator acts as a consolidation hub of video streams close to cameras and users located in a specific boundary. The group of cameras located in the same proximity can be connected to the same aggregator via a high speed network connection that is much faster than the connection of the clients used to directly access to the cloud services. Moreover, the aggregator can include preprocessing functions for video streams before forwarding the streams to destined devices or cloud services for offloading the network bandwidth and cloud services. The aggregator can act as a cache server to store popularly accessed and recently received video streams which can additionally enhance the CVM system performance.

The SDN layer provides functions to dynamically adjust the network configuration according to the current network status and the amount of arrival traffic (e.g., data from video streams). The configuration includes routing, traffic scheduling, congestion control, and network bandwidth allocation. With an appropriate network configuration, the overall performance of the CVM system can be significantly improved.

The total delay in the CVM system based on the framework (denoted by d^*_{total}) for transferring a piece of video streams to or from the client is mathematically expressed as follows:

$$d^*_{total} = d_{client} + d_{service} + d_{aggre} + d_{sdn} \qquad (2)$$

where d_{aggre} and d_{sdn} denote the delays incurred in the SA and SDN layers, respectively. With the optimal control of SA and SDN services, the delays in the SA and SDN layers can be greatly diminished (i.e., $d_{aggre} + d_{sdn} << d_{network}$). As a result, the total delay incurred in the framework can be optimized as well. The optimization approach to achieve the optimal control of SA and SDN services which is out of scope in this paper will be addressed and presented in the future work.

In Fig. 1, a layer provides a service to the adjacent layer above it and is served by its lower adjacent layer. Next, the five layers of the framework are discussed from the bottom layer to the top layer as follows:

3.1 Cloud Resource Layer

This cloud resource layer provides services to access a pool of cloud computing resources and services such as servers, networks, and storage for operating the cloud services located in its above layer. Basically, the CVM provider can rent resources from other public cloud providers such as Amazon, Microsoft, and Google to reduce the total cost of ownership (TCO). The CVM provider might operate local cloud resources in its private cloud. The CVM providers also can implement the hybrid cloud to gain a larger scalable computing infrastructure [18].

In Fig. 1, the cloud resource layer consists of two sublayers, i.e., resource provision and resource monitor sublayers. The resource provision sublayer is responsible to prepare and allocate cloud computing resources to the cloud services for accommodating requests and processing video streams received from the clients. For reducing the resource allocation cost, the resource provision sublayer should be able to resize the cloud computing resources to sufficiently meet the actual resource demand. Generally, most of the public cloud providers offer the on-demand provisioning option by which the CVM provider can increase or decrease the amount of cloud computing resources on demand. In some public cloud providers (e.g., Amazon and Microsoft), the reservation provisioning option is available which can significantly reduce the resource allocation cost for a long-term usage. Under uncertainties of resource demand from the clients and resource prices offered by the public cloud providers, the resource allocation cost can be efficiently minimized by the Optimal Cloud Resource Provisioning (OCRP) algorithm [19].

The resource monitor sublayer provides a service to monitor the cloud computing resources and get the last status of the resources. According to the monitoring status, the resource provisioning sublayer can dynamically adjust the amount of cloud computing resources. Cloud monitoring platforms and services that can be applied in this sublayer were discussed in [20].

3.2   Cloud Services Layer

The cloud services layer is the layer where different cloud services for the CVM system are available to the clients. These cloud services provide functions to process and store video streams. A number of video processing approaches which could be implemented in some cloud services were reviewed in [21]. Examples of the cloud services shown in Fig. 1 are listed as follows:

– *Adjustment service:* This service provides basic video processing functions such as noise reduction and contrast/sharpness/brightness adjustments.
– *Snapshot service:* A video stream can be transformed to a shorter video stream or a sequence of still images by this service given a specific range of the original stream. This service might be able to capture audio from the video stream as well.
– *Encoder service:* The encoder service provides video and audio codecs [21] for encoding, respectively, video and audio from a video stream.
– *Recognition service:* The recognition service provides functions to identify objects in a video stream. Objects appeared in video streams which could be detected by this service are, for example, human faces [22], animals [23], vehicle license plates [24], and events (e.g., fire and flood [25]).
– *Analytics service:* The (video) analytics service mainly provides surveillance functions to automatically detect events. This service could be applied for detecting and preventing accidents, crimes, and terrorism [26]. Video anomaly identification approaches to detect suspicious activities for addressing security threats which could be implemented in this service were discussed in [27]. The service could be also applied for marketing and other business intelligence [28].
– *Database service:* The video database management system which is specifically designed for organizing and retrieving video data [29] can be offered by this service.
– *Backup service:* This backup service provides backup and recovery functions to maintain video streams in cloud storage.

In Fig. 1, this cloud services layer consists of SDN interface and service management sublayers. The SDN interface sublayer is responsible to interact with services offered by the SDN layer. The service management sublayer provides services for distributing requests (i.e., video streams from the cameras or service requests from the applications) to and monitoring status of the cloud services. According to the status of the cloud services, the cloud computing resources in the cloud resource layer can be efficiently provisioned.

3.3   Software-Defined Networking Layer

The software-defined networking (SDN) layer provides functions based on the SDN approach [9]. This SDN approach decouples control and data planes and provides programmability in the control plane. Hence, this approach allows application developers to simply and flexibly manage the control plane, which is related to the routing control of data packets, from their applications. With the SDN approach, the network configuration can be programmatically controlled and dynamically optimized, and the network performance can be improved [9].

Basically, the SDN approach consists of three layers, namely infrastructure, control, and application layers. The infrastructure layer which is the lowest layer consists of switching devices (e.g., routers and switches). These devices operate in the data plane, and provide functions to process and forward packets. They could also provide functions to collect and report network status. The control plane provides services (for example, as the form of application programming interface or API) for accessing functions of the switching devices. The functions can be provided for traffic scheduling, packet routing control, and congestion control. The application layer is the top layer where SDN applications access and control the switching devices by invoking the services in the control layer. In Fig. 1, the SDN layer of the proposed framework consists of the control and infrastructure sublayers equivalent to the two layers in the basic SDN approach, while the application layer is equivalent to the SDN interface sublayers existing in the cloud services and stream aggregation layers.

The control sublayer in this SDN layer can provide services for adaptive routing and virtual network management which are controllable by the SDN interface sublayers. Hence, the SDN interface sublayers can retrieve the last status of the virtual network such that appropriate traffic scheduling, congestion, and routing controls, which could significantly reduce the network latency and increase the system scalability, can be made for transferring video streams or service requests.

In the control sublayer, ISPs and network operators could offer reservation and on-demand options to the CVM provider for allocating network bandwidth to both cloud services and aggregators. Network bandwidth allocated by the reservation option is generally cheaper than that of the on-demand option for the long-term utilization. With the reservation option, the amount of bandwidth needs to be purchased in advance and usually cannot be refunded. In contrast, the amount of bandwidth can be dynamically provisioned at the moment when the bandwidth is needed with the on-demand option. While network bandwidth demand and price might be uncertain, the reserved bandwidth could be either overprovisioned or underprovisioned. Furthermore, the higher cost of the on-demand option will be unavoidable when the reserved bandwidth is underprovisioned. The optimization approach proposed in [30] to address the SDN-based network bandwidth allocation can be applied, while the two bandwidth allocation options and the uncertainties are taken into account.

3.4 Stream Aggregation Layer

The stream aggregation (SA) layer provides a number of aggregators with high speed network connectivity bridging clients and cloud services. Basically, an aggregator acts as a proxy server close to a group of clients located in the same proximity such that the network latency between clients and cloud services can be greatly diminished.

Aggregators can be provided by ISPs to the CVM provider. In addition, the concept of cloudlets can potentially form an infrastructure for aggregators. Originally, the term *cloudlet* coined in [8] is a resource-rich server or computer cluster that serves nearby mobile devices for mobile computing. The mobile devices could be directly connected to the cloudlet via either wireless telecommunications (e.g., 3G/4G) or wireless LAN (e.g., WiFi) connectivity. The cloudlet can synchronize data with and utilize larger resources from public cloud providers (e.g., Amazon and Microsoft) via high speed WAN connectivity. With this concept, a cloudlet provider could be available to operate computer clusters or micro-datacenters located in different physical locations. Resources from the cloudlet provider can generally serve other applications as well, not just mobile computing. The CVM provider can rent the resources including servers and storage from multiple cloudlet providers for operating the aggregators.

In Fig. 1, the SA layer contains five sublayers as follows:

- *Preprocessing sublayer:* In this sublayer, the aggregator may provide services for preprocessing functions such as video encoding and adjustment to offload both network bandwidth and cloud services.
- *Buffer sublayer:* This sublayer provides queue management system for buffering video streams that can avoid clogging networks interconnecting with cloud services and clients.
- *Cache sublayer:* The aggregator can store frequently accessed and recently received video streams with cache management system provided by this sublayer such that the network latency for accessing the video streams from the cloud computing resources can be significantly lessened. This cache management system might not be available for, especially, security monitoring systems because of some security matters. That is, video streams which are recently received or monitored by a user could be wiped from an aggregator since the streams might contain some sensitive information. In this paper, this cache sublayer is introduced for some other applications, for example, home entertainment and social networking applications. That is, online high-definition movies and video clips shared by social networking users can be managed by the cache management system for better video streaming.
- *Coordination sublayer:* The coordination sublayer provides a service in which the aggregator can interconnect with other aggregators for sharing necessary information among the aggregators. The shared information obtained from this interconnection service is used by the cache management system (in the cache sublayer) and can improve the performance of the CVM system in some situations, for example, the situation when video streams stored in one aggregators will be soon accessed by surveillance monitors connected to other nearby aggregators and the situation when a portable camera (e.g., dashcam or smartglasses) is transferring video streams to a sequence of aggregators by which the camera will pass.
- *SDN interface sublayer:* This SDN interface sublayer provides a service for the aggregator to interact with the SDN layer.

3.5 Client Layer

The client layer is the layer closest to the cameras and users. In Fig. 1, the client layer is divided into stream and application sublayers which are independent of each other. The stream sublayer is the layer where cameras capture and transfer video streams to aggregators. Cameras could be CCTV, IP cameras, webcams, dashcams, and smartglasses. The application sublayer is the layer where applications utilized by the end user are operated. Examples of the applications shown in Fig. 1 are listed as follows:

- *Monitor:* The monitor application can be used as monitoring and surveillance tools. With the value-added cloud services, the application could detect objects, human faces, or interesting events. The application could also distribute video streams encoded in various formats to fit the performance of the user's terminal device.
- *Alarm:* The alarm application can notify all devices that subscribe to specific events. For example, a surveillance camera detects a suspicious person in a restricted area, and then sends an email regarding this detection to all subscribed email addresses.
- *Report:* The report application could be used to produce a summary report about video streams, cameras, or system usage, e.g., the total size of video streams which were recorded and transferred, the current number of malfunctioning cameras, and the number of active users. The report might include the summary of processing results from the recognition and analytics services such as the list of physical areas where anomaly events were identified in the last month and the number of interesting objects found in a specific day and location.

3.6 Overview of Framework Implementation

An approach recommended by this paper to implementation of the proposed framework for a CVM provider is overviewed in Fig. 2. In this approach, a set of cloud computing resources including storage and VMs (as servers) can be provisioned from public cloud providers such as Amazon Web Services (AWS) and Microsoft Azure to operate the cloud services. The number of provisioned VMs should be dynamically resized according to the current load of the VMs and arrival of video streams. The public cloud providers can operate their resources in datacenters located in different geographical locations. The CVM provider should provision the resources from locations close to the clients. For example, Singapore, Ireland, and Oregon shown in Fig. 2 are locations where the CVM provider's clients are served by the CVM system.

ISPs or WAN operators can provide SDN-based virtual networks to the CVM provider. Traffic scheduling, routing and congestion controls can be flexibly managed to fulfill QoS requirements of the CVM system. Aggregators can be provisioned by cloudlet providers. In Fig. 2, a group of clients, i.e., users and cameras in houses, commercial buildings, and vehicles, located in the same proximity can

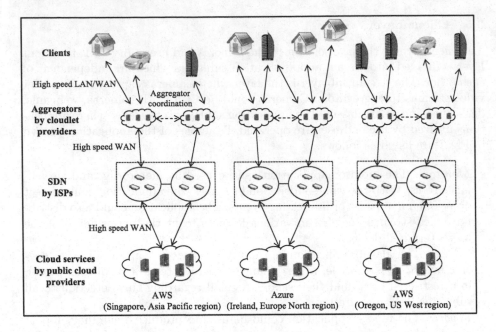

Fig. 2. Approach to framework implementation.

be connected to the same aggregator. Some clients could be connected to multiple aggregators (i.e., multihoming aggregators) to increase the reliability of the network connectivity. Figure 2 shows that the aggregators require the service of the coordination sublayer to exchange information about movable clients (e.g., vehicles) so that the cache management system can be managed dynamically.

Regarding the network connectivity, the high speed LAN and WAN should be allocated to the link between clients and aggregators (e.g., gigabit Ethernet LAN or FTTx for the stationary clients and WiFi or LTE network for the movable clients). The high speed WAN is required for the connection between aggregators and public cloud providers.

4   Usage Scenarios

In this section, two different usage scenarios applying the proposed CVM framework are demonstrated as follows:

4.1   Home Security System

Currently, a CVM system has been applied in the home security system. Value-added services such as motion detection and face detection provide useful information to home users. Dropcam and Ivideon are, for example, CVM providers offering services for the home security system. However, both Dropcam and

Ivideon might not be able to serve numerous users and handle video streams from numerous cameras in some locations where network latency in the network between the clients (i.e., the users and the cameras) and the providers' datacenters are too high. Due to such geographical and size scalability problems, home users might not be satisfied with the system. The proposed CVM framework could be applied in a home security system to improve the overall service performance and also provide a variety of value-added services offered by the cloud services such as fire and flood detection and anomaly identification at home.

4.2 Traffic Monitoring System

A traffic monitoring system can gain benefits from the proposed CVM framework. In this system, a set of CCTV cameras are located in different locations for monitoring streets. The system could be used to trace events on the streets (and their nearby places) and control the traffic. Video streams from the CCTV cameras are consolidated by the aggregators before being sent to cloud services by the SDN. The traffic police and staffs from the traffic authority can get useful information from the cloud services such as accident detection, face detection, license plate detection, and traffic jam prediction for better safety and traffic management.

The traffic authority might invest and deploy the aggregators in this system. The aggregators should be located in different physical areas to cover a group of CCTV cameras which are in close proximity. Then, the SDN service offered by ISPs provides better network performance for delivering the video streams among traffic control centers of the authority and the cloud services.

5   Conclusion

Cloud computing has been applied to a video monitoring system to offer a large pool of storage and processing power for storing and processing video streams captured by cameras. However, the size and geographical scalability problems could be encountered when a large amount of video streams is transferred to or from the cloud. To address the problems, the CVM framework has been proposed in this paper. Two main approaches have been applied by the framework, i.e., stream aggregation (SA) and software-defined networking (SDN). The SA approach can significantly reduce the network latency by providing a number of aggregators close to the clients (i.e., users and cameras). Furthermore, the cache management system and preprocessing functions of the aggregators can even greatly diminish the overall network latency in the clients' network connectivity. The SDN approach for the flexible network management can minimize the network latency in both the clients' and the aggregators' network connectivity. By applying both SA and SDN approaches together, the size and geographical scalability of the CVM system can be significantly enhanced.

For the future work, optimization approaches to achieve the optimal control of SA and SDN services (including cloud computing resources and network bandwidth provisioning, cache management, traffic scheduling, routing and congestion controls) will be studied. A prototype of the proposed framework will be implemented and evaluated with the use of discrete event simulation. Then, we will evaluate and analyze performance matrics (e.g., network latency and service delay) of CVM systems with and without the framework.

References

1. Williams, C.A.: Police surveillance and the emergence of CCTV in the 1960s. Crime Prev. Community Saf. **5**(3), 27–37 (2003)
2. Hildebrandt, P.: Dash-Cams keep record: recording officers' interactions with the public with mobile video isn't enough, SOPs must clarify how video is captured and stored. Law Enforcement Technol. **36**(2), 10–14 (2009)
3. Kurze, M., Roselius, A.: Smart glasses linking real live and social network's contacts by face recognition. In: Proceedings of the 2nd Augmented Human International Conference, p. 31. ACM (2011)
4. Hossain, M.S., Hassan, M.M., Qurishi, M.A., Alghamdi, A.: Resource allocation for service composition in cloud-based video surveillance platform. In: IEEE International Conference on Multimedia and Expo Workshops (ICMEW), pp. 408–412 (2012)
5. Dropcam. http://www.dropcam.com/
6. SmartVue. http://www.smartvue.com
7. Ivideon. http://www.ivideon.com/
8. Satyanarayanan, M., Bahl, P., Caceres, R., Davies, N.: The case for vm-based cloudlets in mobile computing. IEEE Pervasive Comput. **8**(4), 14–23 (2009)
9. Xia, W., Wen, Y., Foh, C.H., Niyato, D., Xie, H.: A survey on software-defined networking. IEEE Commun. Surv. Tutorials (2014)
10. Lin, C.F., Yuan, S.M., Leu, M.C., Tsai, C.T.: A framework for scalable cloud video recorder system in surveillance environment. In: 2012 9th International Conference on Ubiquitous Intelligence & Computing and 9th International Conference on Autonomic & Trusted Computing (UIC/ATC), pp. 655–660 (2012)
11. Saini, M.K., Atrey, P.K., Saddik, A.E.: From smart camera to SmartHub: embracing cloud for video surveillance. Int. J. Distrib. Sens. Netw. (2014)
12. Chen, W., Cao, J., Wan, Y.: QoS-aware virtual machine scheduling for video streaming services in multi-cloud. Tsinghua Sci. Technol. **18**(3), 308–317 (2013)
13. Huang, Z., Mei, C., Li, L., Woo, T.: CloudStream: Delivering high-quality streaming videos through a cloud-based SVC proxy. In: 2011 Proceedings IEEEINFOCOM, pp. 201–205 (2011)
14. Wu, G., Talwar, S., Johnsson, K., Himayat, N., Johnson, K.D.: M2M: From mobile to embedded internet. IEEE Commun. Mag. **49**(4), 36–43 (2011)
15. Kamilova, M.I., Hesselman, C., Widya, I., Huizer, E.: Adding policy-based control to mobile hosts switching between streaming proxies. In: Sixth IEEE International Workshop on Policies for Distributed Systems and Networks, pp. 243–246 (2005)
16. Egilmez, H.E., Dane, S.T., Bagci, K.T., Tekalp, A.M.: Koc University Istanbul, Turkey. In: 2012 Asia-Pacific Signal & Information Processing Association Annual Summit and Conference (APSIPA ASC), pp. 1–8. IEEE (2012)
17. Kurose, J.F., Ross, K.W.: Computer Networking: a Top-Down Approach, 6th edn. Pearson Education, Upper Saddle River (2013)

18. Sotomayor, B., Montero, R.S., Llorente, I.M., Foster, I.: Virtual infrastructure management in private and hybrid clouds. IEEE Internet Comput. **13**(5), 14–22 (2009)
19. Chaisiri, S., Lee, B.S., Niyato, D.: Optimization of resource provisioning cost in cloud computing. IEEE Trans. Serv. Comput. **5**(2), 164–177 (2012)
20. Aceto, G., Botta, A., De Donato, W., Pescapè, A.: Cloud monitoring: A survey. Comput. Netw. **57**(9), 2093–2115 (2013)
21. Dasu, A., Panchanathan, S.: A survey of media processing approaches. IEEE Trans. Circuits Syst. Video Technol. **12**(8), 633–645 (2002)
22. Connolly, J.F., Granger, E., Sabourin, R.: An adaptive classification system for video-based face recognition. Inf. Sci. **192**, 50–70 (2012)
23. Burghardt, T., Ćalić, J.: Analysing animal behaviour in wildlife videos using face detection and tracking. IEE Proc.-Vis., Image and Sig. Proc. **153**(3), 305–312 (2006)
24. Du, S., Ibrahim, M., Shehata, M., Badawy, W.: Automatic license plate recognition (ALPR): a state-of-the-art review. IEEE Trans. Circuits Syst. Video Technol. **23**(2), 311–325 (2013)
25. Lai, C.L., Yang, J.C., Chen, Y.,H.: A real time video processing based surveillance system for early fire and flood detection. In: Instrumentation and Measurement Technology Conference Proceedings, IMTC 2007, pp. 1–6. IEEE (2007)
26. Regazzoni, C.S., Cavallaro, A., Wu, Y., Konrad, J., Hampapur, A.: Video analytics for surveillance: Theory and practice [from the guest editors]. IEEE Signal Process. Mag. **27**(5), 16–17 (2010)
27. Saligrama, V., Konrad, J., Jodoin, P.M.: Video anomaly identification. IEEE Signal Process. Mag. **27**(5), 18–33 (2010)
28. Shan, C., Porikli, F., Xiang, T., Gong, S. (eds.): Video Analytics for Business Intelligence. SCI, vol. 409, pp. 309–354. Springer, Heidelberg (2012)
29. Ardizzone, E., La Cascia, M.: Automatic video database indexing and retrieval. Multimedia Tools Appl. **4**(1), 29–56 (1997)
30. Chase, J., Kaewpuang, R., Wen, Y., Niyato, D.: Joint virtual machine and bandwidth allocation in software defined network (SDN) and cloud computing environments. In: Proceedings of IEEE ICC, Sydney, Australia (2014)

Context-Awareness in Task Automation Services by Distributed Event Processing

Miguel Coronado[1]([✉]), Ralf Bruns[2], Jürgen Dunkel[2], and Sebastian Stipković[2]

[1] Grupo de Sistemas Inteligentes, Universidad Politecnica de Madrid,
Calle Ramiro de Maeztu, 7, 28040 Madrid, Spain
`miguelcb@dit.upm.es`
[2] Department of Computer Science, Hochschule Hannover -
University of Applied Siences and Arts, Ricklinger Stadtweg 120,
30459 Hannover, Germany
`{Ralf.Bruns,Jurgen.Dunkel,Sebastian.Stipkovic}@hs-hannover.de`

Abstract. Everybody has to coordinate several tasks everyday, usually in a manual manner. Recently, the concept of Task Automation Services has been introduced to automate and personalize the task coordination problem. Several user centered platforms and applications have arisen in the last years, that let their users configure their very own automations based on third party services. In this paper, we propose a new system architecture for Task Automation Services in a heterogeneous mobile, smart devices, and cloud services environment. Our architecture is based on the novel idea to employ distributed Complex Event Processing to implement innovative mixed execution profiles. The major advantage of the approach is its ability to incorporate context-awareness and real-time coordination in Task Automation Services.

Keywords: Distributed Task Automation Services · Complex Event Processing · Personalized services · Context-awareness · Mobile services

1 Introduction

Nowadays, most users of smartphones, smart devices, social platforms, and cloud services use these emerging technologies to coordinate their private and business tasks (and, of course, for other purposes). However, the numerous coordination tasks are still performed *manually* to provide different technical platforms and human participants with new information or to trigger appropriate actions. To overcome with this cumbersome and time-consuming procedure, Task Automation Services (TAS) platforms have been introduced recently.

Task Automation Services allow the users to automate their tasks by defining simple rules instead of performing manually all the required steps of a task. If these automation rules are matched by events that are emitted by smartphones or by services (such as Twitter or Dropbox), they trigger a desired reaction. For instance, some users may want to "post in Twitter their Facebook status as

© Springer International Publishing Switzerland 2015
B. Benatallah et al. (Eds.): WISE 2014, LNCS 9051, pp. 190–203, 2015.
DOI: 10.1007/978-3-319-20370-6_15

soon as they publish it". Others may also need to "update their Twitter profile picture any time they change their Facebook's".

Currently, several TAS platforms are available to provide this type of functionalities. We can distinguish two types of TAS's depending on the platform they are running on:

- *Web-based TAS's* such as Ifttt[1], Zapier[2] and Elastic.io[3] are deployed as cloud services. They collect personal events by accessing appropriate web services on behalf of the user and provide a simple rule editor.
- *Smartphone-based TAS's* such as AutomateIt[4] and Tasker[5] run on a smartdevice and have access not only to data via web services, but also to the local resources of the device, e.g. the embedded smartphone sensors.

Task Automation Services rules may be executed according to different *execution profiles* that define where rule execution takes place. According to the above mentioned TAS types, we may distinguish:

1. A *web-driven execution profile* centralizes the rule execution on a server, allowing lightweight clients at the cost of requiring Internet connection. Typically, clients setup and manage the rules by a web page. Alternatively, smartphone apps could provide the same functionality. Web-driven execution profiles may have to cope with a huge amount of incoming events; they may have access to a large set of channels and may coordinate events from different users.
2. A *device-driven execution profile* executes all rules on the device itself, allowing offline rule execution (when only local resources are involved). Usually, when we talk about device-driven TAS, we refer to smartphone apps, although the definition is not restricted to smartphone devices. Rules in a device-driven execution profile can exploit the device-specific data, e.g. provided by the smartphone sensors. Therefore, some rules could derive the users' local context or current situation.
3. A *mixed execution profile* benefits from the advantages of both previous profiles. It distributes the execution of automation rules between clients (smart devices) and servers. However, mixed execution profiles require a distributed and, therefore, more complex system architecture and more complex rules.

Note that current TAS systems are still rather restricted: they allow only the definition of very simple rules. Furthermore, they cannot combine web-driven and device-driven execution profiles, i.e. mixed execution profiles are yet not available.

In the following, we will present an innovative architecture for Distributed Task Automation Services supporting mixed execution profiles. Our approach

---

[1] http://ifttt.com.
[2] http://zapier.com.
[3] http://www.elastic.io/.
[4] http://automateitapp.com/.
[5] http://tasker.dinglisch.net.

is based on the employment of Complex Event Processing (CEP). CEP is a novel software technology for processing continuous streams of data in near real-time [9]. The basic concept of CEP is in-memory pattern matching, which means to identify in data streams those patterns of data that represent a meaning-full situation in the application domain.

In our approach, we use CEP to build a Distributed TAS system that is capable of coordinating peoples' tasks in real-time. The approach provides the following features:

- *Context-awareness:* The current activities, contexts and situations of the participating users can be concluded by correlating sensor data of their smartphones (e.g. accelerometer, GPS) and further domain-specific context information. The corresponding rules are realized in a device-driven execution profile.
- *Coordination:* Appropriate TAS rules coordinate various participants by taking into account their current context and situation information. They are realized according to a web-driven execution profile, which is implemented on a central server.

The paper is structured as follows. In the following section, we present a TAS coordination scenario that motivates our approach, and which is used to explain our approach in the subsequent sections. Then in Sect. 3, we present the basic concepts of Complex Event Processing. In Sect. 4, we describe our general architecture of a Distributed TAS system. In the subsequent sections, we evaluate our approach and present some implementation issues. The related work is discussed in Sect. 7. Finally, we summarize the most significant features of our approach and give a brief outlook on future lines of research.

2   TAS Coordination Scenario

Task Automation Service's (TAS's) are highly flexible platforms that users can use to orchestrate task automation addressing many different situations. The scenario we describe in this section presents a complex use case, where various smart devices determine the current situations of their owners, which are then broadcasted to a central Task Automation Service that performs appropriate coordination tasks. Note that each smart device is capable to orchestrate simple automations on their own, but that a centralized TAS platform is used for coordination purposes.

Consider the following use case: Patricia and Thomas live together. They share the housework, which also includes outside tasks such as shopping, sharing the car, or picking up their children from the kindergarten. Since they work in different parts of the city, they cannot devise a fixed schedule beforehand. In the past, it required a high coordination effort for them to organize these things manually by phone calls or text messages. Sometimes it happened that they didn't notify each other, causing that both of them went shopping at the same time (buying the needed groceries twice) or forgetting to tell that they have already picked up the kids.

Because they both use TAS for their personal automations, they decided to share several rules that help them in coordinating these tasks. They set up rules to automatically inform each other, when they are in a certain situation or doing a certain activity. Using the GPS sensors of Patricia and Thomas' smartphones, the TAS can deduce the concrete situation, in which the two of them are, causing an appropriate action. In the usual TAS terminology, one rule could be read as "When I am at the supermarket, then text my mate that I'm shopping". Then, if Thomas goes to the supermarket after work, Patricia will know he is doing the shopping, so she does not need to go there.

The task "picking up the children" requires that one of them is at the kindergarten shortly before the children are dismissed. Therefore, it requires the TAS to coordinate ahead, taking journey times from their current position to the kindergarten into account. The task could be expressed as "Everyday, either Patricia or Thomas must be at the kindergarten at 17 o'clock. Usual rules for coordinating this task could be "When I'm at home and my mate is still at work, remind me I should pick up the children" and "If my mate was at the kindergarten, inform me that I don't have to pick up the children".

In particular, automatic task coordination avoids manually triggered notifications, which are error-prone and awkward. Furthermore, corresponding messages can take the current situation of the recipient into account, i.e. they are only delivered, when the recipient is in a ready-to-receive mood.

3   Complex Event Processing

Complex Event Processing is an innovative software technology for processing continuous streams of events in near real-time [9,10]. Everything that happens inside or outside of a system is considered as an *event*. CEP analyses streams of incoming events to detect the presence of *event patterns*.

An event pattern is a particular sequence of events with a special meaning for the application domain. A *pattern match* signifies a meaningful situation or state of the environment and causes either the generation of a new *complex event* or triggers a domain-specific action. Complex events correlate between simple events and provide the real power of CEP.

Event stream processing systems manage the most recent set of events in-memory and employ sliding windows and temporal operators to specify temporal relations between the events in the stream. The core concept of CEP is a declarative *event processing language* (EPL) to express *event processing rules*. An event processing rule contains two parts: a *condition* part describing the requirements for firing the rule and an *action* part that is performed if the condition matches. The *condition* is defined by an event pattern using several operators and further constraints [3].

In the following, we use a simplified pseudo language for expressing event processing rules, which is easier to understand than an EPL of a productive CEP system. This pseudo language supports the following operators:

Operators

AND, OR Boolean operator for events or constraints

    NOT Negation of a constraint

      -> Sequence of events

  Timer *Timer(time)* defines a time to wait.

      Timer.at(daytime) is a specific (optionally periodic) point of time

.within defines a time window in which the event has to occur

An *event processing engine* analyses the stream of incoming events and executes the matching rules. Event processing rules transform low level simple events into more complex events in order to gain insight into the current state of the environment.

Luckham introduced the concept of *event processing agents* (EPA) [10]. An EPA is an individual CEP component with its own rule engine and rule base. Several EPAs can be connected to an *event processing network* (EPN) that constitutes a software architecture for event processing. Event processing agents communicate with each other by exchanging events.

4 Architecture

In this section, we present an architecture for Distributed TAS supporting mixed execution profiles. In particular, our architecture exploits the sensor data of the smart devices for achieving situation awareness.

4.1 Architecture Overview

An overview of the overall system architecture is given in Fig. 1. The distributed architecture shows the different TAS rule engines according to the mixed execution profile definition. We can distinguish the following components:

Smart devices: The system consists of numerous smart devices, which have the following responsibilities in the system. First, they collect all events emitted by its sensors and other local resources (the so-called content providers). The streams of events are processed on each smart device by its own CEP rule engine, which contains appropriate rules for providing semantic inference. In particular, the CEP rules filter, process and enhance the observed data events to produce richer situation events that reflect the current users' context. All the situation events are sent to the server to allow cross-user coordination. Furthermore, smart devices can perform conventional task automation rules. These rules can react on responses of the coordination server, or they are either server-independent and can be processed locally.

Coordination Server: The central Coordination Server is deployed to the cloud and responsible for coordinating the smart devices and their users. For this purpose, it also has its own CEP engine with appropriate coordination rules that manage the smart devices taking the users' current context into account.

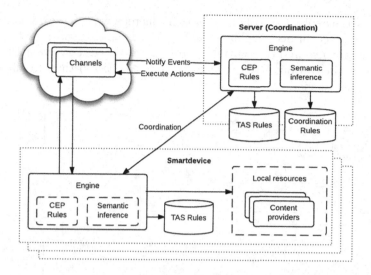

Fig. 1. Architecture overview of a distributed TAS system with coordination

Furthermore, the server provides support for conventional task automation rules, that orchestrate automations between web channels.[6]

Channels: Additionally, both the smart devices as well as the coordination server have access to web services (the so-called *channels*), using specific connectors.[7] These web services can provide the system with more necessary context information, e.g. weather or traffic data.

In our architecture we distinguish CEP rules from Task Automation rules: Because CEP rules allow temporal reasoning, all rules that involve movement, or GPS positioning will be defined as CEP rules. Note that CEP rules provide some form of semantic inference: they shift simple events (e.g. sensor events) to complex events (e.g. situation events) that assign the occurred events a new non-obvious and semantically richer meaning.

4.2 CEP for TAS

In this section, we will explain in some more detail, how Complex Event Pocessing(CEP) in our TAS architecture works (see Fig. 1). In our approach, CEP is based on a multi-staged Event Processing Network (EPN) in order to logically structure and modularize the event processing rules.

---

[6] This is the case for rules like "Whenever I receive an email with attachment save that attachment on my Dropbox", those are out of the scope of our scenario, but they are still supported by our system.

[7] In most cases, they are implemented by API connectors (because most third party web service developers offer it); however, webhooks or pub-sub are even more convenient approaches to work with events on the cloud.

To make the explanation of our approach concrete, we will use our application scenario presented in Sect. 2. The following Fig. 2 shows a set-up with two different smartphones[8] and the central Coordination Server. The Event Processing Network contains various Event Processing Agents (EPAs) that are distributed on the different devices.

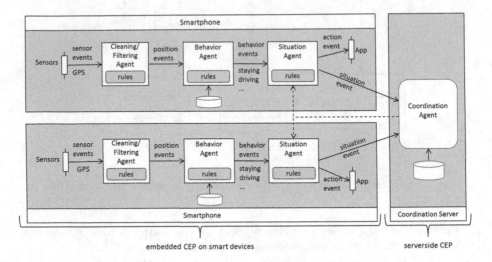

Fig. 2. Event Processing Network for distributed TAS

The EPN defines the archetypal processing stages and the related EPAs, which are common to most TAS systems. However, the particular event processing rules must be adapted to a specific application scenario. In the following we describe the responsibilities of each EPA.

Cleaning/Filtering Agent

The Cleaning/Filtering Agent is deployed to the smartphones and collects all sensor events, such as the *GPS events*. Sensor data is often inconsistent or has redundant information, because sensors are noisy and have a fixed sampling rate. Therefore, in a first step, all technical sensor events have to be pre-processed to overcome inconsistencies or to filter out irrelevant events.

For instance, GPS sensor data is generated with a fixed sampling rate. Thus, many subsequent *GPS events* are logically identical. But the TAS system is only interested in situation changes, and not in the repetition of events carrying similar measured values. Therefore, the Filtering Agent filters out those *GPS events* that are related to the same geographical position. The following event processing rule has the task to find out, if the phone has been moved to a new position.

---

[8] Other types of smart devices like smart home devices are possible, which would have their own domain-specific EPN.

```
rule:"new phone/user position"
CONDITION     GPS-Event AS g1 ->
              GPS-Event AS g2
              AND (Geo.isDifferent(g1,g2))
ACTION        new PositionEvent( g2.x, g2.y)
```

The rule "new phone/user position" expresses a temporal sequence of *GPS events* (by the following operator "->") and assigns the alias names **g1** and **g2** to them. The newer event **g2** represent the current position of the user and is only relevant if the GPS position has significantly changed, which is checked by the service `Geo.isDifferent(...)`. In the action part of the rule, a new *Position event* with the information of the current position is triggered.

Behavior Agent

The incoming *Position events* are correlated with further sensor events (e.g., *Acceleration sensor events*) to determine the particular behavior of the user. New (more complex) *Motion events* are created that characterize the current behavior of the smartphone user. Here we consider the different types of motion such as "walking", "driving", "staying". The following rule derives that the user is staying for a longer time a certain position.

```
rule: "staying"
CONDITION PositionEvent AS pos ->
             NOT (PositionEvent).within(5 min)
ACTION    new StayingEvent(pos)
```

The above rule assumes that the user is staying at a certain position, if a *Position event* is not followed by a new *Position event* within a time interval of 5 min. The operator `.within` defines a time window, in which a certain event has to occur.

The next rule derives a corresponding *Driving event*. The average velocity of a moving user can be calculated by aggregating all *Position events* within the last five minutes and determining the average of the measured speed values. The speed is determined by a method `getSpeed(..)` that is provided by the GPS sensors. If the speed is faster than 15 km/h, it is concluded that the user is driving.

```
rule: "driving"
CONDITION PositionEvent.avg(getSpeed())
             .within:batch(5 min)
     AS avgVelocity
     AND avgVelocity > 15 km/h
ACTION   new DrivingEvent(avgVelocity)
```

In summary, the Behavior Agent processes a correlation step to synthesize *Motion events*. All *Motion events* are subsequently propagated to the Situation Agent.

Situation Agent

In the next processing stage, the Situation Agent is determining the current situation of the smartphone user. The situations of interest depend on the concrete use case scenario. For instance, in our example scenario 'picking up the children from kindergarten', we want to know, where each family member is and if the children have already been picked up.

The incoming *Location* and *Motion events* are carrying only GPS coordinates that have no specific meaning in the TAS domain, and are not sufficient for further processing. Therefore, the GPS data should be transformed to domain locations. A first enrichment step relates GPS coordinates to a real address, which can be done by a reverse geocoding API, e.g. provided by GoogleMaps. Then the address can be mapped to a relevant location of the user, such as "kindergarten", "home" or "work". An example gives the following simple rule that derives a "working" situation:

```
rule: "In Working situation"
CONDITION ( StayingEvent AS stay
            -> NOT PositionEvent )
        AND LocationFinder.getLocation(stay.position) == "work"
ACTION   new WorkingEvent(user)
```

If the system has created a *Staying event*, which is not followed by a new *Position event* (i.e. no significant movement has occurred afterwards), then the GPS position is checked in a utility class `LocationFinder.getLocation(..)`. If the positions corresponds to the users' workplace, a new *Working event* will be created.

All *Situation events* are sent to the TAS server in order to allow task coordination based on the current situations of the users.[9] Therefore, the *Working event* will carry information for identifying the smartphone user.

Coordination Agent

The Coordination Agent is deployed to a central cloud server and responsible for coordination tasks. All smart devices send their *Situation events* to the Coordination Agent that coordinates common tasks and conflicts centrally. In the kindergarten example, the following simplified rule could determine that the person, which is not working, has to pick up the children.

```
rule: "picking up children"
CONDITION
      ( WorkingEvent(u1) -> NOT SituationEvent(u1) ) AND
      ( HomeEvent(u2) -> NOT SituationEvent(u2) )
      -> Timer.at(17 o'clock)
ACTION new PickUpChildrenEvent(u2)
```

---

[9] Detected situations can also generate *Action events* which are sent to an app on the smartphone in order to trigger an appropriate app action.

The rule matches, if for user u1 a *Working event* and for user u2 a *Home event* has occurred. To make sure that their situations haven't changed, no subsequent *Situation events* may have occurred. Furthermore, the current time must be 17 o'clock. If all this holds, then a *PickUpChildrenEvent* is created for the user u2, who is already at home. Additionally, the SituationAgent triggers an *Action event*, which prompts or signals the user u2 to pick up the children from the kindergarten.

Note that this a simplified example. For a realistic coordination mechanism more sophisticated rules are necessary.

4.3   TAS Event Model

The event model of our TAS application is depicted in Fig. 3 showing the different types of events that are used by the event processing rules presented above. Note that the grey boxes represent the generic event types common to most classes of TAS coordinating systems. The various subtypes are more specific, here to our use case described in Sect. 2.

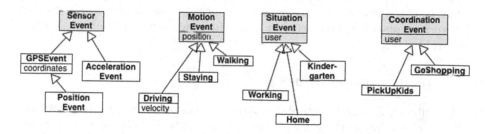

Fig. 3. Event model

The TAS system makes use of the following types of events:

- *Sensor events* are explicit events that are emitted by explicit event sources, here the sensors of the mobile devices. In particular, we can distinguish *GPS events*, *Acceleration events* and *Position events*, which are filtered *GPS events*.
- *Motion events* describe the current motion of a user and are produced by CEP rules that correlate various *Sensor events*. In our example, we distinguish *Driving, Walking* and *Staying events*.
- *Situation events* describe the current situation of a user, which is application specific (in our case we consider *Working, Home* and *Kindergarten* events).
- *Coordination events* are a result of a coordination rule that correlates various *Situation events* from different users/devices. *Coordination events* are sent back to the related mobile devices. They inform the user about task they are obliged to.

5   Evaluation

The presented architecture distributes TAS coordination on different components: the smartphones provide local situation-awareness for each user. The central web server is aware of the global situation and is responsible for coordinating the tasks of all participating users. Our architecture offers the following advantages:

- *Reduced network traffic:* Sensor data is processed directly on the mobile device and not send to the central server. Because the sensors of potentially many users may produce a high volumes of data, the overall network traffic is reduced significantly.
- *Exploiting local processing power:* Processing data on the smart devices also exploits the processing power of mobile devices, which nowadays is reasonable. The central coordination server doesn't have to track each movement of each device.
- *Privacy:* All participants get only the information that is relevant and necessary for them to know: In our scenario, users are not able to track GPS coordinates of other users, which would violate privacy. They only receive messages about what they are obliged to do. Furthermore, private and sensible user data such as working places, kindergarten or home addresses must not be revealed to a central server.

6   Implementation Issues

The Distributed TAS architecture shown in Fig. 1 has been implemented prototypically in order to prove the feasibility of our approach. As smart devices we used smartphones with the Android operating system. The smartphones are the mobile clients of the central coordination server.

The client application (= app) has been developed with the Android application framework that provides access to the local device resources like hardware sensors of the device and the data of all installed applications. So far, commercial CEP engines have not been developed for mobile operating systems. However, the popular open source CEP engine Esper[10] (in version 3.2) has recently been ported to the Android platform: the open source CEP engine Asper[11] is based on Esper 4.9.0. Asper provides the most important features of powerful CEP systems for the Android platform, so that we could use it with minor problems as the code base for our Distributed TAS system.

We identity three different types of communication between actors in out architecture. The mobile devices send their events to the HTTP interface of the central coordination server. On the coordination server the incoming events are processed by the open-source CEP engine Esper.

The coordination server pushes notifications to smarphone devices (e.i. Android applications) using Google Cloud Messaging for Android (GCM)[12]. GCM

---

[10] http://esper.codehaus.org/.
[11] https://github.com/plingpling/asper.
[12] http://developer.android.com/google/gcm/index.html.

enables asynchronous and resource-saving communication from the TAS server to the mobile CEP application. As illustrated in Fig. 1, both the Android application and the central server have access to cloud services by means of so-called channels, which are implemented as web services. By specific connectors, those web services provide further context information like weather and traffic data.

As our implementation responds to a prototype and its objetive it to proof the viability of our architecture and its benefits, we have not considered necessary to include security mechanisns to guarante personal data may not be leaked out from the server. However, it is obvious that the alternative scenario where all GPS information is shared p2p shows more privacy risks. For similar reasons, a rule editor has not been developed. Thus, all user rules are coded according to the pseudo language described in Sect. 3 and stored in-memory.

7   Related Work

The employment of Complex Event Processing for Task Automation Services is a novel field of application, where only very first approaches have been published [5]. In general, related work shows task automation approaches conceived to solved particular problems, that lack of the flexibility and personalization capabilities that characterize Task Automation Service's. Automating business rules correlating events coming from different processes is a good showcase with lots of researches behind [6]. Smarthome automations constitute a renewed usecase where smartdevices can coordinate to work in a desired way e.g. for energy saving [7].

On the other hand, commercial TAS like Ifttt or Zapier lack of CEP i.e. they process incoming events as soon as they arrive, so rules are always triggered by a single event. This is not the case of automations on the IoT field. Several authors propose systems where built-in rules are triggered by correlated events coming from different sensors [2,4,8]. SPITFIRE platform [5] is close to Task Automation Service's vision, since it provides a user interface to set up rules (called queries). However, they only consider connecting sensors and actuators, not cloud services. They do not address task coordination either. CASAS [13] constitutes a different approach, it uses a Machine Learning algorithm to learn from the resident's daily activities and generate automation polices that mimic these patterns.

In general, CEP engines have been primarily developed for the emerging market of business information systems. The engines are deployed on powerful server systems and process high level events from backend business processes. Commercial vendors of CEP engines have focused on this profitable enterprise market segment [15]. Until a few years ago, mobile operating systems were rather inefficient and the computing resources of mobile devices were very limited. As a consequence, vendors have not been interested to develop a CEP engine for this area of use. Along with the rise of computing power of mobile devices, recently, first proposals demonstrate the applicability of CEP for processing data streams emitted by mobile devices, in particular by the embedded sensors. However, either the mobile devices serve merely as special event sources [1,12] or the sensor data are only preprocessed on the mobile device in order to achieve context-aware event filtering [11]. The real event processing of mobile data sources is usually still executed on powerful backend servers. The execution of sophisticated event processing rules directly on the mobile device is still a rather new approach [14]. Consequently, mixed execution profiles for distributed event processing have not been proposed so far.

8   Conclusion

Task Automation Services is an emerging area with multiple application domains and challenging technical implications. In this paper, we presented an innovative system architecture for context-aware and personalized TAS. Applying Complex Event Processing and mixed execution profiles are novel concepts for TAS. The proposed TAS architecture possess the following properties.

- *Situation- and Context-Awareness:* The built-in sensors of smartphones or other smart devices provide the TAS system with a continuous stream of context data. Event processing rules are used to aggregate and correlate the sensor data to more abstract and more meaningful situation data.
- *Coordination:* We introduced a TAS cloud server that provides cross-user coordination exploiting the context data of each participant.
- *Real-time Processing:* The real-time capabilities of CEP are exploited on the cloud-based TAS as well as on the device-based TAS.
- *Distributed Processing:* by mixed execution profiles combine the advantages of formerly separated web-driven as well as device-driven execution profiles.

In summary, our approach leads to a new quality of TAS: Distributed Task Automation Services.

In future work, we intend to investigate more complex task coordination scenarios with advanced mixed execution profiles. In particular, the incorporation of diverse smart devices, such as smart home automation devices or smart vehicles, seems to be very promising.

Acknowledgement. This work was partly funded by the Spanish Ministry of Economy and Competitiveness through the project Calista (TEC2012-32457).

References

1. Amade, D.: Joining oracle complex event processing and J2ME to react to location and positioning events (2010). http://www.oracle.com/technetwork/articles/amadei-cep-090595.html
2. Arcelus, A., Jones, M.H., Goubran, R., Knoefel, F.: Integration of smart home technologies in a health monitoring system for the elderly. In: 21st International Conference on Advanced Information Networking and Applications Workshops (AINAW 2007), vol. 2, pp. 820–825. IEEE (2007)
3. Bruns, R., Dunkel, J.: Event-Driven Architecture: Softwarearchitektur für ereignisgesteuerte Geschäftsprozesse. Springer, Heidelberg (2010)

4. Byun, J., Jeon, B., Noh, J., Kim, Y., Park, S.: An intelligent self-adjusting sensor for smart home services based on ZigBee communications. IEEE Trans. Consum. Electron. **58**(3), 794–802 (2012)
5. Chatzigiannakis, I., Hasemann, H., Karnstedt, M., Kleine, O., Kroller, A., Leggieri, M., Pfisterer, D., Romer, K., Truong, C.: True self-configuration for the IoT. In: 2012 3rd IEEE International Conference on the Internet of Things, pp. 9–15. IEEE, October 2012
6. Daum, M., Götz, M., Domaschka, J.: Integrating CEP and BPM. In: Proceedings of the 6th ACM International Conference on Distributed Event-Based Systems - DEBS 2012, pp. 157–166. ACM Press, New York, July 2012
7. Di Giorgio, A., Pimpinella, L.: An event driven smart home controller enabling consumer economic saving and automated demand side management. Appl. Energy **96**, 92–103 (2012)
8. Domonte, E.P.: An integrated and low cost home automation system with flexible task scheduling. In: XV Workshop of Physical Agents, Leon, pp. 1–10 (2014)
9. Etzion, O., Niblett, P.: Event Processing in Action. Manning (2010)
10. Luckham, D.: The Power of Events: An Introduction to Complex Event Processing in Distributed Enterprise Systems. Addison-Wesley, Boston (2002)
11. Mohomed, I., Misra, A., Ebling, M., Jerome, W.F.: Harmoni: Context-aware filtering of sensor data for continuous remote health monitoring. In: Proceedings of Pervasive Computing and Communications (PerCom), pp. 248–251. IEEE Computer Society (2008)
12. Mouttham, A., Peyton, L., Eze, B., Saddik, A.E.: Event-driven data integration for personal health monitoring. J. Emerg. Technol. Web Intell. **45**, 144–148 (2009)
13. Rashidi, P., Cook, D.: Keeping the resident in the loop: adapting the smart home to the user. IEEE Trans. Syst. Man Cybern. A Syst. Hum. **39**(5), 949–959 (2009)
14. Stipkovic, S., Bruns, R., Dunkel, J.: Event-based smartphone sensor processing for ambient assisted living. In: 2013 IEEE Eleventh International Symposium on Autonomous Decentralized Systems (ISADS), pp. 221–227 (2013)
15. Vidačković, K., Renner, T., Rex, S., Fraunhofer IAO, S.: Marktübersicht Real-Time-Monitoring-Software: Event-Processing-Tools im Überblick. Fraunhofer-Verlag (2010). http://books.google.de/books?id=rvbUXwAACAAJ

Data Streams Quality Evaluation
for the Generation of Alarms in Health Domain

Saúl Fagúndez, Joaquín Fleitas, and Adriana Marotta(✉)

Universidad de la República, Montevideo, Uruguay
{sfagundez, jfleitas, amarotta}@fing.edu.uy

Abstract. In this paper we present a proposal for managing data streams from sensors that are installed in patients' homes in order to monitor their health. It focuses on processing the sensors data streams taking into account data quality. In order to achieve this, a data quality model for this kind of data streams and an architecture for the monitoring system are proposed. Besides, our work induces a mechanism for avoiding false alarms generated by data quality problems.

Keywords: Data quality · Data streaming · Smart home · Health monitoring · Sensors · Data quality model

1 Introduction

The use of sensors has had an enormous increment in last years, becoming a valuable tool in many different areas, such as weather forecasting, driving assistance, water level and quality monitoring, and health monitoring. Sensors produce data streams, which in general have a simple structure but are generated with a very high rate. In this kind of scenario quality of data becomes an extremely important issue, especially in cases where critical decisions must be made based on obtained data. However, not much attention has been paid to this specific topic, existing only few works that focus on it.

Health monitoring through the use of sensors is sometimes used for elderly people care. Different kinds of sensors are installed in their homes and on the patients themselves in order to monitor their behavior as well as their vital signs (blood pressure and temperature). Their behavior is important for example in the case of patients suffering from Alzheimer Disease. Data provided by the sensors are directly transmitted to the hospital, so that the patient can be monitored, avoiding his movement from one place to another. The data received at the hospital are continuously evaluated through a monitoring system, which generates alarms when suspicious data is detected.

This work is situated in the context described in the previous paragraph, and focuses on processing the sensors data streams taking into account data quality. In order to achieve this, a data quality model for health sensors data streams and an architecture for the monitoring system are proposed.

The main contribution of this work is the proposal of a data quality model specific to data streams coming from home and on-patient sensors.

Data quality (DQ) is represented by quality dimensions, each one representing a different quality aspect [1–4]. Our approach is based on a DQ meta-model that consists

B. Benatallah et al. (Eds.): WISE 2014, LNCS 9051, pp. 204–210, 2015.
DOI: 10.1007/978-3-319-20370-6_16

in: a *quality dimension* that captures one aspect of DQ, a *quality factor* that represents a particular aspect of a DQ dimension, and a *quality metric* that defines the criteria for the measurement of the quality factor. Metrics may be applied to data objects at different granularity levels, e.g. a data item or a set of data items. The DQ dimensions that are used along this work are the following: *Accuracy, Completeness, Consistency,* and *Freshness,* which are based on wellknown concepts, about which there is general consensus in the DQ literature [1–4].

According to [5] a data streaming is a continuous and ordered sequence of elements, where elements are presented in real-time. The mechanism for applying dynamic queries to the streams of data is through data windows, which capture certain portions of data from the streams. A window may be logically defined considering the number of elements, or physically defined considering the duration, i.e. the data that arrive to the stream during certain time period [6]. A DSMS (Data Stream Management System) provides a data model for managing dynamic data streams and continuous queries, which are constant queries that process data as they arrive.

As we previously said, some work has been done in the area of sensor data streams quality. In [7] the authors state that quality restrictions in this kind of data must not be ignored and should be carefully managed so that an exhaustive evaluation can be done. This is especially important in applications that directly consume sensor data and their quality becomes a critical issue. In some other applications data from sensors are stored in a database in order to be processed later. In these cases data quality is still essential for decision making supported by data. In [8] a data streaming meta-model is proposed in order to allow the propagation of data quality information towards the corresponding business application. A quality model is presented (five data quality dimensions are managed) and the impact of data stream processing operators on data quality is analysed. The authors focus their analysis on accuracy and completeness quality dimensions. Meanwhile, in [9] the authors present a model that is based on an intuitive notion of the sensor data completeness. They measure the quantity of data that arrive to a consuming point and compare it with the maximum possible quantity of data at that point. On the other hand, in [10] some mechanisms for reducing energy consumption in sensor networks are proposed. These mechanisms assure certain level of data quality, so that they provide a balance between energy efficiency and quality of aggregate data. In [11] a probabilistic approach is used for evaluating the quality of sensor data, modelling the uncertainty in sensor readings. Finally, an event based solution for improving quality in data streams exchanged between health organizations is proposed in [12]. They focus on two quality aspects: data consistency and duplicate detection. They use alerts to notify detected problems.

Our work manages a broad set of quality dimensions and its model and mechanism can be naturally extended with more dimensions. It also distinguishes different quality factors, which allows a more detailed and complete study of the data quality. In addition, besides defining the data quality model, our work induces a mechanism for avoiding false alarms generated by data quality problems.

The rest of the paper is organized as follows. Section 2 presents the proposed system architecture, Sect. 3 focuses on the data quality model and its application, and Sect. 4 presents the conclusions and future work.

2 Health Monitoring System

We consider a smart home with three rooms; a bedroom, a kitchen and bathroom, and a person suffering from Alzheimer's disease. Each room is equipped with two ultrasound distance sensors which measure the distance of some object to the sensor. When the person is in the room, the sensors report the distance to that person. We also have two on-body sensors: one of blood pressure and a thermometer.

At the same time, there is a system which receives and manages data from the sensors in order to detect whether the person has certain variations in his behaviour or in his vital signs. It is a real time and autonomous system, which is able to analyse the data streaming coming from different sensors and to send alarms in predefined situations.

2.1 Proposed Architecture

The proposed architecture consists on different components that are shown in Fig. 1. The user's access point to the system is the *Monitoring* component, where he should first define the requirements, quality parameters, and alarms needed in his particular context. Then, the *Middleware* is responsible for managing the execution of distributed and dynamic queries. The *Data Quality Manager* is responsible for measuring the level of quality of data obtained from the queries and enriching data with quality values. This module interacts with the *Middleware*, so that the *Middleware* is able to return the data window enriched with quality values to the *Monitoring* component. A database containing historical blood pressure data is maintained and queried by the *Data Quality Manager* component in order to evaluate the accuracy of pressure values. The *Monitoring* component is responsible for carrying out the monitoring of the person at home. Some of its functions are to control the temperature and blood pressure of the patient and know in which room of the house he is located. It includes a system of alarms that are activated according to the parameters set and the information obtained from sensors. The *Data Processing* component has the functionality of managing information obtained from the *Middleware* and returning the result to the *Monitoring* component.

3 Data Quality Model and Management

Several data quality issues must be considered in the proposed scenario: (1) Possible errors locating the person in the house because of wrong sensor measurements. (2) Absence of sensor measurement during a predefined time period. This problem encompasses all types of sensors. (3) Blood pressure sensor values whose measures are higher than normal values that are expected according to historical data of person's blood pressure. This may be due to a health problem in the patient (an alarm should be sent, see Sect. 3.1) or due to a data quality problem. (4) For both blood pressure sensors and temperature sensors data, there are a maximum and a minimum valid value that should be respected. (5) Adequate sensor measurement rate. When increasing sensor measurement rate, energy cost and network traffic increase, therefore, this rate should balance the data frequency needed and the energy and traffic supported by the system.

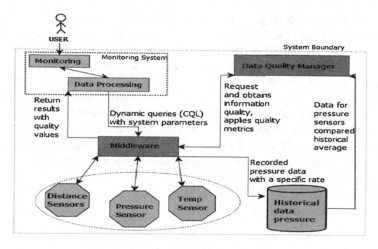

Fig. 1. Architecture

Taking into account the previously described problems and in order to manage them, we define a data quality model that specifies a set of metrics to be applied to the involved data. Table 1 shows the defined data quality model. A metric is defined for each quality factor applied to a kind of sensor, for example, *Dist-Prec* metric is defined for *Precision* factor applied to *distance* sensors data.

Dist-Prec verifies if the sensor satisfies the minimal distance between the sensor and the person from which the sensor values have enough precision (issue 1).

Table 1. DQ model

Dimension	Factor	Sensor	Metric
Accuracy	Precision	Distance	*Dist-Prec*: Satisfaction of minimum distance supported by the sensor
			Result range: (0..1)
	Semantic Accuracy	Pressure	*Pres-SAcc*: Satisfaction of a maximum threshold calculated from historical personal pressure data
			Result range: (0..1)
Completeness	Density	Distance	*Dist-Dens*: Non-null values quantity
			Result range: (0..1)
Freshness	Currency	Distance, Temperature, Pressure	*Dist-Curr, Temp-Curr, Pres-Curr*: Time period between two consecutive data windows issued by a sensor
			Result range: (0..1)
Consistency	Domain Integrity	Distance, Temperature, Pressure	*Dist-Dom, Temp_Dom, Pres-Dom*: Correspondence of the sensor values to a pre-defined domain: positive integer in a pre-defined range
			Result range: (0..1)

Pres-SAcc evaluates if blood pressure values are out of the expected values, in which case there can be a data quality problem or a situation that deserves special attention (issue 3). *Dist-Dens* is applied to distance sensors because a minimum quantity of non-null sensor values are needed for calculating a person location in a room (issue 1). Each sensor should issue data with a minimum frequency that is defined in the system; the metrics for *Currency* factor are used to verify the satisfaction of this requirement (issues 2 and 5). The metrics for *Domain Integrity* factor control if the sensor values belong to certain integer ranges, which are defined in the system (issue 4).

The granularity for all defined metrics is: data window. Note that *Pres-SAcc* and *Domain Integrity* metrics calculate the result considering the quantity of the window values that satisfy the required condition.

DQ information must be attached to the data streams. Figure 2 shows the conceptual schema corresponding to the data window and the DQ information attached to it.

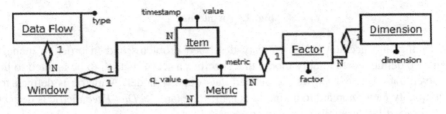

Fig. 2. Data window with DQ information

Example: Consider the distance sensors in the home rooms. Each data stream sent from the Middleware to the Data Processing component has the format shown in Table 2.

Table 2. Distance data stream with quality information

Timestamp	10	20	30	40	50	60	70	80	90
Distance value	2,5	2,5	2	2	0,3	0,4		2,5	2,5
Precision	1			0,3			1		
Density	1			1			0,7		
Currency	2			2			2		
Domain Integrity	1			1			1		

Quality values are calculated using the proposed quality model applying the respective quality metric for distance sensors over the data windows. In this example, in the second data window there is a problem of sensor precision, since some of its values are lower than the minimum for the sensor, so Precision value = 0,3. Meanwhile, in the third window there is a NULL value, so Density value = 0,7.

The Data Processing component integrates data from all distance sensors of the rooms, detecting where the person is located in the home and calculating associated quality information. Table 3 shows an example of the generated data stream.

We consider a range of 10 min and the rooms of the house: Bedroom "Be", Kitchen "K" and Bathroom "B". In the table we can see that the system returns the location of the patient, and the corresponding quality values, using a window of size 3.

Table 3 Data stream generated by Data Processing component

Timestamp	10	20	30	40	50	60	70	80	90
Location	Be	Be	Be	K	K	K	B	B	B
Precision	0,8			1			0,9		
Density	0,8			0,7			0,8		
Currency	1			0,8			1		
Domain Integrity	1			0,8			0,9		
Inter-sensor consistency	1			1			1		

3.1 Alarms Generation

The system's main function is to monitor the person at home using the installed sensors. This is achieved through the analysis of the data streams, considering the parameters set by the user as well as the quality of the data. Depending on this analysis, different outputs will be obtained. If sensor errors are detected certain alarms will be generated, while if potential patient health problems are detected other alarms are generated. The following is an example of a possible situation that generates alarms:

In order to detect where the person is located in the house, two distance sensors are placed in a room so that the system can get the position of the person.

- If information is missing from one or both sensors (metric *Dist-Dens*) then the system returns a **DQ alarm** that indicates the DQ problem encountered.
- If the person is located in two rooms simultaneously (metric *Dist-Dom*) then the system returns a **DQ alarm** that indicates the DQ problem encountered.
- Otherwise, if two distance sensors locate the person in a room, and in a pre-established time period other two sensors detect the person in another room, and this behaviour is repeated for another pre-established time period, then this could be a risk of agitation of the person, so the system returns a **health alarm**.

4 Conclusions

In this paper we present a proposal for managing data streams from sensors that are installed in patients' homes in order to monitor their health.

A set of possible problems in the sensors data are described and taking into account these problems, a DQ model is proposed. In addition, an architecture for the system that is in charge of processing sensor data is proposed. Finally, an example of the generation of alarms is presented.

The DQ model presented in this work was specifically designed for a particular context with particular kinds of sensors. However, this proposal can be seen as a step towards the definition of a general DQ model for sensor data streams.

As future work, a deeper study on general problems in sensor data streams and on the most appropriate DQ dimensions, factors and metrics for this kind of data may be carried out. Also, quality metrics implementation using the particularities of DSMSs should be deeper studied.

References

1. Batini, C., Scannapieco, M.: Data Quality: Concepts, Methodologies and Techniques. Springer, Heidelberg (2006)
2. Strong, D.M., Lee, Y.W., Wang, R.Y.: Data quality in context. Commun. ACM **40**, 103–110 (1997)
3. Pipino, L., Lee, Y.W., Wang, R.Y.: Data quality assessment. Commun. ACM **45**(4), 211–218 (2002)
4. Wang, R.Y., Strong, D.M.: Beyond accuracy: what data quality means to data consumers. J. Manage. Inf. Syst. **12**(4), 5–33 (1996)
5. Golab, L., Tamer Özsu, M.: Issues in data stream management. SIGMOD Rec. **32**(2), 5–14 (2003)
6. Hebrail, G.: Data stream management and mining. Mining Massive Data Sets For Security, Paris, pp. 89–102 (2008)
7. Klein, A.: Incorporating quality aspects in sensor data streams. ACM first Ph.D. (2007)
8. Klein, A., Lehner, W.: Representing data quality in sensor data streaming environments. J. Data Inf. Qual. **1**(2), 10:1–10:28 (2009)
9. Bitwas, J., Naumann, F., Qiu, Q.: Assessing the completeness of sensor data. In: 11th International Conference on DASFAA, Singapore (2006)
10. Sharaf, M.A., Beaver, J., Labrinidis, A., Chrysanthis, P.K.: Balancing energy efficiency and quality of aggregate data in sensor networks. VLDB J. **13**(4), 384–403 (2004)
11. Kuka, C., Nicklas, D.: Quality matters: supporting quality-aware pervasive applications by probabilistic data stream management. In: Proceedings of the 8th ACM International Conference on Distributed Event-Based Systems, New York, NY, USA, pp. 1–12 (2014)
12. Berry, A., Milosevic, Z.: Real-time analytics for legacy data streams in health: monitoring health data quality. In: 17th IEEE International Enterprise Distributed Object Computing Conference (EDOC), pp. 91–100 (2013)

Multilayer and Multi-agent Data Fusion in WSN

Sheng Zhang[1,2], Xiaodong Liu[1], Xiaoling Bao[1],
and William Wei Song[2(✉)]

[1] School of Information Engineering, Nanchang Hangkong University,
Nanchang, China
zwxzsl68@126.com, technology12@163.com,
bxl007315@sina.com
[2] Business Intelligence and Informatics, Dalarna University, Borlänge, Sweden
wso@du.se

Abstract. In the wireless sensor networks, the hardware limitations of sensor nodes cause high transmission failure rate. We usually increase the density of nodes to improve the quality of information transmission. However, it is difficult for the limited energy supply, storage, and communication bandwidth to transfer large amount of redundant sensory data. So we use data fusion technology to remove the redundant data as much as possible before the data transmission. Data fusion becomes a research hotspot in recent years. In this paper we propose a multilayer and multi-agent data fusion mode, and analyze the proposed mode performance in three aspects: hops, energy consumption and network delay.The simulation experiments show that, if reasonably suitable parameters, such as the network scale, the number and size of agents, the data processing cost, are selected, the mobile agent mode is much better than the client/server mode.

Keywords: Wireless sensor networks · Data fusion · Multilayer · Multi-agent

1 Introduction

A wireless sensor network (WSN) is composed of a large number of tiny sensor nodes to monitor physical and/or environmental conditions, such as temperature, sound, and pressure. The nodes are usually tiny in volume, limited in energy supply, and limited in resources (e.g. the CPU, the amount of memory, radio bandwidth and coverage). Meanwhile a WSN usually is deployed in dangerous or unattended places, which always causes high transmission failure rate. To overcome the hardware limitations, researchers usually deploy large amount of redundant sensor nodes to increase a high data transmission quality. However, a large number of redundant sensor nodes bring a new problem: it is difficult for the limited energy and communication bandwidth to transfer large amounts of redundant sensory data.

The related researches show that the energy consumption of communication is much more than that of calculation in wireless sensor networks. According to analysis by Gregory [1], if the distance is 100 m between two wireless sensor nodes, the energy used to transfer 1 bit data from one node to another with radio mode is equal to that of executing 3000 CPU instructions. Therefore, if we can remove the redundant data as

© Springer International Publishing Switzerland 2015
B. Benatallah et al. (Eds.): WISE 2014, LNCS 9051, pp. 211–225, 2015.
DOI: 10.1007/978-3-319-20370-6_17

much as possible before the data transmission, the communication load will reduce tremendously. On the other hand, we can combine, integrate, or compress the sensory data from different type sensors in a node to a consistent, accurate data packet, which may cost fewer resources of WSN than before. All such information processing technologies are called data fusion in general. Data fusion is the process of integration of multiple data and knowledge representing the same real-world object into a consistent, accurate, and useful representation. Therefore, data fusion becomes more and more important for WSN research.

Instead of focusing on specific data fusion method, in this paper, we investigate a sensory data collection mechanism. We put forward a multilayer and multi-agent data fusion strategy. The main ideas are (1) abstracting a real WSN as a multilayer logical network, (2) setting one or several mobile agents in different layers to gather and fuse sensory data, (3) setting a static agent in each sensor node to filtrate or combine sensory data from many kinds of sensor nodes (e.g. the temperature sensor, the humidity sensor, the pressure sensor, etc.). We map a real WSN into a multilayer and multi-agent logic network. In this logic network, all agents run in parallel model for respective tasks. Our objectives are to delete the redundant data, reduce the network overhead, improve the data collection efficiency, and increase the lifetime of the WSN.

The rest of the paper is organized as follows: In Sect. 2, we discuss related work. In Sect. 3, we describe the multilayer and multi-agent data fusion network architecture and the possible data fusion methods in different logic layers. Then we analyze the MA mode vs. the C/S mode in three metrics of hops, energy consumption and network delay. We give an evaluation through some simulation experiments in Sect. 4, and conclude and discuss future work in Sect. 5.

2   Related Work

Up to now, there are many data fusion methods proposed by researchers [2]. All the methods can be divided into two main kinds: a traditional client/server (C/S) mode and a mobile agent (MA) mode. See Fig. 1, the picture on the left side shows the C/S mode, while that on the right side shows the MA mode.

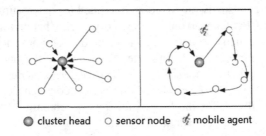

● cluster head   ○ sensor node   ⚡ mobile agent

Fig. 1. The C/S mode and MA mode

In the traditional C/S mode, all sensor nodes send raw sensory data to the sink node, where the data is fused centrally. In the MA mode, a mobile agent is created by the sink node, is dispatched to a neighbor senor node for gathering and fusing raw sensory data, then jumps to the next node to perform the same operation, and one after another, and finally returns to the sink node with the result data. As indicated by Qi, Xu and Wang [3], the advantages of the MA mode can be briefed as follows:

- Scalability: the performance of the network is not affected when the number of sensor nodes is increased or reduced.
- Reliability: mobile agents can be sent when the network connection is alive and can return results when the connection is re-established.
- Extensibility and task-adaptability: mobile agents are programmed to carry different task specific integration processes for the functionality of the network.
- Energy-awareness: the itinerary of the mobile agent can be dynamically determined based on both the information gain and energy constraints.
- Progressive accuracy: a mobile agent partially merges results as it visits more nodes, improving the accuracy of the integrated result at each visited node.

The MA mode saves both network bandwidth and computation time by avoiding unnecessary migrations. The researchers have done many works for using MA to gather senor data in WSN. In 2003, Qi, XU and Wang [3] and Xu and Qi [4] proposed signal and information processing with multi-agent in sensor networks, then proposed a model based on mobile agent in WSN for target tracking in 2008. It has been proposed the optimal mobile agent routing with fusion cost in WSN in [5]. Researchers also studied data gathering algorithm based on mobile agent for emergent event monitoring in [6]. Gavalas put forward a nearly optimal distributed data fusion method for WSN based on the Agent in 2010 [7]. It computes an approximate solution to the problem by suggesting an appropriate number of MAs that minimizes the overall data fusion cost and constructs near-optimal itineraries for each of them. Earlier this year, we also proposed a hierarchical data fusion conception in WSN based on MA [8].

3   Our Approach

3.1   Multilayer and Multi-agent WSN Mode

In a typical WSN application architecture, see Fig. 2, there are sensor nodes, deployed in a target monitoring area, and a special node, sink node, which gathers sensory data from other normal sensor nodes. Users can get information from the target monitoring area.

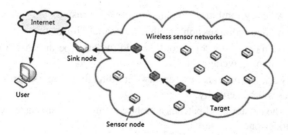

Fig. 2. A typical example of WSN

A WSN is composed of many clusters, and each cluster includes a cluster head node (CH) and several senor nodes. A cluster head can not only gather sensory data from other senor nodes in its own cluster, but also senses the monitoring environment like a normal sensor node. We set a static agent in each normal sensor node, at the same time, and give each cluster head the rights of creating and dispatching a mobile agent in its own cluster. The sink node gathers information from all the clusters by dispatching one or more mobile agents. Figure 3 shows a WSN mapping into a multilayer and multi-agent logic network.

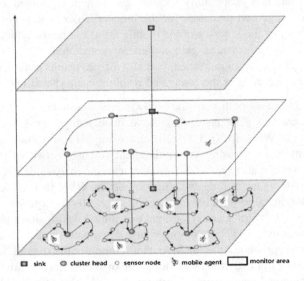

| ◼ sink | ◎ cluster head | ○ sensor node | 🦅 mobile agent | ▭ monitor area |

Fig. 3. A multilayer and multi-agent network mode

In Fig. 3, there are three logic layers: the sink layer, the cluster head layer and the normal sensor node layer. We can select different data fusion methods for different layers. A possible data fusion scenario for each layer is shown in Table 1.

Table 1. The possible data fusion methods

Node layer	A possible data fusion method
Normal node	(1) A "copy inhibition" method in time dimension;
	(2) A "data compression" method in spatial dimension;
	(3) A "merger" or "operator" method in data type dimension (e.g. maximum, minimum, average, etc.).
Cluster head	(1) Each node sends raw sensory data directly to the cluster head, cluster head fuses data centrally;
	(2) The cluster head patches a mobile agent to gather sensory data from normal nodes one by one.
Sink	Data fusion method just like a cluster head.

3.2   Modes Analysis

We choose three metrics, (1) hops, (2) energy consumption, (3) network delay, to evaluate the performance of the C/S mode and MA mode.

(1) **Comparison of hops.** A hop is defined to be that a node sends a message packet to another node. The total number of the hops of a network is the sum of hops made by all sensor nodes in WSN when the sink node receives successfully all messages from nodes. The factors that can affect the total hops include the data file size s_f (the size of the raw data that each node collects), the mobile agent size s_a, the number of sensor nodes N, the number of mobile agents m, and the number of sensor nodes n that each mobile agent migrates.

(a) Hops of C/S Mode. We consider the hops of a cluster first, then the whole WSN. We assume that a cluster has n nodes $(S_1, S_2, S_3, \ldots, S_n)$, S_n is the cluster head, and the other n-1 nodes send messages $\left(s_{f1}, s_{f2}, s_{f3}, \ldots, s_{f(n-1)}\right)$ to the cluster head at the same time. If the node $i(S_i)$ occupies the cluster head's communication channel, the cluster head only receives s_{fi} packets from S_i, and the other n-2 nodes need to resend their messages at next time. Without loss of generality, we assume that the cluster head receives messages in the order from the $(n-1)^{th}$ node to the 1st node, and the size of message packet is 1 unit.

When the cluster head receives the message of the $(n-1)^{th}$ node, the hops are

$$H_1 = \sum_{i=1}^{n-1} s_{fi} \tag{1}$$

When the cluster head receives the message of the jth node, the hops are

$$H_j = \sum_{i=1}^{n-j} s_{fi} \quad (1 \le j \le (n-1)) \tag{2}$$

When the cluster head receives the message of the first node, the hops are

$$H_{n-1} = s_{f1} \tag{3}$$

So, the total network hops in this cluster are

$$H_{cs-c} = \sum_{i=1}^{n-1} H_i = H_1 + H_2 + \cdots + H_j + \cdots + H_{n-1}$$
$$= \sum_{i=1}^{n-1} s_{fi} + \sum_{i=1}^{n-2} s_{fi} + \cdots + \sum_{i=1}^{n-j} s_{fi} + \cdots + s_{f1} \tag{4}$$

Specially, if $s_{f1} = s_{f2} = s_{f3}, \ldots, = s_{f(n-1)} = 1$, that is, each sensor node sends only one packet to the cluster head, the total network hops in this cluster are

$$H_{cs-c} = \sum_{i=1}^{n-1} H_i = H_1 + H_2 + \cdots + H_j + \cdots + H_{n-1}$$

$$= (n-1) + (n-2) + \cdots + (n-j) + \cdots + 1 = \frac{n(n-1)}{2}$$

(5)

There are m clusters in the WSN. Each cluster will send the gathered result from its own cluster to the sink node. The method of calculation of hops in the whole WSN is similar to that for a cluster. In order to simplify the calculation, we assume that each sensor node contains the same data file size (s_f). Therefore, the total network hops of the C/S mode are

$$H_{cs} = \sum_{j=1}^{m} (H_{cs-c})_j + H_{cs-s} = m\frac{n(n-1)}{2}s_f + \frac{m(m+1)}{2}ns_f$$

$$= \frac{mn(m+n)s_f}{2}$$

(6)

where, $(H_{cs-c})_j$ indicates the total hops of the jth cluster and H_{cs-s} the total hops that all clusters send messages to the sink node of the C/S mode.

(b) *Hops of MA Mode.* Since the mobile agent usually fuses data from normal sensor nodes when it jumps from one node to another, we assume that the data fusion rates are $p_1, p_2, \ldots, p_{n-1}$ in n-1 nodes $(S_1, S_2, \ldots, S_{n-1})$ respectively. Then $1 - p_1, 1 - p_2, \ldots, 1 - p_{n-1}$ are the un-fusion rates, denoted as $q_1, q_2, \ldots, q_{n-1}$. The mobile agent has its own overhead such as identification, service code, itinerary, and so on. So we assume that the mobile agent visits the sensor nodes from S_1 to S_{n-1}, and return to the cluster head S_n at last. The agent visiting path is $S_1 \rightarrow S_2 \rightarrow S_3 \rightarrow \ldots \rightarrow S_n$.

The messages which need to be transferred from S_1 to S_2 include the un-fusion data packets and the agent size in S_1, so the number of hops from S_1 to S_2 is

$$H_1 = s_{f1}q_1 + s_a$$

(7)

The messages which need to be transferred from S_2 to S_3 include three parts: the data from S_1, the un-fusion data of S_2, and the agent overhead. The number of hops becomes

$$H_2 = s_{f1}q_1 + s_{f2}q_2 + s_a$$

(8)

And the hops from S_{n-1} to S_n are

$$H_{n-1} = s_{f1}q_1 + s_{f2}q_2 + \cdots + s_{f(n-1)}q_{n-1} + s_a$$

(9)

Then, the total hops in this cluster in the MA mode are

$$H_{\text{ma-c}} = \sum_{i=1}^{n-1} H_i + s_a = (n-1)s_{f1}q_1 + (n-2)s_{f2}q_2 + \cdots + s_{f(n-1)}q_{n-1} + ns_a$$

$$= \sum_{i=1}^{n-1} (n-i)s_{fi}q_i + ns_a \tag{10}$$

In order to simplify the calculation, we assume that each sensor node contains the same data size s_f, and uses the same un-fusion rate q $(0 < q < 1)$. Therefore, the total network hops in the MA mode are

$$H_{\text{ma}} = \sum_{j=1}^{m} (H_{ma-c})_j + H_{ma-s}$$

$$= m\left(\frac{n(n-1)}{2} s_f q + ns_a\right) + \frac{m(m+1)}{2} ns_f q + ms_a \tag{11}$$

$$= m(n(m+n)s_f q/2 + (n+1)s_a)$$

where, $(H_{\text{ma-c}})_j$ indicates the total hops of the jth cluster, and $H_{\text{ma-s}}$ represents the total hops of all the clusters to the sink node in the MA mode.

(2) **Comparison of Energy Consumption.** A sensor node is normally composed of four basic units: a sensing unit, a processing unit (including CPU and memory), a communication unit, and a power unit. Among these units, communication and sensing consume the most of the energy. However, since the energy consumed in sensing is the same for both modes, we choose not to include this factor in the following comparison.

The energy consumption involves these three components: (1) energy consumed in data transfer (E_{tran}), (2) overhead processing (E_{oh}), and (3) data processing (E_{pro}). We introduce that e_{tr} is the coefficient indicating the amount of energy consumed by transferring one byte of data, e_{rw} the coefficient indicating the amount of energy consumed in reading or writing one byte of data, and e_{pro} the coefficient indicating the amount of energy consumed in processing one byte of data.

(a) *The Energy Consumption in the C/S Mode.* We assume that there are n-1 nodes sending sensory data to the cluster head in a cluster, so the transfer energy consumption is

$$E_{tran} = s_f e_{tr} \frac{n(n-1)}{2} \tag{12}$$

In the C/S mode, the overhead processing is the energy consumption on the file access. The file access operates not only in the sensor nodes, but also in the cluster head. So,

$$E_{oh} = 2(n-1)s_f e_{rw} \tag{13}$$

The energy consumption of data processing is

$$E_{pro} = n(s_f/v_d)e_{pro} \tag{14}$$

Thus, the total energy consumption in a cluster is

$$\begin{aligned} E_{cs-s} &= E_{tran} + E_{oh} + E_{pro} \\ &= s_f e_{tr} n(n-1)/2 + 2(n-1)s_f e_{rw} + n(s_f/v_d)e_{pro} \end{aligned} \tag{15}$$

where, v_d is the data processing rate.

Therefore, the total energy consumption of the whole network in the C/S mode is

$$\begin{aligned} E_{cs} &= mE_{cs-c} + E_{cs-s} = m(s_f e_{tr}\frac{n(n-1)}{2} + 2(n-1)s_f e_{rw} + n\frac{s_f}{v_d}e_{pro}) \\ &\quad + ns_f e_{tr}\frac{m(m+1)}{2} + 2mns_f e_{rw} + m\frac{ns_f}{v_d}e_{pro} \end{aligned} \tag{16}$$

(b) The Energy Consumption in the MA Mode. We assume that there are n nodes in a cluster (including cluster head node), the cluster head creates and dispatches a mobile agent to gather sensory data. The agent in each node fuses sensory data with the fusion rate $p(0 < p < 1)$. So the transfer energy consumption is

$$E_{tran} = (n-1)(1-p)s_f e_{tr} + ns_a e_{tr} \tag{17}$$

where, s_a is the size of the mobile agent.

In the case of the MA mode, the overhead processing is the energy consumption of creating, dispatching, and receiving the mobile agent. So,

$$E_{oh} = n(s_a/v_d)e_{pro} \tag{18}$$

The energy consumption of data processing is,

$$E_{pro} = (n-1)((1-p)s_f/v_d)e_{pro} \tag{19}$$

Thus, the total energy consumption in a cluster is

$$\begin{aligned} E_{ma-c} &= E_{tran} + E_{oh} + E_{pro} \\ &= (n-1)(1-p)s_f e_{tr} + ns_a e_{tr} + n(s_a/v_d)e_{pro} \\ &\quad + (n-1)((1-p)s_f/v_d)e_{pro} \end{aligned} \tag{20}$$

Therefore, the total energy consumption of whole network in MA mode is

$$\begin{aligned} E_{ma} &= mE_{ma-c} + E_{ma-s} \\ &= m((n-1)(1-p)s_f e_{tr} + ns_a e_{tr} + n(s_a/v_d)e_{pro} \\ &\quad + (n-1)((1-p)s_f/v_d)e_{pro}) + mn(1-p)s_f e_{tr} \\ &\quad + m(s_a/v_d)e_{pro} + mn(1-p)s_f/v_d e_{pro} \end{aligned} \tag{21}$$

(3) **Comparison of Network Delay.** The network delay is the time spent to gather sensor data from a WSN. In the MA mode, it starts from the time a mobile agent is created to the time the mobile agent returns with results. In the C/S mode, it is from the time the clients send out data to the time the data processing is finished and results are generated at the sink node.

Similar to the energy consumption, the network delay consists of three components: t_{tran}, t_{oh}, and t_{pro}, where t_{tran} represents the time spent in transferring the migration unit from one node to the other, t_{oh} the overhead time (In the case of C/S mode, it is the time spent on file access. In the case of MA mode, it is the time used to create, dispatch, and receive the mobile agent.), and t_{pro} the processing time. There are a few factors which affect the network delay, including the network transfer rate v_n, the overhead of file access t_f (the time used to read and write a data file), and the overhead of mobile agent t_a.

(a) The Network Delay in the C/S Mode. In a cluster, the transmission time is $t_{tran} = (n - 1)s_f/v_n$, in which n-1 nodes send data to the cluster head. The overhead time is $t_{oh} = 2(n - 1)t_f$, in which the cluster head and the normal sensor nodes need to access data file. The processing time is $t_{pro} = ns_f/v_d$.

Therefore, the total network delay in a cluster in the C/S mode is

$$t_{cs-c} = t_{tran} + t_{oh} + t_{pro} = (\text{n - 1})s_f/v_n + 2(n - 1)t_f + ns_f/v_d \qquad (22)$$

So, the total network delay of the whole network in the C/S mode is

$$\begin{aligned} t_{cs} &= mt_{cs-c} + t_{cs-s} \\ &= m((\text{n - 1})s_f/v_n + 2(n - 1)t_f + ns_f/v_d) \\ &\quad + mns_f/v_n + 2mt_f + mns_f/v_d \end{aligned} \qquad (23)$$

(b) The Network Delay in the MA Mode. In the MA mode, the transmission time is the time used to transfer the mobile agent in a cluster. So,

$$t_{tran} = n((1 - p)s_f + s_a)/v_n \qquad (24)$$

The overhead time is used for creating, dispatching and receiving an agent, so it is

$$t_{oh} = 2(n - 1)t_a \qquad (25)$$

The processing time is,

$$t_{pro} = ns_f/v_d \qquad (26)$$

Thus, the total network delay in a cluster is

$$\begin{aligned} t_{ma-c} &= t_{tran} + t_{oh} + t_{pro} \\ &= n((1 - p)s_f + s_a)/v_n + 2(n - 1)t_a + ns_f/v_d \end{aligned} \qquad (27)$$

So, the total network delay of whole network in the MA mode is

$$t_{ma} = mt_{ma-c} + t_{ma-s}$$
$$= m(n((1 - p)s_f + s_a)/v_n + 2(n - 1)t_a + ns_f/v_d)$$
$$+ (m + 1)(n(1 - p)s_f + s_a)/v_n + 2mt_a$$
$$+ mn(1 - p)s_f/v_d$$

$$(28)$$

4 Experiment and Evaluation

We assume the simulation conditions of WSN as follows.

- Each node has the unique identifier in the WSN.
- They can communicate each other among the neighbor nodes, i.e. if node A can communicate with node B, the node B must communicate with node A.
- All nodes have the same power at the initial stage of network.
- All nodes are located statically in the monitor area.

The experiments are simulated in the MATLAB platform. The type of sensor node is Telosb, and the communicated chip is CC2420. The basic network consists of 100 wireless sensor nodes randomly distributed within a 100×100 m^2 area. The related parameters in the simulation experiments are shown in Table 2.

Table 2. Parameters of the network

Sign	The means of parameters	Notice
N	The number of sensor nodes	N = mn
m	The number of mobile agents	
n	The number of nodes that each agent migrates	Initial value: 10
v_n	The network transfer rate	Ref. CC2420 250 kbps
v_d	The data processing rate	128000 kbps
s_f	The data file size	1 k
s_a	The mobile agent data buffer size	1 k
t_f	The time of reading or writing data packet	0.0125 s
t_a	The time of mobile agent proccessing data	0.05 s
e_{tr}	The energy of transfering 1 byte in sensor node	0.06 w
e_{pro}	The energy of proccessing 1 byte in sensor node	0.000726 w
e_{rw}	The energy of reading or writing 1 byte in sensor node	0.000726 w
p	The data fusion rate	0.7

We design four kinds of experiments to evaluate the effect on the network hops, energy consumption and network delay using the two computing modes. The four parameters are the number of nodes, the number of mobile agents, the data size of mobile agent, and the agent processing data cost. In each experiment, we only change the value of one parameter but keep the others fixed. The results and discussion are described as follows.

4.1   Effect of Hops

In this experiment, we change the number of nodes from 2 to 100 and use one mobile agent. The result is shown in Fig. 4. We observe that the network hops increase in both the C/S mode and MA mode. But the hops in the C/S mode grow much faster than that in the MA mode. The reason is that several clients (sensor nodes) compete to control the server (the cluster head) communication channel, when all clients send messages to the server at the same time. But there is only one client winning to transfer messages, other clients have to try for next chance. On the other hand, the MA mode is less influenced by the number of nodes because there is no conflict during a mobile agent jumping from one node to another along the itinerary. Another reason is that the number of sensory data packets decrease, since the mobile agent fuses sensory data on the way.

Figure 5 is a zoom-in of Fig. 4, showing that the C/S mode performs a little better than the MA mode, when the node number is less than 2. This happens because in the MA mode it needs more connections than the C/S mode in order to send and receive mobile agents. It also happens when the overhead of the mobile agent surpasses the overhead of the C/S mode.

We fix the node number to 30, and change the number of mobile agents from 1 to 15. Without loss of generality, we assume that each mobile agent migrates the same number of nodes. From Fig. 6, we can observe that the hops in the C/S mode do not change significantly and are far greater than that in the MA mode, while the hops increase slowly with the increasing number of the mobile agents.

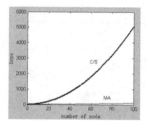   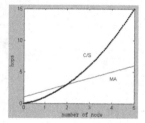   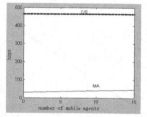

Fig. 4 Hops vs. No. of nodes   **Fig. 5.** Zoom-in of Fig. 4   **Fig. 6.** Hops vs. No. of agents

4.2   Effect of Energy Consumption

In this experiment, we change the number of nodes from 2 to 100 and use one mobile agent. The result is shown in Fig. 7. We observe that the energy consumption in both modes grows as the number of nodes increases. But the energy consumption of the C/S mode grows more quickly than that of the MA mode, because there are more hops in the C/S mode, and the transfer energy consumption is the most main factor in the WSN, thus the C/S mode consume more energy than the MA mode.

We can also see that the MA mode consumes a little more energy than the C/S mode when the number of nodes is less than 7 (the point of intersection in Fig. 7). This happens because the MA mode needs more connections than the C/S mode in order to send and receive the mobile agents. It also happens when the overhead of the mobile agent surpasses the overhead of the C/S mode. In other words, mobile agents need extra energy when they run in the network. This extra cost is obvious when the network scale is small, for example, the number of nodes in the network is less than 7.

We fix the node number to 100, and change the number of mobile agents from 1 to 100. The result is shown in Fig. 8. We can see that the energy consumption of the C/S mode does not change, while the energy consumption decreases first and increases later in the MA mode. There are two intersection points at a and b. The energy consumption in the MA mode is less than that of the C/S mode when the number of agents is between a and b. Otherwise, the energy consumption in the MA mode is more than that of the C/S mode. So, if the network scale does not change, we can choose the number of agents appropriately to get the lowest energy consumption. For example, the suitable number is 10 in this experiment.

We fix the number of nodes to 100, the number of mobile agents to 10, and change the size of the mobile agents. The experiment result in Fig. 9 shows that the energy consumption of the C/S mode does not change, while the energy consumption increases with the agent size getting bigger in the MA mode. When the agent size is less then 5 KB, the MA mode consumes less energy than the C/S mode.

We fix all other parameters and observe the effect of the mobile agent data processing cost. The result is shown in Fig. 10. With increasing of the data processing cost, the energy consumption of the MA mode increases, while the energy consumption of C/S mode does not change. When the cost is less than 0.7 s, the MA mode consumes less energy than the C/S mode.

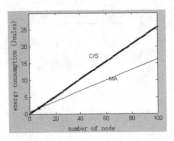

Fig. 7. Energy consumption vs. No. of nodes

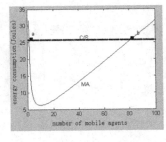

Fig. 8. Energy consumption vs. No. of agents

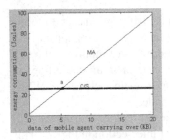

Fig. 9. Energy consumption vs. Size of agent

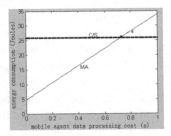

Fig. 10. Energy consumption vs. Data processing cost of agent

We give a summary of the effect of energy consumption in the above four aspects as follows.

- We fix the number of mobile agent to 1 and change the number of nodes from 2 to 100, the MA mode consumes a little more energy than the C/S mode when the number of nodes is less than 7.
- When we fix the number of nodes to 100 and the number of the mobile agents to 10, the MA mode consumes the lowest energy.
- If we fix the number of nodes to 100 and the number of the mobile agents to 10, the energy consumption of the MA mode is less than that of the C/S mode when the agent size is less then 5 KB and the data processing cost is less than 0.7 s.

4.3   Effect of Network Delay

Similarly to effect of energy consumption, we change the number of nodes from 2 to 100 and use one mobile agent. The result is shown in Fig. 11. We observe that the network delay in both modes grows as the number of nodes increases. But the network delay of the C/S mode grows much faster than that of the MA mode. The two lines intersect at point a in Fig. 11. It means that the MA mode performs worse than the C/S mode when the number of nodes in the network is bigger than 60. The reason is the same as discussed in the energy consumption analysis.

We fix the node number to 100, and change the number of mobile agents from 1 to 30. The result is shown in Fig. 12. We can see that the network delay of the C/S mode does not change, while the network delay decreases rapidly first and increases slowly later in the MA mode. There are two points of intersection, a and b, in Fig. 12. The network delay in the MA mode is less than that of the C/S mode when the number of agent is between a and b. Otherwise, the network delay in the MA mode is more than that in the C/S mode. Similar to the effect of energy consumption, the MA mode get the shortest network delay when the number of agents is 10.

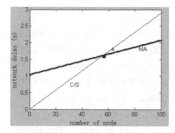

Fig. 11. Network delay vs. No. of nodes

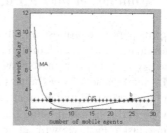

Fig. 12. Network delay vs. No. of agents

We fix the number of nodes to 100, the number of the mobile agents to 10, and change the size of the mobile agents. The experiment result in Fig. 13 shows that the network delay of the C/S mode does not change, while the network delay increases with the agent size getting bigger in the MA mode. When the agent size is less then 11 KB, the MA mode has less network delay than the C/S mode.

We fix all other parameters and observe the effect of the mobile agent data processing cost. The result is shown in Fig. 14. With increasing of the data processing cost, the network delay in the MA mode increases, while the network delay in the C/S mode does not change. When the data processing cost is less than 0.1 s, the MA mode executes less time than the C/S mode.

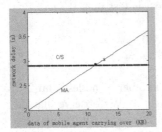

Fig. 13. Network delay vs. Size of agents

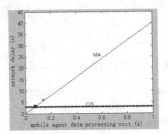

Fig. 14. Network delay vs. Data processing cost of agent

We give a brief summary of the effect of network delay in the above four aspects as follows.

- When we fix the number of nodes to 100 and the number of the mobile agents to 10, the MA mode runs the shortest time.
- If we fix the number of nodes to 100 and the number of the mobile agents to 10, the energy consumption of the MA mode is less than that of the C/S mode when the agent size is less then 11 KB and the data processing cost is less than 0.1 s.

5   Conclusion and Future Work

In this paper we propose a multilayer and multi-agent data fusion network architecture, and analyze the architecture in the MA mode vs. the C/S mode in three metrics: hops, energy consumption, and network delay. The simulation experiments show that the MA mode is not always better than the C/S mode. If we choose suitable parameters for the network scale, the number and size of agents, the data processing cost, etc., the MA mode performs much better than the C/S mode. In the future, we will try to carry out three tasks. First, we will set up a real WSN, and develop software to verify the above results we obtained in this paper. Second, in this paper we mainly compare and analyze the MS mode and the C/S mode. We will extend the analysis methods proposed here to other computing modes and make a broader comparison. Third one is a research question we try to answer after the work done here: if we know the network scale, how do we determine the parameter values to get the lowest network energy consumption and the least network delay?

Acknowledgement. This work is partially supported by the National Natural Science Foundation of China (Grant No.61162002, 61364023) and the Foundation of Jiang Xi Provincial Department of Education (Grant No. GJJ12428, GJJ13516).

Appendix

Here are the figures from Fig. 4 to Fig. 14.

References

1. Iyer, R., Kleinrock, L.: QoS control for sensor networks. In: IEEE International Conference on Communications, ICC 2003, vol. 1, pp. 517–521. IEEE (2003)
2. Chen, Y., Shu, J., Zhang, S., Liu, L., Sun, L.: Data fusion in wireless sensor networks. In: Second International Symposium on Electronic Commerce and Security, ISECS 2009. vol. 2, pp. 504–509. IEEE (2009)
3. Qi, H., Xu, Y., Wang, X.: Mobile-agent-based collaborative signal and information processing in sensor networks. Proc. IEEE **91**(8), 1172–1183 (2003)
4. Xu, Y., Qi, H.: Mobile agent migration modeling and design for target tracking in wireless sensor networks. Ad Hoc Netw. **6**(1), 1–16 (2008)
5. Tu, Z., Wang, Q., Shen, Y.: Optimal mobile agent routing with fusion cost in wireless sensor network. In: IEEE Instrumentation and Measurement Technology Conference, I2MTC 2009, pp. 46–50. IEEE (2009)
6. Yuan, L., Wang, X.: Study on data gathering algorithm based on mobile agent and WSN for emergent event monitoring. In: International Symposium on Computer Network and Multimedia Technology, CNMT 2009, pp. 1–5. IEEE(2009)
7. Gavalas, D., Mpitziopoulos, A., Pantziou, G., Konstantopoulos, C.: An approach for near-optimal distributed data fusion in wireless sensor networks. Wireless Netw. **16**(5), 1407–1425 (2010)
8. Zhang, S., Yang, H.L., Xiong, H.J.: Hierarchical Data Fusion in WSN Based on Mobile Agent. Appl. Mech. Mater. **513**, 1154–1159 (2014)

Strategies for Data Quality Monitoring
in Business Processes

Cinzia Cappiello(✉), Barbara Pernici, and Laura Villani

Dipartimento di Elettronica, Informazione E Bioingegneria,
Politecnico di Milano, Milano, Italy
{cinzia.cappiello,barbara.pernici,laura.villani}@polimi.it

Abstract. The relevance of data quality is continuously increasing in
modern enterprises. This is due to the fact that poor data quality has
often a negative impact on the business effectiveness and efficiency.
Errors, missing or out-of-date data might cause the failure of the business processes and consequently the loss of time and money. In such a
scenario, the adoption of tools and methods able to detect and correct
process data errors is desirable. In this paper we propose the quality-
aware process redesign as a quality improvement method. In particular,
the business process is analyzed and modified at design time in order
to include Data Quality blocks that are components responsible for the
error detection and repair and thus for improving the process reliability.
Note that Data Quality blocks can be added to the process workflow
using different configurations. This paper aims to describe and compare
such configurations. Furthermore, since each configuration impacts in
different ways on the process quality and performance, we provide some
guidelines for the selection of the configuration able to satisfy the business requirements.

Keywords: Data quality · Business process · Data quality monitoring

1 Introduction

The correctness and richness of data in a modern enterprise might influence its
business success and performance. In fact, business daily operations and decisions are influenced by the quality of data on which they rely and the data quality
management can be considered as a "potential source of sustainable competitive
advantage" [16]. Data quality is often defined as "fitness for use" [23] that is
the ability of the analyzed data to meet users' requirements. This definition
suggests that data quality assessment depends on the considered context and
process. Data quality is also a multidimensional concept: different aspects are
analyzed by using different dimensions. This paper focuses on the data quality
dimensions associated with data values, and in particular, on accuracy, completeness, consistency and timeliness.

If an enterprise finds out that its own data are affected by poor quality
problems, it should adopt data quality improvement strategies. The literature

© Springer International Publishing Switzerland 2015
B. Benatallah et al. (Eds.): WISE 2014, LNCS 9051, pp. 226–238, 2015.
DOI: 10.1007/978-3-319-20370-6_18

suggests two improvement approaches: (i) *data-based improvement* for which inspection and correction actions are taken in order to eliminate the errors in data values; (ii) *process-based improvement* in which processes are analyzed in order to detect and eliminate the cause of errors. We focus on the latter type of improvement strategies and we show the ways in which processes can be redesigned in order to guarantee high data quality levels and process reliability. In details, we consider the adoption of Data Quality blocks that are components responsible for checking data and detecting errors. Data Quality blocks can be added to the process workflow with different configurations. In this paper we identify three possible configurations and we compare them also providing some guidelines for their selection.

The paper is structured as follows: Sect. 2 analyzes the previous literature contributions and highlights the novel aspects of the proposed approach; Sect. 3 describes the operations to perform for analyzing processes while Sect. 4 introduces the components (i.e., Data Quality blocks) that we use to redesign the business processes and guarantee high quality levels. The ways in which such components might be inserted in the business process are shown in Sect. 5. Finally, Sect. 6 compares and discusses the different configurations on the basis of the results of simulations performed on a specific case study.

2   Related Work

Data quality for modern enterprises is an important issue since, especially in information-intensive businesses, information has the same role of raw materials for manufacturing enterprises. The value of information depends on the importance of the processes in which it is involved [5]. Most of the times, poor data quality negatively affects organizations' activities by reducing the efficiency of the business processes and the effectiveness of the decisions and causing money losses. Enterprises should adopt a data quality management program to guarantee a suitable data quality level. Such programs might be expensive, but it is worth noticing that error prevention can cost ten times less than its correction [11]. The literature shows that the most effectiveness improvement techniques are the process-based improvement approaches that aim to detect and eliminate the root causes of the errors [12]. In these approaches business processes are analyzed in order to observe the failures, their occurrence and their relationships within data quality issues. In this scenario information is considered a product, i.e., an Information Product (IP) [22]. In fact, the process takes in input raw data and through a series of operations it provides the final output that is the desired information.

The business processes can be better analyzed if they are modelled. The most important notations used for modeling business processes include BPMN and YAWL [1] but none of them support the process designer in the specification of the data quality issues, requirements or activities. For this reason, some researchers defined the Information Production framework (IP-map) that enriches the process modeling with some representations that aim to capture the way in which data are manipulated and transferred in order to provide the desired output. In particular, IP-map introduces the Data Quality blocks as components that are "used to represent the checks for data quality on those data items that are essential in producing a defect-free information product" [19]. Unfortunately, the design, implementation and utilization of Data Quality blocks require additional resources in terms of time and costs [19]. In this paper we use the Data Quality blocks to have a quality-aware redesign of the business processes. We show that there are different ways to use them and each configuration has different impact on business process quality and performance.

Also more recent contributions highlight the need to consider a quality-aware business processes modeling as the starting point for data quality improvement activities. For example, in [15] authors claim the need to consider data quality requirements during the design of a business process. [18] proposes an extension of BPMN to model data quality requirements. Another data quality-oriented BPMN extension to highlight the points of the process in which data quality issues arise is proposed in [7]. In such contribution the proposed notation is the starting point of a comprehensive methodology that aims to support the process designer in a quality-aware redesign of the business processes. Anyway, the cited contributions do not thoroughly consider the data quality improvement activities. They only cite some possible improvement techniques or provide examples without systematically evaluating the impact of their adoption, an aspect that we instead develop in our approach.

Other papers focus on the assessment of data quality dimensions during the process execution. [2] introduces a framework to evaluate process errors that depend on data quality issues. Moreover, some authors identify the data quality dimensions to consider as relevant in a business process. [20] explores inaccurate data values inside the business processes. The author suggests the insertion of data quality blocks after the execution of each activity to check the level of accuracy. A wider set of data quality dimensions is considered in [6,14] and [13]: the data quality dimensions that are considered as relevant in business processes for most of the considered studies are accuracy, completeness and timeliness. Such dimensions together with consistency are the data quality dimensions that can be assessed by using objective metrics and that we consider in this paper. As regards *Accuracy*, it is often defined as "the extent to which data are correct, reliable and certified" [17,23] defines it as "a measure of distance of a data value v to some other values v' that is considered correct". *Completeness* is defined as "the extent to which a given data collection includes data describing the corresponding set of real-world objects" [23]. The *Consistency* dimension refers to the violation of semantic rules defined over a set of data items [4]. Finally, *Timeliness* is "the extent to which the age of data is appropriate for the task at hand" [21]. Timeliness is usually measured by considering other two variables: currency and volatility [3]. The former refers to the age of the data from their last update while the latter is the time interval in which the data can be considered temporally valid.

3   Process Analysis

The approach proposed in this paper aims to enable the quality-aware redesign of the business process. In particular, it suggests the process designer where to insert the Data Quality blocks inside the process. In order to provide such support, more knowledge about the considered business process is needed. In particular, three phases have to be executed:

1. **Process Description:** In order to improve the data quality level within a process, it is necessary to have a deep knowledge about the process structure and the data flows. The process should be described by considering the tasks that compose it and the workflow structure. If the process is not modeled yet, it is necessary to gather information by direct observations or interviewing the process manager. Anyway, the output of this phase is the process model that shows the way in which the different tasks interact along the workflow structure (e.g., parallel, sequential, loop structures).
2. **Data Analysis:** The data analysis is performed in order to identify the set of data that are manipulated in each process task. In particular, it is important to know the data sources from which data are extracted and the operations performed on such data.
3. **Workflow Redesign and Annotation:** The process workflow derived from the first phase is thoroughly analyzed in order to identify the possible causes of errors and consequently the points of the process in which the errors are generated and should be monitored. In order to enable such analysis the process workflow is simplified by enrolling the loops [8] and calculating the probabilities of execution of process branches [11].

The collected knowledge enables the discovery of data dependencies that might cause the *error propagation*. In fact, even if a failure occurs in a specific point of the process, often the cause of the failure is located in a previous activity. For this reason the analysis of the process workflow and the data dependencies can be exploited to identify where are the root causes of the errors and where to put the Data Quality blocks. Furthermore, the identification of data dependencies supports the definition of the repair actions to activate on the basis of the type of fault. The repair actions might include for example: (i) *compensation* to re-establish a correct status of the objects affected by a fault, (ii) *retry* to re-execute the failed activities, and (iii) *substitution* that is used to substitute a process instance with another one.

4   Data Quality Blocks

The exception handlers that we use in this paper are the *Data Quality blocks* that, as described in Sect. 2, have been introduced in the IP-map notation as a procedure able to check and improve the quality level of the data that are exchanged between two process activities. The main issues related to the use of the quality blocks are:

- The design of the quality blocks;
- The position where the quality blocks has to be placed inside the process;
- The quantity of the quality blocks to include in the process.

In this section we discuss the first issue while the other two issues are described in Sect. 5.

It is necessary to consider that a Data Quality block has to be designed on the basis of (i) the quality dimensions that is necessary to monitor and (ii) the considered data sources.

On the basis of the considered data quality dimensions (i.e., accuracy, completeness, consistency and timeliness), it is possible to identify four types of quality blocks, one for each dimension.

Accuracy. As described in Sect. 2, the accuracy dimension reveals the correctness of the data values used in the process. The methods used to assess such correctness, and thus also the corresponding Data Quality block design, depends on the type of data that have to be monitored:

- *Textual data type:* the block adopts string matching algorithms published in the literature [10]. Such algorithms compare the values used in the process with reference values contained in dictionaries and repositories and produce a measure of similarity that mainly highlights the presence of syntactic errors.
- *Numeric data type:* in order to assess the accuracy of the numeric data, we have designed the quality blocks by considering some concepts of the theory of the propagation of uncertainty [9]. In particular, in order to detect errors within numeric values, it is necessary to analyze the quality of the input data but also the operations used to manipulate data. In fact, on the basis of the theory of the propagation of uncertainty the data errors propagate in different ways on the basis of the considered operations performed on the data set. Considering the error contained in the input data and the types of the operations performed, it is possible to calculate the error on the output data.

In general, the accuracy (either for textual or numeric data) is measured in terms of the distance between the considered data value and the reference value (i.e., the correct value) [17]. This definition coincides with the mathematical definition of *absolute error* that is:

$$e_x = \bar{x} - x$$

where $\bar{x}$ is the value used in the process and x the correct one. Starting from this formula, it is possible to calculate the relative error:

$$\xi_x = \frac{\bar{x} - x}{x}$$

from which it is possible to derive the following formulas:

$$\bar{x} = x(1 + \xi_x)$$

and

$$f(\bar{x}) = f(x(1 + \xi_x)) \simeq f(x) + f'(x)x\xi_x$$

$$\xi_f = \frac{f(\bar{x}) - f(x)}{f(x)} \simeq \frac{f'(x)x\xi_x}{f(x)}$$

For the functions with more variables:

$$f(\bar{x}, \bar{y}) = f(x(1 + \xi_x), y(1 + \xi_y))$$

$$f(\bar{x}, \bar{y}) \simeq f(x, y) + f_x(x, y)x\xi_x + f_y(x, y)y\xi_y$$

and

$$\xi_f = \frac{f(\bar{x}, \bar{y}) - f(x, y)}{f(x, y)}$$

$$\xi_f \simeq \frac{f_x(x, y)x\xi_x + f_y(x, y)y\xi_y}{f(x, y)}$$

The propagation on uncertainty on the most used operations suggests the utilization of the formulas listed in Fig. 1 [9].

Mathematical function	Formula
Sum - two variables	$\xi_{x+y} = \frac{x}{x+y}\xi_x + \frac{y}{x+y}\xi_y$
Average - two variables	$\xi_{\frac{x+y}{2}} = \frac{x}{x+y}\xi_x + \frac{y}{x+y}\xi_y$
Sum of sequences:	$\xi_{\sum_{i=1}^{n} x_i} = \sum_{i=1}^{n} \frac{x_i}{\sum_{i=1}^{n} x_i}\xi_{x_i}$
Subtraction - two variables	$\xi_{x-y} = \frac{x}{x+y}\xi_x - \frac{y}{x+y}\xi_y$
Moltiplication - two variables	$\xi_{x*y} = \xi_x + \xi_y$
Product of sequences	$\xi_{\prod_{i=1}^{n} x_i} = \sum_{i=1}^{n} \xi_{x_i}$
Division	$\xi_{x/y} = \xi_x - \xi_y$

Fig. 1. Formulas to evaluate the propagation of uncertainty

We use these formulas inside the quality blocks in order to estimate the accuracy of the data value after the execution of an operation.

Completeness. The quality block associated with this dimension searches for the "null" values inside the data sources that are used by the tasks of the analyzed process. The output of the assessment performed by this block is the degree of completeness that is the percentage calculated on the basis of the ratio between the quantity of not null values and the total number of values.

Consistency. Consistency is a dimension that is strictly related to the process activities. For example, in this paper, we have verified the consistency between the cities and the nations in which the cities are also associated with their postal codes. In order to perform this assessment we rely on additional tables that contain the correct correspondences among such values.

Timeliness. This dimension usually refers to the validity of data in terms of their age and updateness. In details, we evaluate timeliness by assessing currency and volatility parameters described in Sect. 2. Furthermore, as regards the temporal aspects, in this paper we also consider the execution time in terms of the process execution time and the time needed to perform the tasks included in the quality blocks. In fact, for our purpose, it is important to understand how the adoption of quality blocks impacts on the temporal aspects related to the data validity and process performance.

5 Monitoring Strategies

In this section, we describe and compare the possible configurations with which the Data Quality blocks can be added to the process structure in order to detect errors and avoid failures. The Data Quality blocks described above have been designed as activities that have to be inserted inside the business process. In the following, we discuss strategies about the two following issues: (i) where to insert the blocks and (ii) how many quality blocks should be inserted in the process.

Once that the process has been analyzed and the quality blocks have been implemented, it is necessary to identify the most appropriate points where to check data. In the following, we propose a set of possible configurations, with the goal of improving data quality but also avoiding a negative impact on process performance.

Let us consider a process for the order management in an enterprise that has an e-commerce web site (see Fig. 2). The process is composed of three main procedures: (i) the authentication of the user (i.e., Identity Management), (ii) the control of goods availability (i.e., Stock Management) and (iii) the definition of the order (i.e., Order Management) that is responsible for the goods delivery. We will use this simple process to show how it is possible to redesign the process in a data quality-aware way by using the Data Quality blocks.

In particular, we have identified three alternative configurations, which might be combined if applied to different sources of data. These three alternatives manage in different ways the trade-off between high data quality level and process performance (i.e., execution time). In fact, the first configuration is oriented to guarantee high data quality levels with an efficient monitoring but it does not take into consideration the execution time of the process. The other two alternatives instead analyse the whole process considering the execution time, but are less timely in detecting errors than the first alternative.

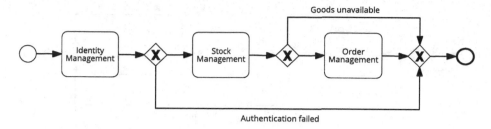

Fig. 2. Analyzed business process

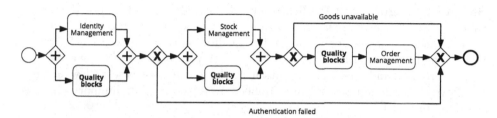

Fig. 3. Quality block insertion according to the first configuration (local check)

First Configuration: Local Check. As a first alternative we propose a solution in which the redesign of the process guarantees optimal results with respect to data quality monitoring. On the one hand, we defined that for all the *activities that update the database* the check should be performed before the activity (sequentually). In this way input data are checked before the update and in case of low quality data the process is suspended. This prevents the upload of data that are incorrect, out-of-date or not reliable. An example is provided for the Order Management activity in Fig. 3. On the other hand, for *reading activities* the check of the values results to be more efficient if performed in parallel with the activity, since parallel execution guarantees a shorter execution time and quality errors (if detected) can be repaired just with the re-execution of that single activity. This strategy enables a timely localization of low quality data and their root causes, favouring the positive effect of repair actions, which is highly dependent on a timely localization of the error. An example is given for the Identity and Stock Management activities in Fig. 3.

This first configuration is suitable for simple processes, since such an accurate monitoring increases the complexity of the process flow and the execution time. Since execution time is an important constraint in many business processes, such a solution is often not appropriate: it might have a negative impact on the user satisfaction and decrease the value and revenue of services.

In order to monitor processes in shorter time, solutions that monitor the whole process and not the single activities can be envisioned. We define two other configurations. Note that such configurations are also the only options if the process is seen as a black box, without any information about its composing activities and their order.

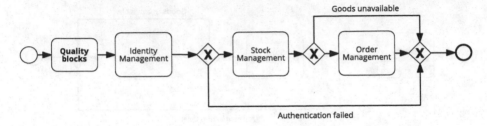

Fig. 4. Quality block insertion according to the second configuration - preliminary check

Second Configuration: Preliminary Check. The second proposed configuration takes into account the impact of quality blocks on execution time, but has also the goal of preventing to insert low quality values in databases. Therefore this configuration envisions that a quality block is inserted before the execution of the process, and that the execution of the process, in case of low quality, is delayed until repair actions are applied. An example of preliminary check is depicted in Fig. 4.

This solution is particularly useful for processes that have often to deal with low quality data since quality is monitored and problems are revealed before the process execution. In this way it is possible to postpone execution until the quality is improved.

Third Configuration: Parallel Check. This last configuration envisions that the quality check is performed in parallel with the process execution, in order to decrease the impact on the execution time. An example is provided in Fig. 5. This solution notifies the presence of errors only at the end of the process, which might compromise the effect and possibility of performing repair actions, but it may be the best solution if quality constraints are most of the time satisfied (e.g., the probability of errors is low). Anyway, the parallel execution might be very useful in particular when the different activities in the process are executed

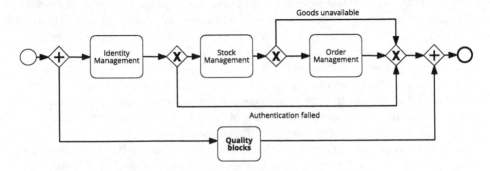

Fig. 5. Quality block insertion according to the third configuration - parallel check

by different organizational units. In fact, in this case, the process is already complex for managing the communication among the different actors involved and the data quality checks do not further overload the process management during the execution time. This should be taken into account in the selection of the most suitable configuration.

The advantages of the different configurations can be also exploited by combining them in order to monitor different databases in different ways. Figure 6 shows a combination of configurations 2 and 3, which is preferable when data sources used within the process have different error probabilities, so that different monitoring configurations should be adopted. In this case, the check of the data characterized by the higher error probability (e.g., the products database) will be performed at the start of the process, while data with lower error probablity (e.g., the customers database) will be monitored during process execution according to the third configuration.

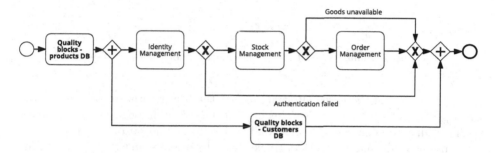

Fig. 6. Example of combination of configurations 2 and 3

6   Results

In this section we discuss experimental results gathered from simulations based on the case study depicted in Fig. 2.

The process has been simplified by identifying three main procedures. Such procedures have been implemented as Web services in Java and the service composition has been realized through the definition of a BPEL process. The database storing the data has been implemented using MySQL.

Also the Data Quality blocks have been implemented as Web services. As described in Sect. 4, four types of quality blocks have been designed. The first Web service checks accuracy. Accuracy is evaluated as the distance between the value in the database and the real (correct) one. For our evaluation, on the one hand real data have been stored in a database with the same structure of the database used in the process. On the other hand errors have been introduced in the database used in the process in order to be able to evaluate accuracy within the process. To verify consistency, it has been necessary to have additional information to the one contained in the database. In the case study, consistency concerns postal codes of towns, and towns and countries. In order to evaluate completeness, the evaluation has been performed considering null values in the database. Finally, for time-related dimensions, we computed currency, volatility, and timeliness on the basis of information associated with the database.

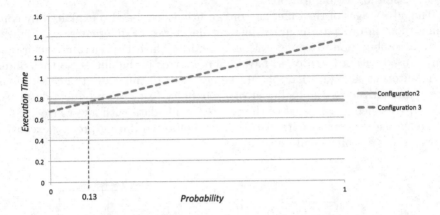

Fig. 7. Simulations of configurations 2 e 3 for the case study

We have tested the three alternatives but the first alternative as proven not appropriate given the eccessive execution time. Most interesting results have been obtained by comparing the second and third configurations. In the second configuration, all quality checks are executed before starting the process. This alternative avoids using low quality data in the process, checking their quality before using them. In this case a delay is introduced for the monitoring and for executing repair actions when needed. Note that we assume that the monitoring activities are executed in constant time while the repair time is not consider in the comparison. In the third configuration, the quality blocks are executed in parallel with the process. In this case, if an error is identified, this might happen at the end of the process and imply re-execution, thus potentially doubling the execution time of the process. Such configurations are also the most interesting ones since they consider the execution time as a critical factor as in most of the real business processes.

In summary, we compared the alternatives taking into account the probability of error and the execution time of monitoring activities. The graph of Fig. 7 shows the behavior of the two strategies according to the probability of error. A threshold is identified above probability 0.13, where the two lines intersect. So, for our case study, above this threshold we would select the second strategy, while the third strategy is preferable with a lower probability of error.

7   Concluding Remarks

The adoption of a data quality management program might have a significant impact on the modern enterprises that use high volumes of data and that need data characterized by quality levels suitable for their processes. Investing on the data quality assessment procedures might help to take decisions and act repair strategies in line with the business requirements.

This paper adopts the Information Product approach and proposes a data quality improvement strategy that aims to identify potential source of errors on the basis of the analysis of the structure of the data and of the process in which data are involved. Taking from the IP-map approach presented in the literature the notion of Data Quality block construct we tried to address the issues related to the design of the blocks and to their positioning inside the process. We proposed the adoption of four types of Data Quality blocks (one for each of the considered data quality dimensions) and we presented three alternatives for the insertion of such blocks inside the process structure. The three configurations differ for their impact on the guaranteed data quality level and on the process execution time. Considering these differences we have defined some guidelines to support a process designer in a quality-aware process redesign based on the adoption of the quality blocks.

Future work focuses on the definition of other monitoring configurations able to take into account other aspects besides the execution time. For example, other KPIs will be considered. Considering several variables, it will be also interesting to analyze how the suitability of the configurations change adding and varying priorities (related to business requirements) associated with such variables.

Acknowledgements. The present work was partially supported by Industria 2015 Project "Sensori".

References

1. Lu, R., Sadiq, W.: A survey of comparative business process modeling approaches. In: Abramowicz, W. (ed.) BIS 2007. LNCS, vol. 4439, pp. 82–94. Springer, Heidelberg (2007)
2. Bagchi, S., Bai, X., Kalagnanam, J.: Data Quality Management using Business Process Modeling. In: IEEE SCC, pp. 398–405 (2006)
3. Ballou, D., Wang, R., Pazer, H., Tayi, G.K.: Modeling information manufacturing systems to determine information product quality. Manag. Sci. 44(4), 462–484 (1998)
4. Batini, C., Cappiello, C., Francalanci, C., Maurino, A.: Methodologies for data quality assessment and improvement. ACM Comput. Surv. 41(3), 1–52 (2009)
5. Batini, C., Cappiello, C., Francalanci, C., Maurino, A., Viscusi, G.: A capacity and value based model for data architectures adopting integration technologies. In: AMCIS (2011)
6. Bringel, H., Caetano, A., Tribolet, J.M.: Business process modeling towards data quality: a organizational engineering approach. In: ICEIS, vol. 3, pp. 565–568 (2004)
7. Cappiello, C., Caro, A., Rodríguez, A., Caballero, I.: An approach to design business processes addressing data quality issues. In: ECIS (2013)
8. Cardoso, A.J.S.: Quality of service and semantic composition of workflows. PhD thesis

 9. Clifford, A.A.: Multivariate error analysis: a handbook of error propagation and calculation in many-parameter systems. Wiley, New York (1973)
10. Cohen, W.W., Ravikumar, P., Fienberg, S.E.: A comparison of string metrics for matching names and records. In: KDD Workshop on Data Cleaning and Object Consolidation (2003)
11. Console, L., Picardi, C., Dupré, D.T.: A Framework for Decentralized Qualitative Model-based Diagnosis. In: Proceedings of the 20th International Joint Conference on Artifical Intelligence, IJCAI 2007, pp. 286–291. Morgan Kaufmann Publishers Inc, San Francisco, CA, USA (2007)
12. English, L.P.: Improving Data Warehouse and Business Information Quality: Methods for Reducing Costs and Increasing Profits. Wiley, New York (1999)
13. Falge, C., Otto, B., Österle, H.: Data quality requirements of collaborative business processes. In: HICSS, pp. 4316–4325 (2012)
14. Heravizadeh, M., Mendling, J., Rosemann, M.: Dimensions of business processes quality (QoBP). In: Ardagna, D., Mecella, M., Yang, J. (eds.) Business Process Management Workshops. LNBIP, vol. 17, pp. 80–91. Springer, Heidelberg (2009)
15. Ofner, M., Otto, B., Österle, H.: Integrating a data quality perspective into business process management. Bus. Proc. Manag. J. **18**(6), 1036–1067 (2012)
16. Powell, T.C.: Total quality management as competitive advantage: a review and empirical study. Strateg. Manag. J. **16**(1), 15–37 (1995)
17. Redman, T.C.: Data Quality for the Information Age. Artech House, Boston (1996)
18. Sánchez-Serrano, N., Caballero, I., García, F.: Extending BPMN to Support the Modeling of Data Quality Issues. In: ICIQ, pp. 46–60 (2009)
19. Shankaranarayanan, G., Wang, R.Y., Ziad, M.: IP-MAP: representing the manufacture of an information product. In: IQ, pp. 1–16 (2000)
20. Soffer, P.: Mirror, Mirror on the Wall, Can I Count on You at All? Exploring Data Inaccuracy in Business Processes. In: Bider, I., Halpin, T., Krogstie, J., Nurcan, S., Proper, E., Schmidt, R., Ukor, R. (eds.) BPMDS 2010 and EMMSAD 2010. LNBIP, vol. 50, pp. 14–25. Springer, Heidelberg (2010)
21. Wand, Y., Wang, R.Y.: Anchoring data quality dimensions in ontological foundations. Commun. ACM **39**(11), 86–95 (1996)
22. Wang, R.Y.: A product perspective on total data quality management. Commun. ACM **41**(2), 58–65 (1998)
23. Wang, R.Y., Strong, D.M.: Beyond accuracy: what data quality means to data consumers. J. Manage. Inf. Syst. **12**(4), 5–33 (1996)

Quality Improvement Framework for Business Oriented Geo-spatial Data

Xiaofeng Du[1(✉)] and William Song[2]

[1] British Telecom, London, UK
xiaofeng.du@bt.com
[2] Dalarna University, Falun, Sweden
wso@du.se

Abstract. In the past few years, Geo-spatial data quality has received increasing attention and concerns. As more and more business decisions are made based on data analytic result from geo-spatial related data, low quality data means wrong or inappropriate decisions, which could have substantial effects on a business's future. In this paper, we propose a framework that can systematically ensure and improve geo-spatial data quality throughout the whole life cycle of data.

1 Introduction

Traditionally, geo-spatial data are only collected and provided by government related organizations or agencies. This type of data is usually used for some specific usage, such as mapmaking, government planning, land survey, and military purpose. However, in the past decade, especially when the online mapping applications, such as Google Maps become a part of our daily life, the perception of geo-spatial data has revolutionarily changed. Now people can easily access geo-spatial data through their personal computer, handhold devices such as mobile phones, and GPS navigation devices etc. They can download geo-spatial data from organisations like Ordnance Survey or even collect their own geo-spatial data if they need. As geo-spatial data become ubiquitous, more and more businesses start embedding geo-spatial information into their business data and use them as decision making tools.

Whoever uses the geo-spatial data tends to assume the data are correct and accurate. However, it is almost never in reality. Decision makers and data analysts should keep the limitation of the data in mind and understand the potential impact of data quality. The potential impact of poor quality data can be summarised in following aspects (Loshin 2011a):

1. Financial Impacts, in the geo-spatial data case, could be associated to investment in the wrong geographical areas, marketing strategy targeting wrong customers, and therefore increased operational cost etc.
2. Confidence and satisfaction-based impacts, in the geo-spatial data case, could be associated to reduced confidence to forecast sale and decreased customer satisfaction as wrong location information used in the previous forecasting and sale, and the result was unsatisfactory.

B. Benatallah et al. (Eds.): WISE 2014, LNCS 9051, pp. 239–249, 2015.
DOI: 10.1007/978-3-319-20370-6_19

3. Productivity impacts, in the geo-spatial data case, could be associated to increased workload and product to market time as the wrong group of customers are targeted due to inaccurate location information.
4. Risk and compliance impacts, in the geo-spatial data case, could be associated to local government policy violation due to wrong location information.

From the above discussion, we can see that it is vital for a business to have fit for purpose accuracy of the geo-spatial data, otherwise, the potential negative impact to the business can be significant.

Data quality improvement as a research topic has been well studied. In Batini et al.'s survey (Batini 2009), a wide range of data quality assessment and improvement methods are discussed, such as data-drive techniques (Bertolazzi et al. 2003; Lenzerini 2002) and process-drive techniques (Muthu et al. 1999; Hammer 1990) based data improvement methods. Caprioli et al. (2003a, b) discussed the rules and standards that specifically for ensuring the quality of spatial data. Veregin (1999) discussed what parameters should be used to measure the quality of spatial data. Stankute and Asche (2011) proposed a data conflation based method to improve spatial data quality. Tadakaluru et al. (2005) introduced a framework for cleaning spatial data used in ARCGIS[1] engine. However, the existing works are mainly focusing on particular methods for data quality improving and assessment, none of them propose a systematic way of tackling the geo-spatial data quality issue throughout the whole life cycle of data, i.e. from data acquisition to producing analytic result for making business decisions.

In this paper, we propose a geo-spatial data quality ensuring and improvement framework. This framework focuses on the geo-spatial data that are for assisting business decisions and analytics, not for mapmaking or other geographical purpose. It tackles the data quality issue in stages. It has a set of components to ensure geo-spatial data quality at the data acquisition stage, a set of components to ensure geo-spatial data quality at the data storing stage, and a set of components to ensure continuous data quality improvement even after the analytic result has been produced. As the framework targets the geo-spatial data for business, improving the location accuracy, temporal accuracy, and currency are the main focuses. The details of the framework will be discussed later in the paper.

The rest of this paper is organized as follows. In Sect. 2, the common geo-spatial data quality elements and possible sources of errors in geo-spatial data are discussed. In Sect. 3, the details of the geo-spatial data quality ensuring and improvement framework are discussed. Finally, we conclude the paper and point out the future direction of the work.

2 Geo-spatial Data Quality

The concept of quality in general is *"features of products which meet customer needs and thereby provide customer satisfaction"* and *"freedom from deficiencies"* (Juran and Godfrey 1999). In data quality case, quality is, according to SDTS[2], *"an essential or*

---

[1] www.esri.com.

[2] Spatial Data Transfer Standard, http://mcmcweb.er.usgs.gov/sdts/.

distinguishing characteristic necessary for cartographic data to be fit for use", i.e. fitness for use (Chrisman 2006). Since data quality is a relative concept, there is no absolute good quality or bad quality data. According to Box's famous say, *"All models are wrong, but some are useful"* (Box 1976). The geo-spatial data is also a model that describe the reality (Longley et al. 2001), therefore, they all have imprecision and inaccuracy at certain levels. In order to know the geo-spatial data's fitness for use, there are list of quality measurement parameters that are used to measure it, which will be discussed in the following section.

2.1 Geo-spatial Data Quality Parameters

In general, geo-spatial data describe geographical information with spatial, temporal and thematic attributes (Berry 1964). The spatial attribute is the information about locations, boundaries, terrain and other geographical features. Temporal attribute is the time when the information of spatial attribute is recorded. Thematic attribute is about the theme of the geo-spatial data. Any geo-spatial data need to have a theme, which tells what it is about, e.g. a country's boundary, a building's location, or a route. Without a theme, geo-spatial data is just pure geometry (Longley et al. 2005). Geo-spatial data quality measurement is mainly around these three attributes. The following list of parameters is usually used to measure the quality of geo-special data (Longley et al. 2005; Xia 2012):

- **Accuracy.** Accuracy is about how accurate the data are. It includes spatial accuracy, temporal accuracy, and thematic accuracy. Spatial accuracy refers to accuracy of spatial features, such as the position and shape of points, lines and areas. Temporal accuracy refers to the accuracy of reporting time associated with the data. Thematic accuracy refers to the accuracy of the attributes of the data.
- **Currency.** Currency is the "use by" date of the data. It is about whether the data are up to date or not. Currency is often mixed up with temporal accuracy. They are two different concepts. A piece of data has very accurate reporting time (temporal accuracy), but may still be out of date (currency). On the other hand, a piece of data is up to date (currency), but may has very inaccurate reporting time (temporal accuracy).
- **Precision** or **Resolution.** Precision or resolution refers to how much detail can be perceived from data. Normally, the higher the precision of data is, the larger space the data storage is required.
- **Consistency.** Consistency refers to giving a dataset, there is no contradictions in it. It also refers to conformance of certain topological rules specified by users (Kainz 1995).
- **Completeness.** Completeness is *"a measurable error of omission observed between the database and the specification"* (Longley et al. 2005).

As in this paper we only discuss the geo-spatial data for business analytics, not for geographical or navigational purpose, some of the quality parameters are out of interest of this paper, such as precision or resolution.

2.2 Source of Error

Errors in data could be caused by many reasons. Mainly, errors are from the following sources (Rasdorf 2000):

- **Data Input Error.** This type of errors can be mistakes of human being. However, it can also be caused by input devices, for example an inaccurate GPS device. Another major data input error source is map digitisation.
- **Data Processing Error.** This type of errors are generated when process data. For example, when converting grid reference coordinate system into longitude and latitude coordinate system, if the converting algorithm has bug, then the converted data will contain errors.
- **Data Display Error.** When geo-spatial data are plotted on maps, errors could be caused by plotting algorithms, maps client interfaces, and display devices.

3 The Quality Improvement Framework

The main objective of developing this framework is to give the data users a systematic way to continuously ensure and improve geo-spatial data quality. As discussed before, have a solution to tackle the data quality issues throughout the whole life cycle of geo-spatial data is crucial. Similar to errors in software development (Westland 2002), data quality issues also propagate themselves through the life cycle of the data. The later stage the quality issues are dealt with, the more expensive the cost will be. The cost can be both the cost to improve data quality and the cost to the business due to data quality issues. Therefore, it is important to deal with the data quality issue at the very beginning of data collection stage and continuously improve data quality.

The framework proposed here divides geo-spatial data quality improvement into three linked stages: data acquisition stage, data storing stages, and data application stage, see Fig. 1. At the data acquisition stage, it is important to ensure the newly collected data are correct and complied with data quality standards and rules. At the data storing stage, it is crucial to ensure the currency of the data. At the data application stage, any data quality issues that have been discovered need to be feed back to the system and dealt with immediately. New data collected in the data application stage will go back to the beginning of the loop, the data acquisition stage. In each stage, several methods are discussed for ensuring and improving geo-spatial data quality. The methods are for business users rather than professional GIS product producers as they have different focuses and interests in geo-spatial data quality.

In the following section of the paper, each stage of the framework will be discussed in details.

3.1 Data Acquisition Stage

The data acquisition stage is the most critical and cost effective stage to tackle the data quality issue. As mentioned before, this framework is mainly focused on geo-spatial data for business purpose. This type of geo-spatial data is normally collected together

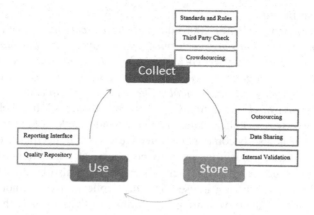

Fig. 1. The structure of the framework

with other business interested data. For example, a summary of sale for a particular shop at a particular time or time period. In this case, the location of the shop and the time when the data is collected would be part of the geo-spatial data. For a network service provider, their interested data could be alarms generated from their equipment. In this case, the location of the alarms and when they happened would be part of the geo-spatial data. The two main quality aspects of the geo-spatial data at this stage are location accuracy and temporal accuracy. The location accuracy is to ensure the collected data's geo-spatial data location information is correct and accurate enough for business purpose. The temporal accuracy is to ensure the time information associated to the geo-spatial data is correct and accurate enough. The following methods are recommended at this stage.

3.1.1 Standards and Rules

Standards and rules are the first check-point for the collected geo-spatial data before they are stored. For any business, they should have a set of predefined standards and rules for the minimum quality criteria of the geo-spatial data. In Caprioli et al.'s work (Caprioli et al 2003a, b), several organisations that for making GIS data standards have been mentioned, such as Open GIS Consortium, Inc. (OGC), ISO/TC 211, CEN/TC 287, and Digital Geographic Information Exchange Standards (DIGEST). They mainly deal with geo-spatial data quality in general. However, for each individual business, they need to have their own personalised rules. For example, for a location of a shop, possibly a postcode would be accurate enough as there is no other shop from the same company on that street and for the shop's sale report, time accurate to a day or month should be sufficient. On the other hand, for an alarm generated from a network device, the location information may need to be accurate to longitude and latitude level and the time accurate to a second or even millisecond.

Metadata is also another important aspect of standards and rules for data quality (Loshin 2011a, b). The reason is that without a clear defined metadata, the semantics of the data is vague and therefore, it is very difficult to assess the quality of the data and improve it.

3.1.2   Crowdsourcing

Crowdsourcing, as Howe (Howe 2006) defined, *"represents the act of a company or institution taking a function once performed by employees and outsourcing it to an undefined (and generally large) network of people in the form of an open call. This can take the form of peer-production (when the job is performed collaboratively), but is also often undertaken by sole individuals. The crucial prerequisite is the use of the open call format and the large network of potential labourers."* It is believed to be a cheap and effective way to collect data. When the handhold devices with GPS enabled become popular, it is also become a cost effective way of collecting geo-spatial data. However, crowdsourcing does not have to be a way of outsourcing. If number of workers is not an issue for a business, crowdsourcing can also be done internally.

Traditionally, crowdsourcing is used as a data collection and annotation method. There are few commercial crowdsourcing platforms that doing exactly that, such as the Amazon Mechanical Turk[3]. However, recent works (Karam and Melchiori 2013a, b) show that the crowd wisdom can also be used to improve data quality once the data are collected. This can be done through a crowdsourcing pattern called *Find-Fix-Verify* (Acosta et al. 2013), which represents finding problem in data, fixing the problems, and verifying the fixes. Different groups of crowd are assigned for Find, Fix, and Verify. This pattern reduces the negative effects caused by low quality workers and at the same time remains cost effective.

3.1.3   Third Party Validation

Third party validation is to use third party services to validate the geo-spatial information in the collected data before store them in database. This is mainly for validating the accuracy of the location. There are several popular geocoding services available, such as Google geocoding service[4], Bing map geocoding service[5], and Gisgraphy[6]. The most common functionality of geocoding services is converting a human readable address to a geographic coordinates, such as longitude and latitude. The converting result can be compared with the geo-spatial information in the collected data to validate its accuracy according to the accuracy rules.

3.2   Data Storing Stage

The data storing stage is when the business interested data with geo-spatial information have been collected and store in databases. As geo-spatial data can be very dynamic, such as the constituency boundaries, road layout, distribution of retail shops of a business, and customer interests in a particular area, at this stage, one of the key tasks is to ensure that all the data are up to date. Any analysis and decisions made based on out of date information will lead to failure and extra cost to business.

---

[3] https://www.mturk.com/.

[4] https://developers.google.com/maps/documentation/geocoding/.

[5] http://msdn.microsoft.com/en-us/library/ff701715.aspx.

[6] http://www.gisgraphy.com/.

Another key task at this stage is to efficiently and effectively manage geo-spatial data resources. This involves how the internal geo-spatial data are shared across the whole business and keep them up to date. This also involves how to manager geo-spatial data from external data resources.

Certainly, other aspects of the geo-spatial data quality can still be improved and some of the methods discussed previously can also be applied at this stage, such as crowdsourcing and third party validation. However, as at this stage, the information base has been built up, therefore new methods can be applied here to improve data quality, such as internal cross validation. We will discuss it later.

At this stage, the following methods are recommended to improve geo-spatial data currency and location accuracy.

3.2.1   Referential Geo-spatial Data Outsourcing

This method is for manage external geo-spatial data resources. Referential geo-spatial data are the geo-spatial data that are useful and important to a business, but not produced or collected by the business itself. For example, the postcode, constituency boundaries, police force boundaries, local crime locations etc. are typical referential geo-spatial data. They can be relatively static, such as police force boundaries, or very dynamic, such as the local crime data. However, as most of referential geo-spatial data are updated regularly, it is very expensive and prone to errors to maintain local copies. Therefore, to eliminate the currency issue of self-maintained referential geo-spatial data, it is recommend outsourcing the management of this type data to external organisations and accessing the data directly from their provided interfaces.

There are many organisations that provide geo-spatial data services, such as Ordnance Survey[7], UK Data Service[8], National Statistics[9], GeoNames[10], and Unlock Places[11]. The data are provided through Web services, programming APIs or direct data access. By using these services, the business can focus on their own geo-spatial data management.

3.2.2   Geo-spatial Data Sharing

This method is for managing internal geo-spatial data resources. By sharing data across different divisions of a business, the currency issue of data quality can be improved if it is due to data being updated in one part of the business not reflected in other parts. Data sharing can also happen between businesses and their partners. To effectively share data, there are three key elements need to be addressed:

1. **Data Sharing Management.** This is about what to share and sharing to whom. Some information may not be suitable for sharing, some information may only be shared to a small group of people, and when data are out of date, only a small group

---

[7] http://www.ordnancesurvey.co.uk/.

[8] http://census.ukdataservice.ac.uk/use-data/guides/boundary-data.aspx.

[9] http://www.ons.gov.uk/ons/index.html.

[10] http://www.geonames.org/.

[11] http://edina.ac.uk/unlock/.

of people may be able to update the data. Therefore, to effectively share data, a business needs to have clear data sharing management strategies and policies.

2. **Data Sharing Structure.** This is about how data are shared. There are mainly two ways of sharing data, the centralised structure and the distributed structure. A centralised structure is that the data are hosted on a central server and can be accessed by multiple clients simultaneously. A distributed structure is that the data are hosted at multiple locations (Tamer Ozsu and Valduriez 2011).

3. **Metadata.** When data are share across a business or between businesses, the most common issue is data semantics inconsistency. This often causes the difficulties to retrieve, interpret and integrate data. By having clearly defined metadata, the business can benefit from, improved data quality, increased usage of existing data set as they become easier to identify, reduced data redundancy, improved data analytic result as the semantics of the data is clearer, and quicker and more confident decision making etc.

3.2.3   Internal Data Validation

Internal data validation is to use the data store in the data repository to validate itself. For geo-spatial data, this method is mainly for validating the consistency of location and compliance of standards and rules.

More often than not in a business's data repository, the same information is described under different context in different data set. For example, a building's coordinates on map is described formally in a data set called company buildings. However, in the computer devices data set, the buildings location may be described again as the devices are hosted in the building and therefore has the same location coordinates on map. In this case, the devices' locations information can be used to validate the building's location and vice versa. This method works especially well under big data. As in big data, the information quantity is huge and therefore, there is better chance to find one piece of information to validate another. Ansolabehere and Hersh (2012) demonstrated in their work how to take the advantages of big data for data validation.

Another focus of internal data validation is to examine the compliance of standards and rules of geo-spatial data.

3.3   Data Application Stage

At this stage, the geo-spatial data start being used in business analysis and decision making. The key focus of this stage is on how to quickly react to the data quality issues that are discovered during the usage of data in order to minimise their impact. Data quality issues can be categorised according to their potential impacts (Loshin 2011a, b). For high impact issues, for example, the issues that could cause financial, reputation, or safety related impacts, predefined procedures should be in place to deal with them in order to prevent future impact from the same issues. The procedures should specify how the geo-spatial data related quality issue can be raised and solved step by step for different data users in different parts of a business.

Another focus of this stage is to communicate with data users about the data quality. Quality specifications for different sets of data should be available to data user, which allows users to assess whether certain data are fit for their needs (concept of "fitness for use") (Chrisman 1984; Agumya 1997).

To systematically improve geo-spatial data quality, all the methods discussed in the data storing stage are all applicable in this stage. However, due to the special characteristic of this stage, quality issues need to be resolved in a fire-fighting style. The following methods are recommended for this stage.

3.3.1   Issue Reporting Interface

Data quality issues could be discovered by any data users in a business. Similar to issue tracker in software development, it is important to have a simple interface for reporting, logging and tracking data quality issues. Once data issues are notified through the interface, quality issue resolving processes should be kicked off and remediation plans should be provided to the data user. Remediation plans can be process reengineering if data quality issue is due to system design, e.g. location conversion error at the data acquisition stage cause location inaccuracy, or simple data corrections. If issues cannot be resolved immediately, workaround should be suggested through the interface to the data users. An effective data quality issue reporting interfaced should have the following features:

- Web based and easy to use
- Flexible interface for users with different technical levels
- Automatically triggering quality issue resolving processes and reporting process outcomes
- Quality issue root cause analysis capability

3.3.2   Quality Information Repository

It is impossible to find absolutely "perfect" geo-spatial data with 100 % accuracy. They are all inaccurate, incomplete, and possibly out of date, at certain levels. Therefore, it is important for data analysts to know the quality specifications of the data and whether the data are fit for purpose to produce analytic results. It is recommended to have a data quality information repository for data users to search for data quality specifications for a particular data set. The quality information can be communicated back to data users through different ways (Devillers and Jeansoulin 2010).

- **Metadata.** Textual metadata is the most common way to communicate data quality information to data user. Several standards (e.g. ISO 19113 and ISO 19115) are in place to define how the quality information should be documented in metadata. The key purpose of metadata is to allow the data user to examine the suitability of datasets.
- **Visualisation.** Visualization provides an effective means of presenting complex information and therefore, it is a suitable approach to communicate data quality information to the data users. In a simple way, the parameters of geo-spatial data quality can be visualised against expected value, then the data uses can judge whether the data quality is fit for purpose or not. Beard et al. (1991), Mcgranaghan (1993), and Fisher (1993) have proposed more sophisticated frameworks for

visualising data quality by using location, size, value, texture, colour, shape, colour saturation and even animations. In those frameworks, the data user can compare the data quality in more details with their expectations.   .

4 Summary

In this paper, we introduced a geo-spatial data quality improvement framework. This framework tackles the geo-spatial data quality issue in a systematic manner throughout the whole life cycle of data. Geo-spatial data quality issue are addressed through three stages in the framework. At each stage, several methods are discussed for ensuring and continuously improving data quality.

In the future work, we will look at how to evaluate and improve the framework. Our next step will be implementing the framework into a software system for geo-spatial data quality management.

References

Batini, C., Cappiello, C., Francalanci, C., Maurino, A.: Methodologies for data quality assessment and improvement. ACM Comput. Surv. **41**(3) (2009)

Caprioli, M., Scognamiglio, A., Strisciuglio, G., Tarantino, E.: Rules and standards for spatial data quality in GIS environments. In: Proceedings of the 21st International Cartographic Conference (ICC), Durban, South Africa, 10−16 August 2003

Veregin, H.: Data quality parameters. In: Longley, P.A., Goodchild, M.F., Maguire, D.J., Rhind, D.W. (eds.) Geographical Information Systems: Principles, Techniques, Applications and Management, 2nd edn., vol. 2, ch.12 Wiley, New York (1999)

Caprioli M, Scognamiglio A, Strisciuglio G, Tarantino E.: Rules and standards for spatial data quality in GIS environments. In: Proceeding of the 21st International Cartographic Conference, Bern, Durban, South Africa 10–16 August 2003

Loshin, D.: The Practitioner's Guide to Data Quality Improvement, 1st edn. Morgan Kaufmann Publishers Inc., San Francisco (2011a)

Howe, J.: 'Crowdsourcing: A Definition', Crowdsourcing: Tracking the Rise of the Amateur, weblog, 2 June 2006. http://crowdsourcing.typepad.com/cs/2006/06/crowdsourcing_a.html. Accessed 26 June 2014

Tamer Ozsu, M., Valduriez, P.: Principles of Distributed Database Systems, 3rd edn. Springer Publisher, New York (2011). ISBN 1441988335

Loshin, D.: Evaluating the Business Impacts of Poor Data Quality (2011b). http://www.sei.cmu.edu/measurement/research/upload/Loshin.pdf

Chrisman, N.R.: The role of quality information in the long term functioning of a geographical information system. In: Proceeding of the Auto-Carto 6, Ottawa, Canada, pp. 303−321 (1984)

Agumya, A., Hunter, G.J.: Determining fitness for use of geographic information. ITC J. **2**(1), 109–113 (1997)

Beard, M.K., Buttenfield, B.P., Clapham, S.B.: NCGIA Research initiative 7: visualization of data quality. Technical report 91-26, Santa Barbara, USA, NCGIA (1991)

Mcgranaghan, M.: A cartographic view of data quality. Cartographica **30**(2/3), 8–19 (1993)

Fisher, P.F.: Visualizing uncertainty in soil maps by animation. Cartographica **30**(2/3), 20–27 (1993)

Box, G.E.P.: Science and statistics. J. Am. Stat. Assoc. **71**(1976), 791–799 (1976)

Longley, P.A., Goodchild, M.F., Maguire, D.J., Rhind, D.W. (eds.): Geographical Information Systems and Science. Wiley, New York (2001)

Berry, B.: Approaches to regional analysis: a synthesis. Ann. Assoc. Am. Geogr. **54**, 2–11 (1964)

Longley, P.A., Goodchild, M.F., Maguire, D.J., Rhind, D.W.: New Developments in Geographical Information Systems: Principles, Techniques, Management and Applications, 2, Abridged edn. Wiley, New York (2005)

Chrisman, N.: Development in the treatment of spatial data quality. In: Devillers, R., Jeansoulin, R. (eds.) Fundamentals of Spatial Data Quality, pp. 21–30. Iste, London (2006)

Xia, J.: Metrics to measure open geospatial data quality. J. Issues Sci. Technol. Librarianship (2012). doi:10.5062/F4B85627

Kainz, W.: Logical consistency. In: Guptill, S.C., Morrison, J.L. (eds.) Elements of spatial data quality, pp. 109–137. Elsevier Science, Oxford (1995)

Rasdorf, W.: Spatial data quality. Technical report- not held in TRLN member libraries, Raleigh, N.C.: Department of Civil Engineering, North Carolina State University (2000)

Bertolazzi, P., Santis, L.D., Scannapieco, M.: Automatic record matching in cooperative information systems. In: Proceedings of the ICDT International Workshop on Data Quality in Cooperative Information Systems (DQCIS) (2003)

Lenzerini, M.: Data integration: a theoretical perspective. In: Proceedings of the 21st ACM Symposium on Principles of Database Systems (PODS) (2002)

Muthu, S., Withman, L., Cheraghi, S.H.: Business process re-engineering: a consolidated methodology. In: Proceedings of the 4th Annual International Conference on Industrial Engineering Theory, Applications and Practice (1999)

Hammer, M.: Reengineering work: don't automate, obliterate. Harvard Bus. Rev. 104–112 (1990)

Stankute, S. Asche, H.: Improvement of spatial data quality using the data conflation. In: Proceedings of the 2011 International Conference on Computational Science and Its Applications, Santander, Spain, 20–23 June 2011

Tadakaluru, A., Bowling Green, K.Y., Mostafa, M., Andrew, K., Ernest, A.: In: Proceedings of the 2005 International Conference on Computational Intelligence for Modelling, Control and Automation, and International Conference on Intelligent Agents, Web Technologies and Internet Commerce (CIMCA–IAWTIC 2005) (2005)

Westland, J.C.: The cost of errors in software development: evidence from industry. J. Syst. Softw. **62**(2002), 1–9 (2002)

Karam, R., Melchiori, M.: Improving geo-spatial linked data with the wisdom of the crowds. In: Proceedings of the Joint EDBT/ICDT 2013 Workshops, Genoa, Italy, 18–22 March 2013a

Karam, R., Melchiori, M.: A crowdsourcing-based framework for improving Geo-spatial open data. In: 2013 IEEE International Conference on Systems, Man, and Cybernetics (2013b)

Acosta, M., Zaveri, A., Simperl, E., Kontokostas, D., Auer, S., Lehmann, J.: Crowdsourcing linked data quality assessment. In: Alani, H., Kagal, L., Fokoue, A., Groth, P., Biemann, C., Parreira, J.X., Aroyo, L., Noy, N., Welty, C., Janowicz, K. (eds.) ISWC 2013, Part II. LNCS, vol. 8219, pp. 260–276. Springer, Heidelberg (2013)

Ansolabehere, S., Hersh, E.: Validation: what big data reveal about survey misreporting and the real electorate. Polit. Anal. (Autumn 2012) **20**(4), 437–459 (2012)

Devillers, R., Jeansoulin, R.: Fundamentals of Spatial Data Quality, 1st edn. Wiley-ISTE, London (2006)

Author Index

Printed in the United States
By Bookmasters